DIGITAL
BUSINESS

Annmarie Hanlon

DIGITAL BUSINESS

STRATEGY, MANAGEMENT & TRANSFORMATION

§ Sage

S Sage

1 Oliver's Yard
55 City Road
London EC1Y 1SP

2455 Teller Road
Thousand Oaks
California 91320

Unit No 323-333, Third Floor, F-Block
International Trade Tower
Nehru Place, New Delhi – 110 019

8 Marina View Suite 43-053
Asia Square Tower 1
Singapore 018960

Editor: Matthew Waters
Development editor: Rhoda Ola-Said
Assistant editor: Charlotte Hanson
Production editor: Imogen Roome
Copyeditor: Neil Dowden
Proofreader: Leigh Smithson
Marketing manager: Camille Richmond
Cover design: Francis Kenney
Typeset by: C&M Digitals (P) Ltd, Chennai, India

Library of Congress Control Number: 2023947994

British Library Cataloguing in Publication data

A catalogue record for this book is available from the British Library

ISBN 978-1-5296-2423-6
ISBN 978-1-5296-2422-9 (pbk)

CONTENTS

LIST OF FIGURES

LIST OF TABLES

ABOUT THE AUTHOR

Annmarie Hanlon PhD, is the Course Director for MSc Marketing and Leadership, and teaches digital marketing at the Cranfield School of Management. As an early adopter, working in 'online business' since 1990, she has led digital strategy and planning projects in sectors including legal and financial, software and IT, health and manufacturing. She is a Fellow of the Chartered Institute of Marketing, a Member of the Marketing Institute Ireland and a Liveryman of the Worshipful Company of Marketors. Annmarie's research interests include ethics in the digital environment and digital transformation within organisations.

Follow her updates on X (previously Twitter) via @AnnmarieHanlon

CONTRIBUTOR

Graham Bell contributed to Chapter 11, Digital Customer Experience Management, due to his knowledge on the metaverse and is responsible for Cranfield School of Management's digital education strategy. Graham is working on a PhD exploring how future technologies such as the metaverse will impact organisations, society, and people in the context of the future of work and education.

ACKNOWLEDGEMENTS

Digital Business is all around us, whether working or studying from home on Teams, Zoom, the Metaverse or in our augmented real life or our actual real life. Mobile phones are a necessity, screens are everywhere, and goggles are moving into our daily life. Writing a book is a journey and needs a team, so I want to acknowledge and thank some special people who helped along the way.

Let me start with my gratitude to you, the reader. Wow! You opened the book and amazingly you are reading this page – keep turning those pages, I have written this book just for you.

Each book has a fantastic team from Sage: Matthew Waters, for the book idea and many conversations to refine and shape the contents; Rhoda Ola-Said, whose relevant editing kept me on track and gave me global inspiration; Charlotte Hanson, for navigating the complex area of permissions to use several graphics; Imogen Roome, for producing this book in double-quick time; Francis Kenney for his consistently creative and eye-catching cover designs.

My supporting network has been wonderful. Special thanks are due to friends in our WhatsApp groups – you know who you are.

And of course, my innovative Marketor friends, as we participate in events together and discuss the future shape of digital business.

None of this would have been possible without the many businesses used as case examples throughout the book. When at FIU in Miami I was fortunate to visit VISA and was amazed by the levels of data and AI that surround their global ecosystem.

And my many academic colleagues at home and across the globe in Cranfield, Dublin, Ulster, Miami and ESCP in Berlin.

Digital business teachers, tutors, lecturers and professors – thank you for opening this book and for choosing it for your course. If you need help, email me – I will respond!

Especial thanks to my sister, for being with me every step of the journey.

ONLINE RESOURCES

Visit https://study.sagepub.com/digitalbusiness to find a range of additional resources for lecturers, to aid study and support teaching.

FOR LECTURERS

Lecturer's guide outlining the key learning objectives covered in each chapter and provides you with suggested activities to use in class or for assignments.

PowerPoint slides featuring figures and tables from the book, which can be downloaded and customized for use in your own presentations.

Author-selected videos featuring discussions of key concepts to help integrate quality content into your teaching and foster a rich learning environment for your students.

PART 1

DIGITAL BUSINESS ESSENTIALS

CONTENTS

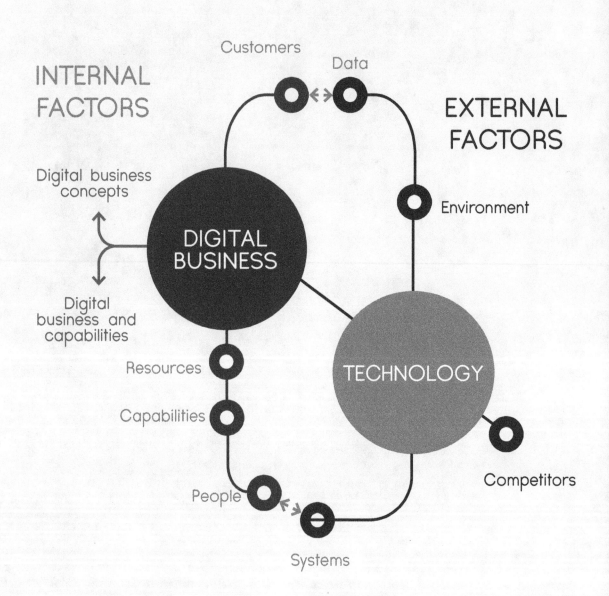

INTERNAL
FACTORS

EXTERNAL
FACTORS

Customers

Data

Digital business
concepts

DIGITAL
BUSINESS

Environment

Digital
business and
capabilities

Resources

TECHNOLOGY

Capabilities

Competitors

People

Systems

1

THE DIGITAL BUSINESS ENVIRONMENT

LEARNING OUTCOMES

When you have read this chapter, you will be able to:

Understand the role of sustainability in digital business

Apply the digital business framework

Analyse types of value for customers

Evaluate competitors using the framework for competitor identification

Create a plan to overcome barriers to the adoption of digital business

PROFESSIONAL SKILLS

When you have worked through this chapter, you should be able to:

- Demonstrate an understanding of the digital business environment
- Deliver initiatives that contribute towards an organisation's environmental, social and corporate governance policies

1.1 INTRODUCTION TO DIGITAL BUSINESS

Technology has changed our world in how we study, work, relax, shop, travel, plan and communicate. For many organisations, the COVID-19 pandemic accelerated the move to digital business as visiting the office, seeing customers face to face or going to places in person became challenging.

For example, healthcare jumped ahead 10 years by offering virtual appointments, companies allowed more employees to work from home, governments adapted to permit online processes, universities moved from classrooms to screens and many organisations digitalised their business operations.

Digital business means applying technology to create or transform a business. Gartner (2022a: 1) suggests it involves creating 'new business designs by blurring the digital and physical worlds'. The first telephone call was made around 150 years ago, but it took decades for telephones to be available in our homes. Yet today, who do you know without a mobile phone? The cost of technology has decreased and internet access is becoming faster, making digital part of our everyday lives. Our mobile phones are hand-held computers that enable us to message friends, pay for drinks, buy products, track deliveries, order food, watch films, manage bank accounts, buy train tickets, check in for flights and remind us what time to be in class.

For businesses, the move from analogue manual processing to a digital environment brings opportunities and challenges.

There are opportunities to rework and review current systems. Do they work for the company? Or for the customers? Older legacy systems tended to focus on the process, driven by the company, which didn't always provide the best customer experience. Newer systems can place the customer in the centre, which we'll explore further throughout this textbook.

But first, the challenges. Back in 1972 at a United Nations conference in Stockholm, Sweden, the concept of sustainability was discussed. It took a further 20 years and another conference in Rio de Janeiro in Brazil before an agenda was set with goals towards sustainability. Eventually, the United Nations created the Global Goals for Sustainable Development (SDGs) in 2015. Their website explains that the SDGs are 'a universal call to action to end poverty, protect the planet, and ensure that by 2030 all people enjoy peace and prosperity' (United Nations, 2015: 1). There are 17 goals, as shown in Figure 1.1, and Appendix A provides more information about the SDGs.

Let's examine how the SDGs are relevant to digital business. Many organisations have signed up to the SDGs, such as the tech companies Meta, Google (under its trading name of Alphabet), PayPal, Alibaba, Huawei, Samsung and Xiaomi, as well as other well-known brands including LEGO, Nike, McDonald's and Unilever.

It's not just about companies signing up to pledge they will do more for the environment, as within a digital context the United Nations has recognised that jobs in the future will demand new skills. One of the SDGs is Quality Education to ensure students gain these skills and to promote lifelong learning (United Nations, 2022). But not all students in all countries can access education online, widening the digital inequality gap. Similarly, not all businesses are ready to go digital. Pre-pandemic there were (and maybe still are) businesses that received your online order, but manually processed the order acknowledgement, filled in forms for the shipping and needed employees to check who had processed the order.

This chapter provides an overview of digital business and its opportunities and challenges. The digital business framework is also introduced as a helpful structure to consider all aspects of digital business. Throughout this textbook we will also explore the relevant SDGs and their application to digital business.

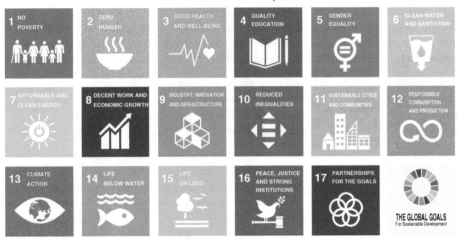

Figure 1.1   The United Nations Sustainable Development Goals

Source: United Nations (2015)

Smartphone Sixty Seconds® – Adoption of the SDGs

- To understand the adoption of the SDGs, take out your mobile phone and search for the name of your favourite company + SDGs.
- Have they adopted the SDGs? If not, why is this?
- What do you think of the action they are taking?

1.2 DIGITAL BUSINESS CONCEPTS

1.2.1 VALUE FOR CUSTOMERS

In digital business, technology acts as an enabler to improve processes and experiences. For any business to be successful, it must offer value to customers or stakeholders. According to Bowman & Ambrosini (2000), value can be considered on 3 levels:

- Total monetary value: The amount the customer is prepared to pay for the product
- Perceived use value: Defined by customers based on their perceptions
- Exchange value: Realised when the product is sold

The total monetary value is straightforward – it's what you're prepared to pay for the goods. In some cases, you might spend some time considering your possible purchase, such as a festival ticket or a holiday. In other situations you might not think about the purchase, but just buy the item, for example a bottle of water. The difference in the consideration of the goods depends on the cost, along with why they're needed. So you might not *need* a festival ticket but want to spend time with friends over the summer and have to figure out the total costs involved. A bottle of water may be needed when you're thirsty and you don't need a long decision-making process.

The perceived use value is based on your personal situation and the benefit you feel you will gain. So this could be a ride with Uber – will you get home quicker or perhaps your bank balance is low and you need to walk? If surge pricing is happening, perhaps you will compromise and take the bus instead as you don't feel the taxi fare is worth it.

The exchange value is the amount received by the organisation when the item is sold – the difference between what it cost to make and how much you paid. The exchange value requires effort to take an item and find a way to add more value and sell it for a higher rate. For example, if you have your own webpage, you could hand code the design, or you could buy a template online from a third-party software site. The template seller has to buy the materials to produce the template (hardware, software), pay a member of staff to create the template and cover the business running costs (electricity, office space or working from home allowance), as well as promoting their services. The software site converts their efforts and costs into value when people download and buy their templates. The challenge in a digital setting is the volume of software sites selling these goods and the effort required to gain new customers before any form of value is realised.

DIGITAL TOOL　Themeforest

The Australian business Envato launched the Themeforest portal which contains thousands of website templates. Some are free and others are chargeable, they are created by members of the community.

- You can explore it here: themeforest.net

1.2.2 VALUE FROM THE 7PS

Value is often created for digital business by changing one of the 7Ps (Booms & Bitner, 1980). The 7Ps are well known in marketing and are also called the extended marketing mix. They are a useful business framework and ensure organisations consider each element in the marketing mix. Table 1.1 explains the 7Ps and shows how they can be adapted to provide opportunities for digital business, with examples.

Table 1.1   Opportunities for digital business using the 7Ps

7Ps element	Potential opportunities for digital business	Examples
Product	Offering a digital version of physical products	The Louvre art gallery in Paris launched 'Louvre at home', enabling audiences to explore works of art from anywhere in the world
Price	Pricing changes based on demand or buyer behaviour	Uber increases its charges (known as surge pricing) when there is greater demand
		Online retailers issue coupons for goods left in shopping carts, or offer discounts for newsletter sign-ups
Place	Goods are available online, via mobile or app	Spotify provides music via its app, it has no physical stores and no physical products
Promotion	Promotion such as advertising takes place online	*Filter Nyheter*, an independent online newspaper in Norway, uses Meta to promote its stories and gain subscribers
People	Virtual people are available 24/7 to support your purchase and may include chatbots	US airline WestJet's chatbot is known as Juliet – Westjet's travel assistant and works on the website and via Messenger
Physical evidence	Website or app is visually pleasing and easy to use	Kaartje2go, a website in the Netherlands for making personalised greetings cards, was named 'DHL Best Online Store 2022' at the annual Dutch Shopping Awards
Processes	Online orders goods are available for collection from delivery points, not just home delivery	The Danish company Bring offers delivery to home, collection points and parcel boxes

1.2.3 VALUE CO-CREATION

Value is not created by organisations alone – customers and stakeholders are often involved in the process. According to Carvalho & Alves (2022), it was about personalising the experience. The difference in a digital setting is that more people are involved (Saha et al., 2022). For example, travel forums allow tourists to ask questions from the hotel, or guests and other people can add their feedback too (Carvalho & Alves, 2022). This allows holidaymakers to build their own holiday with advice from others, not just the hotel or destination.

DISCOVER MORE ON VALUE CO-CREATION

Professors Prahalad and Ramaswamy proposed the idea in 'Co-creating unique value with customers' (2004) published in *Strategy & Leadership*. Although it's an older article it explains the background of the concept with useful examples.

Activity 1.1   Analyse types of value

Consider a purchase you made recently when you had to think before spending the money. Analyse the type of value gained from the purchase:

- Was this based on monetary, perceived use or exchange value?
- Can you identify whether the value was related to the 7Ps and, if yes, which elements?
- Were you involved in the co-creation of the value?
- How could more value have been added?

Having considered digital business concepts, the next section proposes a framework to capture the components of digital business.

1.3 INTRODUCING THE DIGITAL BUSINESS FRAMEWORK

The digital business framework is an ecosystem containing the key elements of digital business. It is in 2 parts: internal and external factors. The internally focused elements can be managed by organisation. These are its assets, including the customers, the organisation's capabilities, its resources, and the people working for and around the organisation.

Technology is at the core of the external factors where these elements are outside the organisation's control. This includes data such as information about the market and consumer behaviour, the external environment, the competitors and the third-party systems used to make things happen. Figure 1.2 shows the digital business framework.

1.3.1 THE DIGITAL BUSINESS FRAMEWORK INTERNAL FACTORS

CUSTOMERS

Looking at the internal factors, the customers vary depending on the product offered. Not all products are suitable or relevant for all customers. For example, an app such as OnTheSnow, showing the snow forecast, may be useful for winter sports or if you live in countries where snow falls, such as Norway or Denmark, but if you live in Miami in the USA or Mumbai in India this app would have no value for you.

While we are considering customers in a digital setting where the focus is on access to the product online, via mobile or via app, this excludes the 2.9 billion people in the world who have no access to the internet (International Telecommunication Union, 2021). We will explore digital products and customers further in Chapter 3, 'E-commerce'.

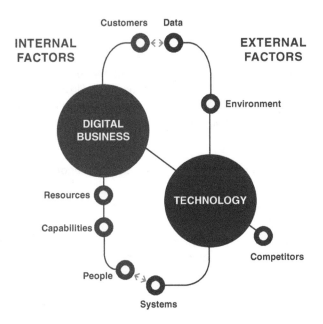

Figure 1.2   The digital business framework

RESOURCES

The idea of resources having value inside an organisation was a theory proposed by Wernerfelt in 1984. Wernerfelt suggested that a resource inside the organisation could be a strength or a weakness, and included tangible physical products or intangible assets. For example, a brand name represents an intangible asset: you can't touch it, but you recognise it. One example is Apple's brand name, which acts as an asset when new products are introduced and is already trusted by their customers. There is a sense of excitement and fun when Apple introduces new technology. The dates for their new mobile phone releases are keenly anticipated and there can be waiting lists for some products. This is all about the power of a strong brand which has become an asset.

CAPABILITIES

Capabilities are the organisation's skills and talents. For example, Amazon.com's capabilities are having an efficient logistics process, being able to offer next-day or same-day delivery through its network of distribution centres. Another skill that Amazon has developed is understanding buying behaviour through its data. So if you buy an item online from Amazon.com the **recommendation engine** (see Key Term) within the business can suggest other relevant products, based on massive amounts of data from other customers.

KEY TERM   RECOMMENDATION ENGINE

A recommendation engine, also known as a recommender system, is an aggregator of suggestions for specific services, based on a user's profile or interests. Aggregators collect different materials and curate them. Recommendation engines collect or aggregate sources of potential followers, news or other information which is then shared. For example:

- X (formerly Twitter) uses its own recommendation engine to suggest who to follow
- News recommendation engines aggregate news from different sources to deliver a summary
- The tourism sector uses recommender systems for hotels and restaurants using factors such as where the person is located

---

DISCOVER MORE ON RECOMMENDATION ENGINES

Professor Rula Hamid and colleagues explored the literature concerning smart tourism recommendation systems and identified the key factors within smart tourism in their paper 'How smart is e-tourism? A systematic review of smart tourism recommendation system applying data management' published in *Computer Science Review* (Hamid et al., 2021).

PEOPLE

'People' refers to the workers and the stakeholders. The workers may be those who work exclusively for the organisation, or they may be temporary or gig workers. This is an area we'll explore further in Chapter 2 which looks at the digital workspace.

1.3.2 THE DIGITAL BUSINESS FRAMEWORK EXTERNAL FACTORS

Moving into the external factors, these are outside the organisation's control and may be dependent on third parties. While the organisation is unable to control these factors, they can identify them and prepare plans to reduce any negative impact or benefit from a positive gain.

DATA

The first of these elements is data. Data is collected with every online purchase. This includes the amount spent, the time and date the purchase took place, whether it is a recurring or one-off purchase, whether it's combined with other similar items, whether you're a registered (and known customer) or whether you're not known to the organisation. The transaction data may be collected in a **customer relationship management system** (see Key Term) inside the organisation but when combined or blended with other data it becomes more useful. For example, VISA, the global digital payments company, uses its analytics to provide advice to destinations. Although it can't see the individual's details, it can see patterns in the data and use these trends to help its partners provide more relevant marketing. So it may see that 1,000 people in Miami paid for their parking at 07:00 and another 500 people paid for a train ticket. This data can contribute towards urban planning and can help local governments understand the peak times when transport is required.

Data is often held by organisations in **customer relationship management (CRM) systems** as this enables organisations to automatically respond to specific events; for example:

- Send an email after a purchase to confirm the purchase
- Request a review around 5 days after the goods have been delivered
- Send reminder emails to customers who have not made a purchase for some weeks
- Better understand which groups of customers make purchases at certain times (e.g. when they've been paid or gained a bonus)
- Connect social media accounts to registered email addresses and respond faster to queries if certain customers have many followers

---

KEY TERM CUSTOMER RELATIONSHIP MANAGEMENT (CRM)

There is no consensus on the definition of customer relationship management (CRM). An abbreviated version taking a management perspective is that CRM is 'a disciplined approach to managing the customer journey from the initial acquisition of a customer, to that customer becoming a high spending, profitable advocate' (Buttle & Maklan, 2019: 4).

But collecting data requires rules to be followed. In the UK and Europe the General Data Protection Regulation (GDPR) applies, while in Australia and New Zealand it's the privacy principles. These principles exist to protect your personal data, let you know when data is being collected and being shared, and allow you to make changes if it's wrong.

Activity 1.2   Access your data

Social media platforms store your data in large CRM systems. You can access your data to see the information they hold about you:

(Continued)

- Select one of your social media accounts (e.g. Instagram, LinkedIn, X, TikTok) and open the app.
- You now need to find how to access your data. All apps vary and typically this involves looking at the settings and privacy. There may be an option in your account that says 'my data' with an option to download an archive or request a copy of your data. If you can't see where to find it, search online for the name of the platform and 'download my data', then follow the instructions.
- It may take a short while for the data to arrive. When it does, do you have any challenges opening the information? How do you feel about the data that's stored about you?

Data also flows back to customers. If an organisation subscribes to data from a dataset management company such as CACI, they can augment their existing customer profiles by trialling different advert types and seeing who responds to which types of content. It's also possible in social media to access lookalike audiences; these are groups of potential customers who have similar characteristics to your existing customer base. By targeting lookalike audiences organisations can increase the number of conversions – whether that's sales, donations or downloading data from their website. But there's a dark side too, as shown in Ethical Insights **Bias in Lookalike Audiences**.

ETHICAL INSIGHTS   Bias in lookalike audiences

Meta's lookalike audiences and LinkedIn's matched audiences are based on algorithms – formulas that identify similar characteristics and save time for organisations. For example, Facebook allows advertisers to select audiences based on their current customer base and LinkedIn enables recruiters to target people matching their criteria for a specific role based on expertise or experience.

But the algorithms can enable bias and lead to discrimination. In the USA the National Fair Housing Alliance legally challenged Facebook for allowing advertisers to discriminate against people based on their gender, religion, familial status and ethnicity. The impact was that accommodation might only be offered to people who were married, male or middle income. Facebook lost the case and had to change how advertisers could assess and categorise 'lookalike audiences'.

Yet bias still exists as the programmers creating the algorithms may have their own biases which may be unconsciously introduced into the system. A programmer creating an algorithm may rely on their own knowledge pool, which may be limited and favour people from a similar background to themselves. A human resources (HR) professional might look at results on LinkedIn and if the first 5 respondents are men, LinkedIn might then only show male candidates as it believes (based on its algorithm) these results are preferred.

- How can bias in algorithms be addressed?
- How can organisations ensure they do not adopt bias in areas such as recruitment?
- What guidelines could be provided to tech companies creating algorithms?

ENVIRONMENT

Organisations cannot operate without considering the wider external environment as this impacts on every aspect of how they operate. To frame the external environment we refer to an earlier marketing model, PESTLE, which stands for political, economic, socio-cultural, technological, legal and environmental/ecological. PESTLE helps organisations to identify risks or challenges before they occur and find ways to reduce the impact. For example, as organisations become more aware of the environmental impact of their products, this is changing behaviour.

CASE EXAMPLE 1.1   IKEA's changing business environment

The Swedish furniture retailer IKEA operates in over 50 countries and has had over 5 billion visits to its website. It has seen many changes and one growing issue is recycling and disposal of old furniture. When customers buy new household goods, their old tables and chairs may end up as waste that can't easily be recycled. To address this, IKEA introduced its 'Buyback & Resell' programme in some countries and a recycle programme in others.

Buyback & Resell allows customers to look for their item online, calculate its value and return it to the store in exchange for cash or vouchers. The store can repair and resell the goods at a cheaper rate in their Circular Hub.

This is one example of addressing the environmental/ecological issues within PESTLE. Table 1.2 provides more explanations with examples of how IKEA addresses the different PESTLE elements.

Table 1.2   PESTLE with explanations and examples

PESTLE element	Explanation	Examples of how this applies to IKEA
Political	Regional governing bodies National government Federal/local government Lobby groups Trade associations Pressure groups	IKEA needs to be aware of political factors in the different countries in which it operates, working with regional governments to create employment and ensuring its goods do not encourage attention from pressure groups.
Economic	Inflation (wages, prices) Taxes Gross domestic product (GDP) Exchange rates Quotas, duties	Economic factors need to be considered when price setting, for example IKEA varies its restaurant pricing based on country regions, so its veggie offering in London is more expensive than in Hyderabad.
Socio-cultural	Acceptable and non-acceptable factors within a national or local community	Meat products such as pork and beef are acceptable in some countries and included in many foodstuffs, in other countries it is considered inappropriate, so IKEA adapts its local menus.

(Continued)

Table 1.2 (Continued)

PESTLE element	Explanation	Examples of how this applies to IKEA
Technological	The availability and use of technology	IKEA is removing the use of its paper catalogue in favour of its website, but not all customers may be happy with this approach as they prefer to browse through a physical copy.
Legal	Product legislation Pricing legislation Place legislation Promotion legislation People legislation Processes legislation Physical evidence legislation Codes of Practice	IKEA needs to follow legislation in each country where it operates. This may mean some products are not for sale in some locations.
Environmental/ ecological	An awareness of environmental issues which may impact an organisation	IKEA produces a sustainability report to demonstrate its actions to mitigate climate change and has introduced recycling programmes in all stores.

To manage the different PESTLE factors, IKEA assesses the risks that could damage the business and organises frameworks and tools to reduce and manage the risks. The company's annual report recognises that practices vary in different locations and addresses key issues in its Code of Conduct which is shared and followed by all its managers, whether they're online or in stores.

Case questions

- IKEA is an international company with a large group of managers and access to expert lawyers. How can small organisations ensure they address all the PESTLE factors?
- IKEA stores take up large spaces, yet customers can easily order online. Is there still a place for the physical stores and, if so, why is this?
- Having considered the different PESTLE factors, which do you think is the most important for your college or university and why?

Activity 1.3   Identify risks and challenges with PESTLE

Using the PESTLE framework, identify potential risks or challenges for a clothing or food organisation that you know. Ensure the elements apply specifically to the organisation, with examples where possible.

COMPETITORS

Competitors are part of the digital business environment. According to Peteraf & Bergen (2003), they might address the same types of customers or they may have the same capabilities. Figure 1.3 presents the framework for competitor identification.

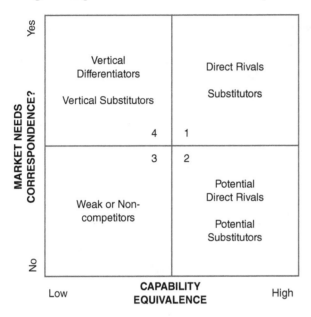

Figure 1.3   A framework for competitor identification

Source: Peteraf & Bergen (2003: 1034). Printed with permission of John Wiley

Let's unpack the framework for competitor identification. Boxes 4 and 1 are those where the market needs or customers are similar. Boxes 1 and 2 are where the organisation has the capabilities to fulfil these needs. Looking at box 1, this competitor has the same capability and the same customers, which makes it a direct rival or potentially a substitute product. For IKEA this could include the US-based company Wayfair or Amazon which can supply many home goods. These organisations are the greatest threats as they have the capability and may share the same market.

Box 2 is where the competitor has the capability but different types of customers; for example, a local furniture shop where personal service matters more. Box 4 is where the market or customers may be similar, but the organisation does not have the capabilities to manufacture and deliver at scale. This could include smaller online flatpack furniture companies who do not have physical stores or the ability to group several items together and buy online.

Finally, box 3 is where the company lacks the ability to compete and serves different markets. This could include a bespoke furniture maker.

SYSTEMS

The last part of the digital business framework is the system which incorporates the different aspects of technology. We'll explore this in more depth in Chapter 4 'Digital

Platforms, Payment Models and Pricing' and Chapter 6 'Enabling and Emerging Digital Technologies'.

1.4 BARRIERS TO ADOPTION OF DIGITAL BUSINESS

As over 5 billion people in the world have access to the internet, digital business should be everywhere. But it's not the case. Some organisations are slow to adopt digital processes for several reasons. Researchers Wilson & Mergel (2022) identified structural and cultural barriers within governments. Structural barriers consider how the government or individual departments are structured; one example given is legal frameworks as it may not be legally permissible to provide certain services via digital means. Read more about overcoming these barriers in Case Example 1.2, 'Estonia's digital government'.

Cultural barriers are more concerned with institutional processes, where the individuals are nervous of sharing material or have a mindset that digital is not to be trusted due to a lack of knowledge or awareness.

At a conference on computer and information science, researchers shared their work on the barriers to adoption by businesses (Rehman et al., 2021). The main structural barriers concerned investment and skills, as well as having the infrastructure in place to enable better digital processes. In businesses this may be an issue with the age of the technology – it's not just about buying one new computer, it may involve buying 100 or 1,000, which requires significant investment. Plus even when the new technology is in the organisation, it's about staff training to ensure the employees can use the systems well.

Looking at individuals, there are differences in internet usage based on age. According to Statista (2021: 3), 'over 30% of online users worldwide were aged between 25 and 34 years' and this contrasts with just 5.5% for those aged 65 or older. Researchers Neves & Mead (2021) looked at barriers to usage with older people and found they may lack access to the technology needed. This is echoed by other research that investigated the use of technology by older people during the COVID-19 pandemic (Murciano-Hueso et al., 2022). These researchers discovered that more older people adopted technology during the pandemic, yet there are still people with slower internet speeds which makes online access difficult. Murciano-Hueso et al. (2022) also found that sometimes it was the size of the technology, as using mobile phones to book appointments was not always helpful as the screens are too small.

DIGITAL TOOL   ITU DataHub

The International Telecommunication Union (ITU) is the United Nations' specialised agency for information and communication technologies – ICTs. It gathers statistics and data about ICTs worldwide. Its website allows you to search by indicators, such as connectivity and sustainability and country.

- You can explore it here: https://datahub.itu.int/

It may seem that it's only older people who don't adopt digital systems, but the European Commission also notes that 1 in 5 younger people lack digital skills (European Commission, 2021).

A summary of the different barriers is shown in Table 1.3.

Table 1.3   Barriers to adoption of digital processes

Sector	Structural barriers	Cultural barriers
Government	• Finances • Human resources • Legal frameworks • Lack of skills • Lack of technology • Lack of integration between departments	• Management support • Lack of awareness • Ethical concerns • Too busy to implement • Concerned about the risks
Organisations	• Finances • Lack of infrastructure • Lack of training • Lack of skills	• Concerned about the risks • Threats to jobs • Fear of change
Individuals	• Speed of technology • Device limitations • Lack of skills • Lack of training	• Concerned about the risks • Lack of understanding • Lack of support

Table 1.3 demonstrates that many of the structural and cultural barriers are the same, regardless of whether they're applied to governments, organisations or individuals.

CASE EXAMPLE 1.2   Estonia's digital government

Estonia is a European country with a population of around 1.3 million. It borders Latvia and Russia, with its capital Tallinn across the Gulf of Finland from Helsinki.

The country had little technological infrastructure in place and in 1994 prepared the 'Principles of Estonian Information Policy', which was a blueprint for IT development. This was followed by the Tiger Leap Initiative, which built capability by making computer skills a priority in schools.

As a commitment to a digital first society, in 2000 the Estonian government declared internet access to be a human right. Combining a country-wide IT infrastructure with skilled people allowed the government to digitalise many processes. This approach was known as e-Estonia.

Instead of building the whole infrastructure and the apps themselves, the government used existing technology from other countries. They stored the data in a **blockchain** (see Discover More). Part of the key to success was removing cultural barriers such as fear of data being shared or stolen and the lack of control. Each individual controls their own data and can decide what is shared, where and when. Plus every time data is requested, the individual is notified and accessing data without permission is a crime. When Estonia had a cybersecurity attack, the government went public very quickly. These steps helped to build trust about personal data and encouraged citizens to adopt the digital systems.

(Continued)

Having removed barriers to adoption of a digital system, citizens had access to many aspects of government online. This included tax records, identity cards and health records. Other processes were also digitalised, including voting and vehicle registration. If you called an emergency ambulance, they could check any medication you might be taking to ensure you had the right treatment at the right time. These online government services saved taxpayers both time and money as the administration was streamlined and centralised. A further benefit when dealing with government departments is that citizens need to provide their information only once, not constantly repeating the same details to several people. This also means when any forms have to be filled in, most of the data is already in place.

The government removed the structural barriers, enabling commercial organisations to offer digital services. This was led by banks and later legal services which traditionally had to take place face to face.

When the COVID-19 pandemic occurred, for Estonia it was business as usual. Many services were already online, internet access was stable and in the education sector many teachers were trained in digital education. The University of Tartu flipped to online teaching within a single day.

Although it is one of the smallest countries in Europe, it's considered as one of the most entrepreneurial countries in the world. Plus its strategic vision to build digital competence, capabilities and capacity places Estonia at the top of Europe's Digital Economy and Society Index.

Case questions

- What do you notice about how the Estonian government approached their plans for accessing digital services? Do you feel this could work in your country – why is this?
- What might be done to remove barriers for citizens to adopt e-government processes?
- How much of your personal data is online? Who controls or manages this data? How do you feel about this?

DISCOVER MORE ON BLOCKCHAIN

Read 'Blockchain Technology: Benefits, Challenges, Applications, and Integration of Blockchain Technology with Cloud Computing' by Habib et al. (2022). This article provides the background and explanations as to where and how blockchain is used.

1.5 DIGITAL BUSINESS AND SUSTAINABILITY

At the start of this chapter, we considered the United Nations' Global Goals for Sustainable Development (SDGs). Before the development of the SDGs, organisations considered corporate social responsibility (CSR). While this sounds like taking a responsibility for the social space where they were operating, the economist Milton Friedman argued that corporations did not have responsibilities, only people had responsibilities. Friedman's perspective was that companies had a duty to 'make as much money as possible' (Friedman, 1970: 1). While organisations need to make profits to survive, this was a binary view that considered enterprises as money machines, without considering their wider environment – the people employed, their location and local legislation which may hold company directors responsible for certain actions.

Since this time the concept of CSR has evolved. Researchers have defined it as an 'umbrella term that encompasses policies, processes, and practices (including disclosures) that firms put in place to improve the social state and well-being of their stakeholders and society (including the environment) whether undertaken voluntarily or mandated by rules, norms, and/or customs' (Zaman et al., 2022: 692).

This is still a complex area and was fraught with difficulties. For example, the McDonald's restaurant chain claims to be socially responsible yet tempts children with free toys. Fast food is recognised as a contributor to obesity in children which results in poor health.

The German car manufacturer Volkswagen had CSR policies in place, but still covered up carbon emissions (Zaman et al., 2022). The Italian oil company Eni claimed its diesel was green and helped the environment! In these cases the directors were legally challenged, had to pay large fines and manage damage to the brand name.

These examples show that CSR lacked meaning and was difficult to measure. Companies could say one thing and make false claims through **colour washing** practices (see Key Term). To ensure organisations took responsibility more action was needed. The United Nations in partnership with financial institutions issued the ground-breaking 'Who Cares Wins' report, which aimed to develop 'guidelines and recommendations on how to better integrate environmental, social and corporate governance' when assessing a company's performance (The Global Compact, 2004: i). To further strengthen the concept of environmental, social and governance (ESG) issues, this report recommended that companies should share details on their ESG policies. Plus, the report was endorsed by most major banks, investors and investment managers – it carried more importance.

Researchers have provided some helpful definitions of the different factors and what these include (Li et al., 2021: 2):

- **Environmental factors** that negatively impact on energy consumption and efficiency, air pollutants, waste production and management, and their impact on biodiversity and ecosystems
- **Social factors** such as workforce freedom, child labour, health and safety at work, discrimination and diversity, poverty and community impact
- **Governance factors** such as business principles, accountability, transparency and disclosure, board diversity and structure, stakeholder engagement

All the ESG factors relate to digital business, from energy consumption and data storage, to keeping photos, contacts and posts safe, workforce freedom and the diversity of boards. ESG has had an impact on many organisations that include an ESG report in the investor relations area of their website.

Smartphone Sixty Seconds® – Find the ESG reports

- To see who's reporting on ESG, take out your mobile phone and search for the name of your favourite company + ESG.
- Do they have an ESG report or ESG goals?
- How do you feel about their ESG goals? Are they credible?

KEY TERM   COLOUR WASHING

Washing cleans clothes and companies make claims to 'wash' their brand or products, signalling support for certain values. This is a deceptive practice that hides the reality, which may be the opposite.

Examples of colour washing include:

- Greenwashing – claim to be environmentally friendly. For example Drax, an energy company promoting itself as a renewable energy company, but burning wood pellets and releasing harmful chemicals outside factories in the USA
- Brownwashing – claim to support people of colour and combat racism. For example, New Balance footwear supporting the Black Lives Matter campaign while its CEO was funding a politician making racist statements
- Pinkwashing – claim to support women or breast cancer. For example, the manufacturer 3M (which is better known for their Post-it® notes) holds breast cancer awareness events. Yet in some of their manufacturing processes they still use toxic chemicals (PFAs) that can contribute to cancer

---

Digital business and sustainability are closely connected. At the same time, colour washing is growing as organisations try to improve their external appearance. The United Nations' SDGs provide a useful framework to assess sustainability within all organisations.

JOURNAL OF NOTE

Government Information Quarterly looks at the connections between policies, information technology, government and the public across different countries. When new technologies are proposed, this journal explores the potential impact on the government, as well as the public served.

CASE STUDY

PAYPAL'S DIGITAL BUSINESS ENVIRONMENT

This case study continues in all chapters.

Launched in 1998, the online payment system PayPal became well known when they partnered with eBay to take and make payments in the buyer and seller community. Before PayPal, purchases on eBay needed a cheque or money order to be sent, before the goods were despatched.

PayPal has nearly 450 million active accounts, processes over 5 billion transactions and trades in over 200 markets. This means that its external environment is complex as it has to obtain regulatory licences to operate in every single jurisdiction – over 200 permissions, regulation systems to follow and adhere to.

Several aspects of PESTLE are addressed by PayPal, in particular the political, technological, legal and environmental issues.

Within the political environment, changing policies and legislation can provide an opportunity, or a potential threat. In order to manage possible threats, PayPal participates in lobbying activity.

It recognises the technological environment that created the business opportunity but also raises potential threats, and as noted in PayPal (2021: 17): 'Many areas in which we compete evolve rapidly with innovative and disruptive technologies, shifting user preferences and needs … and frequent introductions of new products and services.'

From a legal perspective, the key elements to be addressed by this online payment provider are anti-money laundering, counter-terrorist financing and sanctions. These are managed at a global level, as well as at a local compliance level to ensure the company does not infringe on the law in a particular area. Breaking the law through a misdemeanour, or failure to address and carefully monitor these issues, could result in the company gaining negative publicity, brand damage, being asked to pay large fines or, at worst, being closed down in some countries.

Compliance and ensuring the organisation follows the rules create risks. In its annual report PayPal (2021: 13) notes that: 'Our business is subject to extensive government regulation and oversight. Our failure to comply with extensive, complex, overlapping, and frequently changing rules, regulations, and legal interpretations could materially harm our business.'

It may seem that the main risks to the business are political, legal and technological, but PayPal also faces ecological/environmental issues. Its annual report (PayPal, 2021: 12) lists many risks due to environmental issues, including 'earthquakes, hurricanes, floods, fires, and other natural disasters, public health crises (including pandemics)'.

Extending its consideration of environmental factors, PayPal has conducted a materiality assessment of how it responds to social and governance (ESG) issues. To do this, the company has mapped out the increasing importance of factors from an external stakeholder perspective and an internal perspective. This is shown in Figure 1.4 (PayPal, 2021: 33).

(Continued)

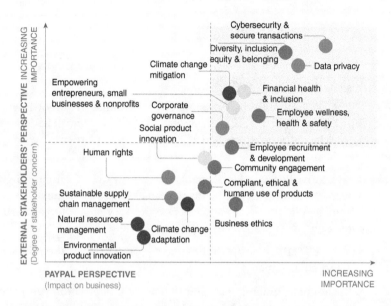

Figure 1.4   PayPal Environmental, Social and Governance (ESG) Materiality Assessment

Source: PayPal (2023a: 40). Printed with permission of PayPal

As Figure 1.4 shows, these areas of concern are categorised into several groups. Two of the three areas of greatest concern are in responsible business practices: cybersecurity and ensuring data privacy is maintained, involving a breach of the secure platform or the customers' data. Both of these factors would have a material impact on the business with fines for data breaches, and a temporary halt of the business due to cybersecurity.

The next area of greatest concern in the top right-hand corner is diversity, inclusion, equity and belonging, in the employees and cultures category. To make this happen, PayPal has allocated $15 million towards ensuring under-represented groups are featured more in their recruitment and promotion processes.

CASE QUESTIONS

PayPal has identified several areas of concern based on their impact on the business and their stakeholders. They have decided some elements are more important than others. The critical factors are shown in the top right-hand corner of Figure 1.4.

- Is PayPal right that these are the most important factors or do you feel other items should be more important?

- Adapting to climate change seems to be lower on the list of elements that would have an impact on PayPal. Why is this?

- How often should this assessment be updated and why?

FURTHER EXERCISES

1. Apply the digital business framework to an organisation of your choice. Use Figure 1.2 as a template to evaluate the different internal and external factors that impact on the organisation.

2. Create a plan to overcome the main cultural barriers to the adoption of digital business raised by individuals.

3. For an organisation of your choice, create an initiative that will demonstrate its environmental, social and corporate governance policies.

4. In the future, all government services will be digital. Discuss.

SUMMARY

This chapter has explored:

- The notion of value for customers and from the 7Ps
- The digital business framework, its internal and external factors
- The structural and cultural barriers to the adoption of digital business
- The connection between digital business and sustainability

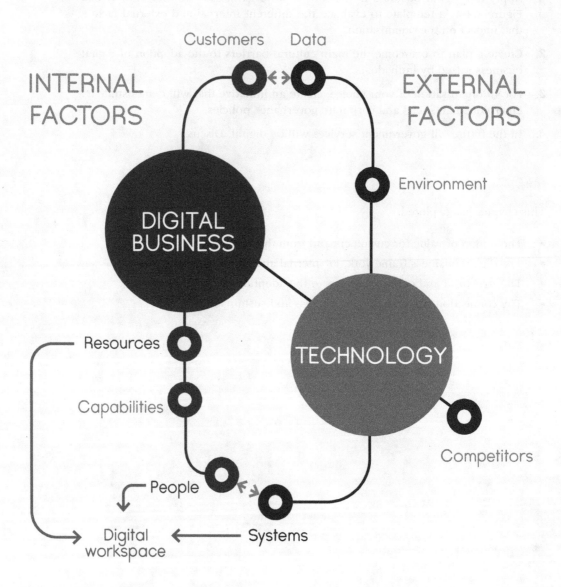

2
THE DIGITAL WORKSPACE

PROFESSIONAL SKILLS

When you have worked through this chapter, you should be able to:

- Write and create digital content for different audiences
- Interpret, communicate and brief internal or external stakeholders on digital business requirements

2.1 BACKGROUND TO THE DIGITAL WORKSPACE

Technology has transformed how people work and has created the digital workspace. Our digital workspace can be defined as 'a way of describing the broad set of connected technologies that employees use on a daily basis to do their jobs' (Marsh, 2018: 16). This means that we no longer need to visit a physical office as we can connect to all our resources, from work files to customer data, through **cloud computing** (see Key Term) using our laptop on the kitchen table, in a coffee shop or in a collaborative workspace.

KEY TERM   CLOUD COMPUTING

According to researchers at the National Institute of Standards and Technology (Mell & Grance, 2011: 2), 'Cloud computing is a model for enabling ubiquitous, convenient, on-demand network access to a shared pool of configurable computing resources (e.g., networks, servers, storage, applications, and services) that can be rapidly provisioned and released with minimal management effort or service provider interaction'. It means that your files and other materials are stored centrally so you can access them from anywhere. So whether you're at uni, work or home you can log on to any device to access your OneDrive or GoogleDrive.

It wasn't always this way and it isn't possible for everyone to work from home as not everyone has access to cloud services (see Digital Tool: **The Global Cloud Ecosystem Index**). Traditional workplaces were formally organised, centralised, one-dimensional environments. The workplace included assigned workstations or personal offices that contained your work computer which connected to a server based inside the office. This was not somewhere to have fun or relax, but somewhere to be serious and work. This changed when the early dot.com companies in Silicon Valley in the USA (e.g. Google, Facebook) started to provide free fruit, games rooms and casual dress codes. But work still happened in the physical office.

DIGITAL TOOL   The Global Cloud Ecosystem Index

The Global Cloud Ecosystem Index tool shows the availability of cloud services in 76 countries. It considers the technology and regulations and the ease of access to cloud computing.

- You can explore it here to see how your country compares to others' technology: review.com/2022/04/25/1051115/global-cloud-ecosystem-index-2022

The digital business framework (see Figure 1.2) illustrated that key internal factors are people, resources and capabilities which are often framed in a recognised working environment. It is no longer about a workplace but a *workspace*, as one of the major phenomena that occurred during the pandemic was the idea of working from home. Suddenly free from the daily commute, thousands of people started working from home – or perhaps living at work?

This chapter reviews the challenges and opportunities in the digital workspace, as well as constraints to the adoption and embedding of new technology in organisations.

2.2 HOW WE WORK

The traditional approach to work as an employee working for a single company for many years is becoming unusual. You may be a freelancer, taking projects with specific organisations over a period of time, or you may respond to specific one-off requirements which are added to crowdsourced websites. Or you may work in an agency where an organisation outsources entire functions such as marketing, human resources (HR), facilities management or logistics.

DIGITAL TOOL   LinkedIn as a recruitment platform

Many recruiters and companies use LinkedIn as a recruitment platform, so it's not just a professional social media network.

- As an example you can explore the available vacancies for PayPal here: linkedin.com/company/paypal/jobs

Before the COVID-19 pandemic, most office employees needed to be present in the office to work. We know the role of technology at work was changing, but the pandemic accelerated the process. Reporters called it 'the World's Largest Work-From-Home Experiment' (Banjo et al., 2020). As Banjo and colleagues noted, working from home was once seen as a privilege, rather than a necessity (2020), but this has continued and is widely accepted and recognised as hybrid working.

Figure 2.1 shows how technology has facilitated alternative methods of working, as well as different workspaces.

We'll explore varying worker roles and alternative workspaces in the following sections.

2.2.1 THE GIG ECONOMY

The gig or platform economy is where 'freelancers take flexible or short contracts to undertake pieces of work' (Hanlon, 2022a: 341). Many well-known companies such as Uber, Etsy and Airbnb are part of the gig economy, which can be partly described as the sharing economy as individuals share their cars, talents or homes.

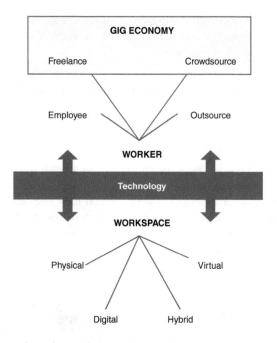

Figure 2.1   Varying worker roles and alternative workspaces

The platform operator matches the provider and the consumer temporarily to make the exchange. Technology facilitates the connections and automates processes. Plus the work is often crowdsourced, open to a pool of providers and allocated to the one that can meet the consumer's needs at that time. Figure 2.2 shows a framework of the different elements in the sharing economy.

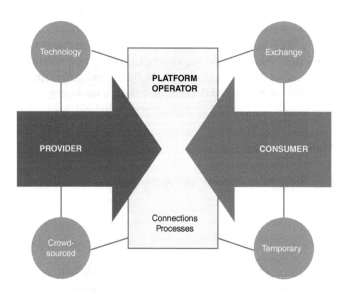

Figure 2.2   Framework of the different elements in the sharing economy

Source: Adapted from Hanlon (2022a: 36)

The advantages of gig work or platform work are the flexibility to choose when to work and what work to take on. But there are downsides, including:

- No employment protection
- No paid time off
- Mainly lower paid work such as delivering food or conducting microtasks
- Less power in the relationship
- Some platforms use algorithms to promote the work
- Dependence on the platform for work
- Most people have at least 2 gig jobs to gain an income

In spite of the downsides, the gig economy is growing. In several countries, from India to the USA, the gig economy is considered so important that it is recognised as making a financial contribution to the country.

DISCOVER MORE ON GIG WORK

Read 'Changing nature of work and employment in the gig economy: The role of culture building and leadership in sustaining commitment and job satisfaction' by Thomas & Baddipudi (2022). This article explores more about the gig economy and its characteristics as well as the issues faced by workers in this environment.

DIGITAL TOOL   Gig work platforms

Some organisations share gig work on platforms that are promoted in one country or across several geographical areas. To understand what's required to share a job or apply for a job explore these platforms here or search for one in your local area:

- Worldwide www.upwork.com
- India www.workflexi.in
- Norway no.gigexchange.com

Activity 2.1   Evaluate the platform economy and gig work

As a student, you may be part of the platform economy and take on gig work to fund your studies. If not, you may know friends or family who are providing gig work opportunities or participating in gig work.

Evaluate the platform economy, either from the perspective of (a) a gig worker or (b) a company needing to outsource small, irregular tasks. What are the advantages and disadvantages that may arise?

2.2.2 THE OUTSOURCE MODEL

An alternative to a gig model that moves from a temporary or one-off situation is outsourcing. Outsourcing is a way for organisations to sub-contract specific services or processes. For example, an organisation might outsource its marketing operations to an agency, its human resource management to an expert firm of HR professionals or manufacturing of its clothing. Outsourcing takes different forms, as Table 2.1 demonstrates.

Table 2.1   Offshoring, nearshoring and onshoring

Outsource format	What this means	Example	Advantages	Disadvantages
Offshoring	Outsourcing to a different country where labour costs may be cheaper	The UK clothing industry moved large amounts of manufacturing production to Morocco, India and Vietnam to produce lower-cost goods	• This can provide local jobs in areas with less employment • There is a cost saving	• Ethically it can be questionable to use cheap labour in another country • As the factory is located in another country, if there are errors they may not be noticed until the goods are in the store
Nearshoring	Outsourcing to a nearby country where running costs or taxes may be lower	High-tech firms have moved customer service to countries like Ireland where there is a highly skilled workforce and lower company taxes	• The location is nearby and easy to monitor • The higher education levels can add value to the business	• This can miss opportunities to develop skills at a local level • It can create unemployment in a local area when the jobs are moved
Onshoring	Domestic offshoring, outsourcing the service to another organisation in the same country due to their expertise and efficiency	Food companies moving food processing and distribution to another company in the same country or large companies moving their HR functions to a specialist third party	• This upgrades processes in the business • There are fewer logistics challenges • This improves efficiency for the business • There may be greater access to expert knowledge	• This can be more expensive, which increases costs to customers • The business no longer controls key processes in the business

DISCOVER MORE ON OUTSOURCING

Read 'Taxonomy of outsourcing alternatives through systematic literature review' by Cesar Augusto López Ramírez and colleagues (2022). This article introduces the purpose of outsourcing with examples, along with the different characteristics of nearshoring and offshoring.

CASE EXAMPLE 2.1 Unisys Australia and the digital workplace

Unisys is a business-to-business (B2B) company that provides IT services to businesses and governments. This includes cloud computing as well as digital services in the workplace: 'We help our clients create the world's leading digital workplace experiences by transforming their end-user experience to engage and retain employees; increase collaboration and innovation; and drive productivity and business growth' (Unisys, 2021: 1).

Founded in the USA, they have over 15,000 employees worldwide of which 32% are female. They are striving to make their workforce more diverse. Unisys has a 'strong presence in Australia, with 900 staff, and has offices that offer managed workforce solutions in Sydney and Melbourne' (iSG Provider Lens, 2022: 25). According to iSG Provider Lens (2022: 4), Australian enterprises increasingly require a flexible, adaptable digital workplace that allows them to change how their employees work, where they work, and how they collaborate.

This means that as the workspace is transitioning from a traditional 'in person, in office' to hybrid and digital working models, new challenges are arising. One of the biggest issues is the security of the data being handled by staff. In a typical office, the data is stored on desktop PCs. But staff are being encouraged to BYOD (bring your own device) and, combined with working from home, the devices may be vulnerable to external threats. Plus other family members may download apps or also share the device. This means that security threats to organisations may accidentally be introduced by staff using their own laptops who inadvertently download viruses or other forms of malware that could compromise the security of client data.

To manage these issues, Unisys has created BYOD policies so that staff understand good practice. In addition to the policies, the firm helps employees implement good practice and share how to configure remote working, regardless of where the employees are based. Part of their solution is a dedicated product, CloudForte®, which they describe as 'a comprehensive suite of digital services to help accelerate the secure move of data and applications to the cloud' (Unisys, 2021: 2).

Security is critical for firms like Unisys which also managed biometric access for the prison service in Australia, although there have been concerns raised by people working in human rights about the use of biometrics in the prison service.

Unisys, like Microsoft, is leading the move to 'workplace as a service' where employees log in to an intranet that takes the user through all the security settings and ensures the websites visited are secure. Commercial market research has recognised the contribution Unisys makes to the market and placed Unisys Australia as a leader in the field of digital workspaces. According to The Insight Partners (2022), the workplace services market is growing and expected to reach US$193 billion by 2028.

Case questions

Unisys Australia is a successful software company employing thousands of people around the work with a recognised presence in Australia.

- How do you think that Unisys manages the balance between offering employers the security that they need, without infringing on the rights of individual employees?
- What do you think about the growth in the digital workplace as a service? Will this continue or will there be a return to traditional office working?
- Where should the use of biometrics be considered with caution?

2.3 THE ROLE OF DIGITAL TECHNOLOGIES AT WORK

2.3.1 NURTURING COLLABORATION

Collaboration is defined by Appley & Winder (1977: 281) as:

> a relational system in which (1) individuals in a group share mutual aspirations and a common framework, (2) the interactions among individuals are characterized by 'justice as fairness', and (3) these aspirations and conceptualizations are characterized by each individual's consciousness of his/her motives toward the other; by caring or concern for the other; and by commitment to work with the other over time provided that this commitment is a matter of choice.

A later definition of e-collaboration by Kock (2005: i) suggests that it is 'collaboration using electronic technologies among different individuals to accomplish a common task'. The common link between these definitions is individuals working together for a shared purpose. But sometimes the workloads vary and some team members may be free riding (Cherney et al., 2018), not doing their fair share yet gaining the same benefits. For example, if you're working on a university group project, some members of the group may put in more effort and more hours than others who do little, but one grade is assigned to the entire group. Worse still, some group members can pull the grades of the others down, by not contributing much. Known as free riding or **social loafing** (see Key Term), some people put less effort into group work than they would do if working alone.

KEY TERM   SOCIAL LOAFING

According to researchers Simms & Nichols (2014), the notion of social loafing was first identified by French engineer Ringelmann in 1913. He noticed that when a group pulled on a rope (this was back in the last century!), presumably to move a large object, the overall effort was lower than when the group members pulled individually. Some group members made less effort as others were doing most of the work for them. Moving to 1974, the term social loafing was introduced by other researchers (Ingham, Levinger, Graves and Peckham) checking to see if this still occurred, which it did.

Digital technologies have evolved to enable greater collaboration in online communication, interaction and materials management, including:

- Workplace communication
- Accessing diaries to check availability for meetings
- Sending instant messages to work colleagues
- Quick calls using online tools
- Online interaction
- Holding meetings regardless of where people are located
- Managing and delivering presentations

- Materials management
- Working on documents, graphic materials and videos together
- Seeing the changes to documents in real time
- Sharing documents and other available materials 24/7

Collaboration software increased during the pandemic (Zandt, 2021) and includes Microsoft Teams, which has the largest share of the market. The number of Microsoft Teams users increased from 2 million worldwide in 2017 to 270 million in 2022 (Vailshery, 2022). Teams is followed by Google and other tools include CISCO, Slack, LogMeIn and Zoom.

Researchers (Jung et al., 2023; Sahakiants & Dorner, 2021) examining online collaboration tools have noted the benefits as:

- Being able to collaborate remotely
- Sharing information
- Gaining soft skills such as people and communication skills
- Building a sense of community

The researchers (Jung et al., 2023; Sahakiants & Dorner, 2021) also identified downsides of online collaboration, including:

- The lack of face-to-face contact
- Internet censorship depending on the region
- Potential connectivity problems
- Lack of technical support
- Fear about data protection and privacy
- Information and communication overload

They recommend that organisations need to provide a digital infrastructure to give users the support needed to manage information overload and other issues that may be encountered. While training in how to use the tools is also recommended, many collaboration tools provide their own online training; e.g. Microsoft Teams has a dedicated support website and Google Workspace has a Learning Centre.

Activity 2.2   Create a collaborative online project

Imagine you are responsible for organising an event at uni to raise money for a charity of your choice. This could be a bake sale, concert, sporting activity or another event of your choice. In a group of 5 to 8 use Trello as an online project management tool.

Trello makes it easy to visualise activities in one place. Each section, such as 'to do', 'doing' and 'done', has a separate list column. In each list there are cards, and individual activities to be completed. As the cards are completed, move them along into the relevant list.

(Continued)

- Organise an online meeting using Zoom, Teams, Google Meet or another desktop tool as you'll need to be able to share screens
- Go to trello.com and sign up for a free account
- Select one of the project management templates (e.g. Simple Project Board)
- Brainstorm ideas for your event
- Agree which one works and discuss why
- Create a Trello Board to manage your idea
- Identify the actions needed to make this happen and who will be responsible
- Plan dates for your next online meeting
- Review how well Trello did or didn't work for your team and why

Smartphone Sixty Seconds® – Find collaboration tools

- Take out your mobile phone and search for 'collaboration tools'
- How many do you find?
- Have you ever used any of these collaboration tools?
- Why do you think this is a growing business?
- What are the best and worst factors about collaboration tools?

2.3.2 MONITORING PRESENCE

Digital technology facilitates many aspects of business but can also feel like ongoing monitoring. In the past, hourly paid factory workers manually recorded the time they arrived at work and the time they finished. This was known as *clocking in* as workers pushed a card into a clock machine to gain a time-stamp for their wages to be calculated. But workers could cheat the system if they 'clocked in' for a friend, putting their friend's card into the machine even though they hadn't arrived at work!

Traditional clocking in has been replaced with biometric access methods such as fingerprint or iris scanning which records entry and exit data. Although this is mainly designed as a record-keeping system, it also acts as a health and safety function, so if there is a fire, the fire fighters know exactly how many people are in the building and it ensures they don't take unnecessary risks.

Organisations have had the ability to monitor employees' activities for some time, even if you're not physically in the office. Technology can track when you access, read or send emails (Becker et al., 2021), or become visible on collaboration tools (e.g. Teams, Slack, Hubstaff). As researcher Debora Jeske (2022) observes, it is a way to mitigate risks and check performance, but also assumes employees are not to be trusted! Introducing monitoring tools into the workplace can have negative effects. For example, employees might not be consulted about the surveillance tools and this could result in counter-productive work behaviour (Jeske, 2022).

Smartphone Sixty Seconds® – Explore biometric access

- Take out your mobile phone and search for 'biometric access'.
- Click on the option to view images.
- Have you ever used biometric access? In what context?
- How do you feel about your fingerprints or irises being stored online?

2.4 CHALLENGES AND OPPORTUNITIES IN THE DIGITAL WORKSPACE

According to the European Commission (EU), technology at work can enhance efficiency. The European Commission also believes that technology has a role to play in improving working conditions (2021b: 7): 'digital technologies can support workers and offer better adapted working environments, with ICT-based personalised systems, wearables and mobile health applications'.

In addition to these opportunities identified by the EU, other issues include the work–life balance and the phenomenon of technostress which is discussed in the next sections.

2.4.1 WORK–LIFE BALANCE

Hybrid working or working from home isn't fun, or available for everyone. Many people struggle to achieve **work–life balance** (see Key Term). Plus any form of working from home may not be available to people without fast internet access or those who care for relatives or young children with constant interruptions at home.

KEY TERM   WORK–LIFE BALANCE

Work–life balance (WLB) is considered to be a situation where individuals gain equal amounts of satisfaction at work and at home (Calvin Ong & Jeyaraj, 2014). It is viewed as a simplistic measure where work and home conflict, competing for attention. If you undertake too much work and your home life suffers, this is having a poor work–life balance.

Within a digital environment, work–life balance has become harder to achieve. Employees who physically go to the office no longer finish work at the end of the day as they may be available at any time via email, direct messages and online tools (e.g. Teams or Zoom). Those working from home may face other challenges, as researchers exploring WLB during the pandemic (Shirmohammadi et al., 2022) identified.

This included stress factors or stressors, as employees had more work to do and for longer hours (work intensity). Many people lacked a dedicated office space and were competing with family members for the kitchen table (workplace limitation).

Shirmohammadi and colleagues identified other factors that impacted on WLB during the pandemic. Employees felt alone (professional isolation) when working without the usual social interaction with colleagues. And in some cases, employees weren't able to deliver the work as needed because they were dependent on other colleagues to deliver some elements of the work (who may have been struggling) and the usual office conversations weren't available (work interdependence).

The WLB also created 'non-work domain stressors' such as having to look after other family members at the same time (care–work intensity). This was especially true when children were not permitted to attend school during the pandemic and the formally organised lockdowns were in place. Working from home – or living at work – created more housework, such as extra cooking and cleaning due to staying at home all the time. This contributed to greater emotional demands and feeling stressed.

In some cases, employees who are unhappy with their work–life balance have started to change their approach to work and focus on only what's needed. This is known as '**quiet quitting**' (see Ethical Insights).

ETHICAL INSIGHTS   Quiet quitting

Quiet quitting has been described as 'opting out of tasks beyond one's assigned duties and/or becoming less psychologically invested in work' (Klotz & Bolino, 2022: 1). Effectively you are still at work, but delivering the bare minimum as detailed in your job description, and you've mentally disengaged from the organisation.

- What examples of quiet quitting have you witnessed and what factors do you think contributed to it?
- How can organisations ensure their staff are fulfilled and happy at work?

On the positive side of working from home, many employees had greater flexibility (job autonomy) and were provided with support from their organisations. Some were able to make changes to accommodate the new way of working (personal adaptability) or gained more support from their families.

Figure 2.3 shows the earlier factors that occur (the antecedents) which can lead to different outcomes in the work–life balance.

Although this research was based on lived experiences during the pandemic, many of the work and non-work domain stressors remain for those working from home. After the pandemic, many employees re-evaluated their workplaces and decided to quit their jobs, which resulted in a phenomenon called **The Great Resignation** (see Key Term).

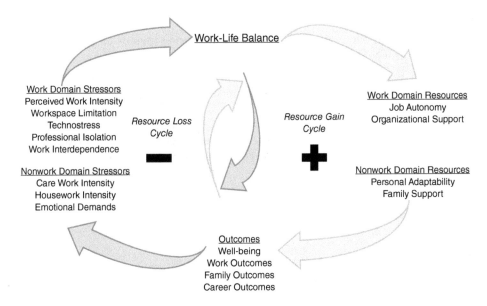

Figure 2.3 An integrative model of the antecedents and outcomes of WLB while working from home during the pandemic

Source: Shirmohammadi et al. (2022: 10)

KEY TERM THE GREAT RESIGNATION

After the COVID-19 pandemic, many people had the opportunity to review their work–life balance and voluntarily quit their jobs; this was termed the 'Great Resignation' as over 47 million Americans left their workplace (Fuller & Kerr, 2022). This didn't just happen in the USA. It was witnessed in many countries in Europe and also recognised in India. In Australia fewer people quit working, but many changed jobs (the great reshuffle). However, there are arguments that this was not because of the pandemic, but due to the Five Rs: retirement, relocation, reconsideration, reshuffling and reluctance (Fuller & Kerr, 2022). The pandemic provided employees with thinking time to decide what they did – and didn't – want to do.

2.4.2 TECHNOSTRESS

As the research by Shirmohammadi et al. (2022) demonstrated, another factor was trying to manage technostress with excessive use of technology, all day, every day.

One way that technostress became evident was with Zoom fatigue. Dr Robby Nadler (2020: 2) calls this computer-mediated communication exhaustion, as having communication between yourself and another person separated by a screen was both mentally and physically tiring, especially as the volume of online meetings has increased.

Other researchers (Fauville et al., 2021) identified other elements of Zoom fatigue, such as:

- Staring at a larger version of colleagues on screen
- The change in non-verbal behaviour such as putting thumbs-up when on mute, which you wouldn't do if you were face to face
- The way that the online video seems like a mirror where you're suddenly looking at yourself and evaluating your appearance

Professor Géraldine Fauville (2021) and colleagues decided to test the concept of Zoom exhaustion and fatigue, and created a scale, which they later refined based on their evidence from 2,724 participants. The final Zoom Exhaustion & Fatigue Scale is shown in Table 2.2.

Table 2.2 Zoom Exhaustion & Fatigue Scale

Constructs	Questions
General Fatigue	1. How tired do you feel after video conferencing?
	2. How exhausted do you feel after video conferencing?
	3. How mentally drained do you feel after video conferencing?
Visual Fatigue	4. How blurred does your vision get after video conferencing?
	5. How irritated do your eyes feel after video conferencing?
	6. How much do your eyes hurt after video conferencing?
Social Fatigue	7. How much do you tend to avoid social situations after video conferencing?
	8. How much do you want to be alone after video conferencing?
	9. How much do you need time by yourself after video conferencing?
Motivational Fatigue	10. How much do you dread having to do things after video conferencing?
	11. How often do you feel like doing nothing after video conferencing?*
	12. How often do you feel too tired to do other things after video conferencing?*
Emotional Fatigue	13. How emotionally drained do you feel after video conferencing?
	14. How irritable do you feel after video conferencing?
	15. How moody do you feel after video conferencing?

Source: Fauville et al. (2021: 5). Printed with permission of Elsevier

Activity 2.3 Apply the Zoom Exhaustion & Fatigue Scale

Using Table 2.2, assess how you feel about online lectures and seminars. Score each item on a scale of 1 = 'Not at all' to 5 = 'Extremely'. For questions 11 and 12 (starred), use 1 = 'Never', 2 = 'Rarely', 3 = 'Sometimes', 4 = 'Often' to 5 = 'Always'. The lowest score possible is 15, and the highest possible score is 75.

This is not a competition to see who gains the highest score, but an evaluation to see how you feel about using video-conferencing tools, such as Zoom or Teams. Test yourself and compare your scores with your classmates.

Consider why some had higher scores than others and what actions could be taken to reduce the higher scores.

2.5 THE FUTURE OF WORK

How work changes over time is an area that Professor Lina Vyas (2022), writing in the journal *Policy and Society*, has considered. Vyas's work forecasts 7 key trends in the labour market and the WLB, which will be accelerated, become part of our normal working life or change in some way. These are shown in Table 2.3.

Table 2.3 Forecasting key trends in the labor market and WLB

Trend	Acceleration	Normalization	Remodeling
Accelerated digital transformation	X		
Emergence of hybrid work	X		
The continued existence of the "office"			X
Changes in organizational infrastructure and labor mobility	X	X	X
The challenges of performance management and atomistic tendencies at work		X	X
Potential exacerbation of existing inequalities	X		X
Managing work–life balance	X	X	

Source: Vyas (2022: 159). Printed with permission of Oxford University Press

Accelerated digital transformation has been evidenced by the uptick in online collaboration tools. This has seen the emergence of hybrid work and, at the same time, the continued existence of the 'office'. Yet there are challenges for those who may have fewer technical skills; this means that existing inequalities become worse rather than better, although there are some organisations, such as the Fundación Cibervoluntarios (see Case Example 2.2), who are trying to support individuals and remove inequalities.

CASE EXAMPLE 2.2   Fundación Cibervoluntarios

One of the challenges with the future of work is existing inequalities, such as those who are less skilled with technology remain at a disadvantage in securing work. In Spain, a group was established in 2001 to help mitigate the difficulties individuals face. This is known as Fundación Cibervoluntarios (the Cyber Volunteers Foundation) which has recruited a network of over 25,000 volunteers who have helped over 2 million people (Fundación Cibervoluntarios, 2022).

Their aims (Fundación Cibervoluntarios, 2021) are:

- To promote the adoption and use of technology
- To promote cyber-volunteering
- To create social awareness of information technology
- To remove barriers to knowledge
- To promote responsible participation

(Continued)

This is a free service and some of the support they provide includes:

- Individual digital skills training
- On-demand video tutorials
- Access to a helpline for urgent queries

Recognised as an exemplar of good practice, the Foundation has won many awards. The *Financial Times* has included the Foundation in its list of Europe's 100 digital champions (Speare-Cole & Mitevska, 2018). The *Financial Times* stated the following:

One of the aims is to alleviate the 'digital divide' between different social groups, and so volunteers focus on reaching communities most at risk of digital exclusion. It works with over 500 grassroots charity associations supporting the elderly, migrants, people with mental health difficulties and the unemployed.

The volunteers who deliver the training can choose when they have time available. The Foundation has created an online management tool so that volunteers can upload their own profile. The online management tool enables volunteers participate in existing activities or suggest new training which may be needed. The volunteers represent a diverse group of people.

The organisation gains funding from the EU and Spanish governments, as well as donations from the Google Foundation and private individuals.

Case questions

The Fundación Cibervoluntarios is run by volunteers who are keen to ensure that people do not miss opportunities due to their lack of digital skills.

- What's your impression of the Fundación Cibervoluntarios? Should it be the responsibility of volunteers to provide digital training?
- What other examples can you think of that support those who need to improve their digital skills?
- Do you volunteer for an organisation and, if so, what motivated you to get involved? How does this make a difference to you, as well as those you help?

FLEXIBILITY VERSUS AVAILABILITY

Your workplace might be a physical environment such as an office, classroom or restaurant, or it may be digital via Zoom or Teams. The trend is moving towards a hybrid model where employees work in the office 1 to 3 days a week and the remainder work from home. This still requires some form of a physical office. While those working from home may benefit from greater flexibility without the commute to work, they may be working longer hours and expected to respond to urgent queries at any time (Vyas, 2022) as they are considered to be always available. This contributes to work domain stressors (Shirmohammadi et al., 2022).

As work–life balance considers work and our personal lives to be separated, an alternative concept is **work–life harmony** (see Key Term) where instead of being 2 distinct areas, the situations complement each other.

KEY TERM WORK–LIFE HARMONY

Work–life harmony is a different concept from work–life balance which recognises how work and home life may be blended. It is defined as 'An individually pleasing, congruent arrangement of work and life roles that is interwoven into a single narrative of life' (McMillan et al., 2011: 15).

This is a holistic perspective which recognises that part of your work life may enter your personal life, such as work colleagues who become friends, which enriches your home life.

Another emerging form of work is operating in mixed environments, working in augmented and virtual reality in the workplace. Mark Zuckerberg and Meta are promoting the use of 'Horizon Workrooms' or workrooms as a way to access **the metaverse** (see Key Term). However, researchers (Cheng et al., 2022) have identified several technical challenges as domestic broadband may not be able to cope with the speeds needed for streaming high-resolution video. Meta's Workrooms are not the only virtual reality environment for work. Google has Project Starline (Jin, 2021) and SK Telecom in South Korea has launched Ifland. The challenge is scaling the technology to enable there to be many people in the same room at the same time whilst maintaining the quality of the experience.

KEY TERM THE METAVERSE

The metaverse is a concept from science fiction and is 'broadly defined as a highly immersive virtual world where people gather to socialize, play, and work, sought to transport communities to other worlds, but within the same physical space' (Hanlon, 2022: 1).

The term was first used in 1992 in the book *Snow Crash* by Neal Stephenson (2011), which used a 'combination of the prefix "meta" (meaning transcending) and the word "universe"' (Cheng, et al., 2022: 141). Yet the idea existed decades beforehand. 'The Veldt', a scary short story by Ray Bradbury (1950), described a 'sentient hyper-realistic room' used by children seeking entertainment which had tragic consequences. In the 1960s, researcher Morton Heilig filed a patent for the Sensorama Simulator, a multi-sensory enclosed cinema booth which incorporated the senses of touch and smell to enrich the user's experience.

DISCOVER MORE ON THE METAVERSE

Read the blog article 'Metaverse – together alone?' published in the *LSE Business Review* (https://blogs.lse.ac.uk/businessreview/2022/06/01/metaverse-together-alone) as this post provides the background to the metaverse, both the opportunities and the challenges.

JOURNAL OF NOTE

The *Journal of Management* considers business strategy and policy, organisational behaviour and human resource management, which makes it a useful resource for looking at the future of work.

CASE STUDY

PAYPAL'S DIGITAL WORKSPACE

PayPal employs over 30,000 people, representing around 150 nationalities, in 30 countries. Just over 40% of staff are based in the USA with the remaining 60% located across the world.

There are indications that PayPal is a great place to work. In 2022 the firm was included on the Forbes list of America's Best Large Employers. On Glassdoor, a worldwide employer review site where employees can feed back anonymously about the company, their salary levels and the recruitment process, PayPal has a rating of 4.4 out of 5, with over 80% who would recommend it to a friend and 98% approving of the CEO.

The company has a Global Wellness Advocate and organises wellness days where staff can take time to recharge their energy levels. To check how staff are feeling, there is an annual survey. This provides feedback for the directors who can decide what action to take as a result of the employee comments.

When applying for jobs, candidates can select their preferences: 'between on-site, fully virtual, and hybrid, we offer a variety of ways to work together. Search by city, country, and region to decide where, and how, you want to work' (PayPal, 2022b: 1). This demonstrates workplace flexibility which is confirmed on the careers website (PayPal, 2022b), which states:

> We champion flexibility. The majority of our roles are virtual flex or fully virtual, providing teams the opportunity to determine the amount of time spent working in-office based on business needs. A small portion of employee roles do require on-site work. We are happy to provide more details about how our working models are applied to the role(s) you are interested in, during the interview process.

The company also recognises work–life balance: 'Whether in or out of the workplace, our employees are living their best life' (PayPal, 2022b: 1). While the company directly employs over 30,000 people PayPal has also outsourced many aspects of its work:

> We rely on third parties in many aspects of our business, including, but not limited to: networks, banks, payment processors, and payment gateways that link us to the payment card and bank clearing networks to process transactions; unaffiliated third-party lenders to originate our U.S. credit products to

consumers, U.S. merchant financing, and branded credit card products; PayPal-branded debit card products issued by an unaffiliated bank; cryptocurrency custodial service providers; and external business partners and contractors who provide key functions (e.g., outsourced customer support and product development functions; facilities; information technology, data center facilities and cloud computing), (PayPal, 2022a: 21).

With such large staff numbers, PayPal is in a constant state of recruitment. If just 5% of the staff change jobs, relocate or retire each year, that's 1,500 vacancies to fill. And 5% is low, so it could be as high as 15%. A search for PayPal jobs on LinkedIn shows there are over 2,000 vacancies. In addition to promoting vacancies on LinkedIn, PayPal has a dedicated recruitment website that acts as a portal to showcase jobs and makes it easy to apply. The firm finds it especially difficult to recruit those working in technology, including software engineers.

This ongoing recruitment partly explains why some services, such as customer support, are outsourced. It's easy to verify prospective employees, by checking references, reviewing their online profile (and being suspicious if they don't have one), but it's more challenging to check the staff working for the third parties. To mitigate potential risk, PayPal has recognised this situation and in a comment to shareholders confirmed:

> while we have policies and procedures for managing these relationships, they inherently involve a lesser degree of control over business operations, governance, and compliance, thereby potentially increasing our financial, legal, reputational, and operational risk, (PayPal, 2022a: 21).

Employee recruitment is increasingly important to PayPal. When vacancies occur, it's important to fill them, as having fewer staff to respond to customer queries means longer waiting times, more unhappy customers and more work for those in the company.

CASE QUESTIONS

PayPal is a growing company that requires large numbers of staff to manage the in-company operations and offers wide flexibility in terms of location, yet they also adopt outsourcing.

- What sensible actions can organisations such as PayPal take to ensure they are perceived as a great place to work?
- PayPal uses its own dedicated recruitment website and LinkedIn to share its vacancies. What other tools do you believe the firm could use to increase its talent pool?
- If you possess the skills PayPal needed, but the job was office based and you preferred a hybrid approach, how could you convince the company to hire you?

(Continued)

FURTHER EXERCISES

1. For an organisation of your choice, analyse its digital workspace and explore whether they are outsourcing and the impact this has on the employees.

2. As we move into different forms of working, such as face-to-face, hybrid and virtual, assess the key challenges for employers in managing employees in different spaces and prepare a presentation to recommend how to mitigate these issues.

3. For a successful organisation of your choice, create an initiative that demonstrates why it is a great place to work.

4. Outsourcing is the way ahead for all businesses. Discuss.

SUMMARY

This chapter has explored:

*   How technology has changed the world of work
*   Types of outsourcing available for organisations and the associated benefits
*   Challenges and opportunities such as work–life balance and technostress
*   The future of work from hybrid to virtual

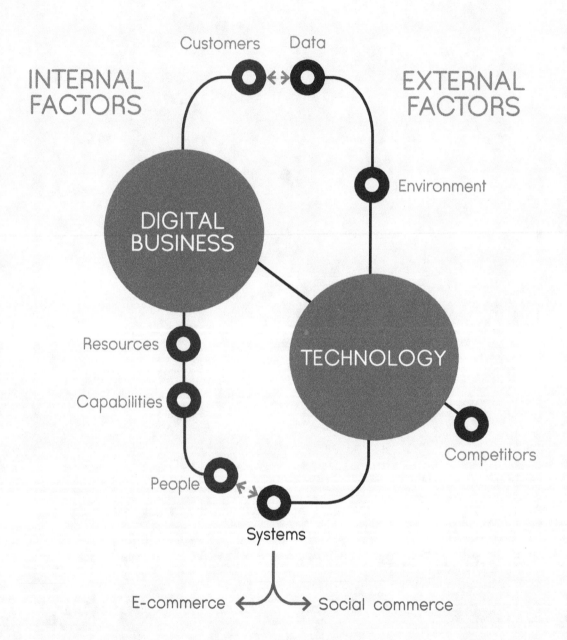

3

E-COMMERCE

PROFESSIONAL SKILLS

When you have worked through this chapter, you should be able to:

- Seek opportunities to drive forward change and improvements for the business
- Horizon scan to identify future trends, technologies, innovations and best practice

3.1 BACKGROUND TO E-COMMERCE

The United Nations holds an e-commerce week in April 'to discuss the development opportunities challenges associated with the digital economy' (United Nations Conference on Trade and Development (UNCTAD), 2022: 4). This demonstrates how important e-commerce has become.

The largest retailer in the world is Alibaba Group, although Amazon is following closely (Chevalier, 2022). E-commerce enables customers to shop online at any time with any device. This chapter looks at the origins and features of e-commerce, along with the challenges such as deshopping, and different business models.

WEB 1.0 THE READ-ONLY WEB

Introduced in the 1990s, 'E-commerce involves the use of digital technologies in business to facilitate online sales and transactions' (Rosário & Raimundo, 2021: 3010). No longer a place to connect a few computers and share information, the possibility of e-commerce was identified with the commercialisation of the internet. With its foundations in information technology, the scientist Tim Berners-Lee who was working at CERN, the European Organization for Nuclear Research, created a proposal to improve communications for large projects (1989). This was a blueprint for the **World Wide Web** (see Key Terms) and used linked text so users could click a link on one page and jump to another related piece of content. The first version of the **internet** (see Key Terms) was called 'Web 1.0' or 'read-only' as this was a static, basic and slow system. This was due to a lack of access to technology, incredibly slow connection speeds and therefore low adoption rates.

KEY TERMS   WORLD WIDE WEB AND INTERNET

The internet is a network of globally connected computers. It is a name created from combining the phrase 'interconnected computer networks'.

The World Wide Web (WWW) is an information system providing materials that can be accessed via the internet.

WEB 2.0: THE READ-WRITE WEB

Moving forward to 2005, Tim O'Reilly, a technical writer, shared a blog post exploring the next generation of the WWW or Web 2.0 (O'Reilly, 2005). Social media had just launched (remember Bebo, MySpace?), Netscape Navigator was the main browser and company websites were little more than brochures. Web 2.0 represented a different way of thinking where applications were created online and accessed online, so there was no need to have a disk to access the software, you found the website and downloaded it. You could comment on posts, and users were part of the content creation process. This was the move from monologues to dialogues and even multilogues where many people could join in the conversation and share their thoughts. Plus it provided opportunities for **disintermediation** (see Key Terms).

> **KEY TERMS** DISINTERMEDIATION AND REINTERMEDIATION
>
> Disintermediation is about removing the intermediary or 'cutting out the middle man' (Sinclair & Wilken, 2009: 94); for example, Amazon selling books instead of traditional bookstores or Dell computers selling directly to home customers, rather than selling through a PC store.
>
> Reintermediation is re-introducing intermediaries where they may be too many choices. There are examples of intermediaries for buying insurance, flights and holidays. Visit one site to get the details from many organisations.

WEB 3.0: THE SEMANTIC AND SOCIAL WEB

As technology improved, Web 3.0 offered personalisation. You re-visit a website, log in and review previous purchases. Your data is stored and easy to retrieve whether you are looking for previous purchases or adding a delivery address. Another change with Web 3.0 was the ability to provide and share information with others in your community on other websites – such as social media.

With the growth of so many websites, consumers were overwhelmed with choices and disintermediation became **reintermediation** in some cases (see Key Terms), especially where consumers had to enter the same details several times. For example, if you are searching for a flight, instead of selecting the dates and airports and waiting for the results on several websites, Skyscanner allows you to enter your details just once and you are presented with options from different airlines. Skyscanner is an intermediary website using reintermediation.

WEB 4.0: THE SYMBIOTIC WEB

The next generation of the web is considered to be one where there is greater collaboration between people and machines. This is based on machine learning and artificial intelligence. Web 4.0 has not yet been fully defined, but includes the concept of the Internet of Things where devices are all connected to the network and intelligently respond to each other. For more on this, see Chapter 6.

Having considered the background to e-commerce, let's explore the business models.

3.2 E-COMMERCE BUSINESS MODELS

According to Statista's research, the highest percentage of online sales take place in the UK, South Korea and Denmark (Chevalier, 2022). There are 8 types of e-commerce business models, which are discussed in this section.

One factor to consider is that it is not always about a product sale. Government (also called administration) to consumer may seem strange as a government may not sell goods to its citizens, but may request forms to be completed or enable citizens to pay for local services online. Table 3.1 clarifies the types of transactions involved in e-commerce with examples.

Table 3.1   E-commerce models with types of transactions and examples

Type of e-commerce model	Types of transactions	Examples
Business to Business (B2B)	Businesses providing goods or services to other businesses	Sharing or buying data, documents, goods, services; e.g. Amazon buying advertising from Google, or local architects buying employee payroll services online
Business to Consumer (B2C), also known as Direct to Consumer (D2C)	Businesses providing goods or services to consumers	Consumers buying goods direct from online retailers; e.g. clothing retailers or buying software for personal use from Microsoft
Business to Government (B2G)	Businesses providing goods or services to government	Governments buying software from businesses; e.g. Microsoft is a supplier of software to many governments which is accessed via their portal
Consumer to Consumer (C2C) also known as peer to peer	Consumers providing goods or services to other consumers	Consumers buying from online marketplaces; e.g. Etsy where consumers make and sell the available goods, or Upwork where consumers sell their services (do walking, gardening, CV writing) to other consumers
Consumer to Business (C2B)	Consumers providing goods or services to businesses	Businesses accessing design services from individuals; e.g. businesses using crowdsourcing to develop a new logo, create a website
Consumer to Government (C2G)	Consumers providing goods or services to government	Citizens providing feedback on government services; e.g. surveys about transport or schools
Government to Business (G2B)	Government providing goods or services to businesses	Businesses accessing government services online; e.g. taxes, employee records
Government to Consumer (G2C)	Government providing goods or services to consumers	Citizens paying online for services; e.g. taxes, waste collection, parking permits

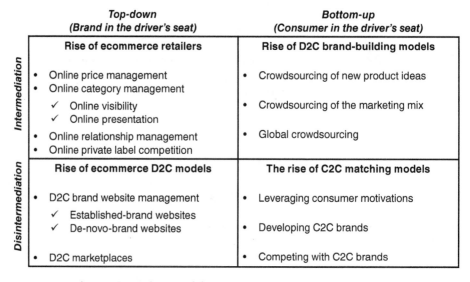

Figure 3.1   Branding issues in the era of disintermediation

Source: Gielens & Steenkamp (2019: 368). Printed with permission of Elsevier

Within each of these models, there are variations for the type of model. Businesses and consumers can enable the transaction directly through their own website, through a marketplace or through other channels such as social commerce. These online business-to-consumer sales, also known as direct-to-consumer (D2C), creates opportunities and challenges for brands as Figure 3.1 shows (Gielens & Steenkamp, 2019).

Figure 3.1 considers disintermediation and intermediation. It also addresses both the brand and the consumer perspective. Let's examine the 4 quadrants of Figure 3.1.

3.2.1 E-COMMERCE RETAIL GIANTS

The top-left hand corner, *Rise of e-commerce retailers*, considers the brand perspective where intermediaries are involved. This can include a bricks and mortar traditional shop that wants an online presence. Yet creating, maintaining and promoting an online store requires a lot of effort. So, depending on the size of the business, it can be easier to use an existing retailer to sell the goods. For example, Amazon provides businesses with a ready-made shop front, they manage the online process and ensure the products are placed in the right areas, and provide greater visibility for businesses who may not otherwise have access to their customer base.

As researchers Gielens & Steenkamp noted, Amazon understands its customers, knows which products matter to them and uses an 'endless aisles model, whereby the retailer's main aim is to add to its catalog and create boundless selection options' (2019: 369), which means that it is always seeking new products to keep the customer on the site. Amazon offers businesses many advantages, including:

- A lower cost structure as businesses pay a monthly fee and a percentage of sales
- Access to a large number of customers
- Easier and faster fulfilment as the packing and despatch takes place from Amazon warehouses
- Better customer experience with instant responses to questions from the Amazon website

The downsides are that Amazon pushes for price discounts to win the sale and changes its prices on a regular basis (see Digital Tool **Keepa.com**). Plus in some cases, Amazon contacts specific brands to offer to sell their goods (Gielens & Steenkamp, 2019). But if the brand does not want to sell direct to Amazon, the firm may find other sellers of the same goods which may ultimately damage the brand and result in online brand competitors.

DIGITAL TOOL   Keepa.com

Keepa captures data on Amazon products' pricing history and has a database of over 3 billion products. This allows consumers to track the price history of a product and whether it's going up or down. Companies pay to use Keepa as a competitor and product analysis tool.

- You can explore Keepa here: keepa.com

3.2.2 DROPSHIPPING AND ONLINE MARKETPLACES

The lower-left-hand corner considers the brand perspective where intermediaries are not involved. This quadrant, *Rise of e-commerce models*, is where businesses are selling direct on their own established websites or creating new websites with wider product ranges which may be from other brands. In some cases, they might not even stock or see the products but simply take the order and ensure it's delivered – this is known as **dropshipping** (see Key Term).

KEY TERM   DROPSHIPPING

Dropshipping is 'where e-retailers advertise products and transfer received customer orders to suppliers while suppliers (dropshippers) manage their inventories and fulfill the orders' (Kim et al., 2022: 1156). Its advantages are that the seller buys and resells the goods quickly, without managing the distribution. It enables smaller businesses to launch a store quickly without the expense of buying stock. The downsides are that the vendor may prioritise some dropshippers over others, giving priority to larger accounts. It's also a competitive space and online consumers might search for the cheapest prices, which impacts on the margins available.

Another e-commerce model is that of marketplaces. Marketplaces offer an intermediary service as they act as a bridge between the buyer and seller.

While Amazon is an online retailer, it is also a marketplace selling a wide assortment of goods. Marketplaces sell a narrow or wide range of goods and are available in all countries. The major players in online marketplaces include Amazon, Alibaba, eBay and Rakuten, but there are many others; for example:

- Etsy (global) sells arts and crafts
- TaskRabbit (global) sells freelance services
- The Iconic (Australia and New Zealand) sells fashion clothing and accessories
- Decathalon (Europe) sells sports goods
- Conforama (France) sells homewares
- Mumzworld (Gulf region) sells baby products
- Morele (Poland) sells electronics
- Jumia (Africa) sells general goods
- Flipkart (India) sells general goods

DIGITAL TOOL   Amazon Seller

Many companies use Amazon to sell their products. Amazon has millions of products available, in over 100 countries. They have a dedicated website that explains how to get started as an Amazon seller which includes a beginner's guide, the options available and how to create a launch plan.

- You can explore the Amazon seller details here: sell.amazon.co.uk/sell-online

As intermediaries, these marketplaces connect buyers with sellers but they can also delist (remove) products and brands in minutes, which could destroy a business overnight. Marketplaces remove products for many reasons. This can include negative feedback, problems with the products, too many returns or perhaps other issues with the suppliers.

Activity 3.1   Evaluate online marketplaces

Imagine you are running a small business and need to increase sales. In groups evaluate the advantages and disadvantages of using online marketplaces to sell your goods.

- The advantages may be clear, but what are the risks?
- What are the alternatives to online marketplaces and how do these compare in terms of the risks involved?
- Does any member of the group have experience working with marketplaces?
- What advice would you give to a small business considering stocking its products on marketplaces?

3.2.3 CROWDSOURCING

The top-left-hand corner in Figure 3.1, *Rise of D2C brand-building models*, considers the consumer perspective where intermediaries are involved. The best example of this is crowdsourcing. According to Steils & Hanine (2022), the benefits of crowdsourcing include new product development, the creation of advertising content and market research. This can take place on a regional or global scale and is a helpful way for organisations to better understand their customers' needs.

Crowdsourcing intermediaries include those shown in Table 3.2, which indicates the target audiences for the platforms and the costs involved.

Table 3.2   Crowdfunding platforms, target organisations and fees

Crowdfunding platform	Target organisations	Popular with	Platform fees	Transaction fees
Kickstarter	Start-ups	Creative businesses	5%	3% + $0.20 per transaction
Indiegogo	Start-ups	Tech companies	5%	2.9%–4.4%
Mightycause	Non-profits	Integrates with CRM systems and social media	$59–$99 per month	1.2% + $0.29
Patreon	Creatives	Podcasters, writers, educators	5%–12% of monthly income	2.9%–5% + $0.10–$0.30 per transaction

Source: Adapted with permission from Hanlon (2022: 305)

Smartphone Sixty Seconds® – Seek crowdfunding sites

- Crowdfunding platforms continue to grow and specialise in certain areas (e.g. personal funding, artistic projects, sports). Take out your mobile phone and search for 'crowdfunding platforms'.
- How many did you find?
- Have you ever participated in crowdfunding? What was this for? How successful was the experience?

3.2.4 THE SHARING ECONOMY

The lower-right-hand corner, *Rise of C2C matching models*, considers the consumer perspective where intermediaries are not involved. Consumers sell goods or services directly to other consumers. This is known as the sharing economy; for example, sharing your car (Uber), spare room (Airbnb) or clothing (Hurr Collective). The consumers are connected through a matching programme, consumers are sharing their goods with others.

The sharing economy has benefits for sustainability. It ensures that clothing is used more than once, rooms are empty less often and cars are shared. The downsides are that consumers are often not trained as retailers, so the process, even via an intermediary, can sometimes go wrong. The idea of consumers sharing goods with other consumers has always existed at a local level, sharing textbooks with classmates, swapping clothes with friends and room sharing when needed. The difference in a digital context is that we share with strangers beyond our local community. Research shows that we share for 'economic, environmental and social' reasons (Gielens & Steenkamp, 2019: 378). While it may be cheaper and have sustainability benefits, we also enjoy the business of sharing.

3.3 SOCIAL COMMERCE

According to researcher Bairbre Brennan (2022), social commerce was recognised as a phenomenon in 2005; it connects e-commerce and social interaction. Social commerce involves consumer-to-consumer interaction (asking questions, liking reviews), adding reviews or recommendations, and asking for help (e.g. on funding platforms), as well as selling goods through social media.

There are different types of social commerce, including:

- Peer to peer, e.g. eBay, Etsy, Uber, Airbnb
- Peer recommendations, e.g. Amazon, Trip Advisor
- Group buying, e.g. Groupon, Living Social
- Participatory commerce, e.g. Kickstarter, GoFundMe, Twitch
- Social network-driven sales, e.g. Instagram, Pinterest

Brennan (2022) considers social commerce along a continuum of activity which moves from being led by social interaction to a transaction-focused activity, as shown in Figure 3.2. In this continuum, the social-interaction-led element is where the purpose is social, but online sales can occur due to recommendations or other discussions. In the centre is where consumers may participate in a community activity, so this is less about commerce and more about working together to achieve a goal; for example, funding a group of people or lowering the total costs of goods for the group. The final element of the continuum is that of activities which are transaction led, such as consumers reading reviews from others before making a purchase, or consumers leaving reviews for others to ensure they do – or don't – buy the goods.

DISCOVER MORE ON SOCIAL COMMERCE

Read 'The relationship between e-commerce and social commerce: subset, evolution or new paradigm?', in *The Sage Handbook of Digital Marketing* by Brennan (2022). This chapter provides the historical context and background to e-commerce as well as further depth on the different types and components of social commerce.

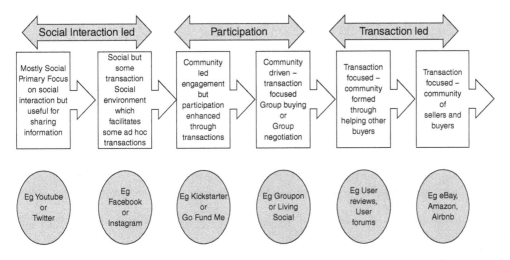

Figure 3.2 Social commerce continuum: breadth of social commerce activity

Source: With permission from Brennan (2022: 244)

Activity 3.2   Create a proposal for an e-commerce idea

Imagine you have an idea about an e-commerce business. Prepare a pitch explaining your idea.

You need to be clear about the target audience, the product offer, pricing, revenue generation, how it works and why it differs from similar offers.

This could be a one-page document, a single slide or a 2-minute video.

3.4 THE MAIN CHALLENGES OF MANAGING E-COMMERCE

In addition to brands having to compete with marketplaces that have larger marketing budgets, managing e-commerce presents several challenges. These include addressing fraudulent reviews and brushing scams, counterfeit websites and deshopping, which are discussed in this section.

3.4.1 FRAUDULENT REVIEWS

Fraudulent reviews exist on many online sites. They can be fake reviews written by the merchant or others paid to fabricate the content. This is an area which many marketplaces are trying to manage (see Case 3.1 'Amazon's Fake Reviews') as they gain more attention from regulators as unfair practice. In many of these situations, third parties organise the reviews and use gig sites such as Amazon Mechanical Turk or social media sites to buy reviews in bulk.

In other examples, fake reviews can be more organised where there is a link between the merchant and the reviewer and goods are exchanged; this is known as **brushing** (see Ethical Insights).

ETHICAL INSIGHTS   Brushing scams

According to J Chen et al. (2022: 1), 'Brushing is online merchants placing fake orders of their own products'. The fake sales may be created by merchants who find 'brushers' and this is a well-organised process:

- Merchants find 'brushers' and send them a small payment
- Brushers pay for goods using some of the money sent to them and then place a fake sale
- Merchants send an empty parcel, so there is a despatch record
- Brushers create fake positive reviews and keep the rest of the payment

Brushing usually occurs within marketplaces such as Amazon, JD.com and Taobao. As payment has been received by the merchant, this is noted within marketplace systems, so the review is noted as 'verified'. This enhances the merchants' products and enables them to stand out in marketplaces. With so many thousands of products it can be difficult to stand out and brushing is seen as a way to appear at the top of the search results.

Amazon and other marketplaces invest heavily to combat brushing. The challenge is that the orders have shipping and delivery details, appearing to be a genuine sale (J. Chen et al., 2022). It is a form of organised fake reviews where products appear to have been dispatched. It is a scam designed to lure the customer into buying products that appear to have good reviews.

- Influencers are regularly sent products which they haven't requested in the hope that they will create a positive review. Should this be considered a form of brushing? Why is this?
- How can businesses without the budget for brushing compete with organisations who employ these tactics routinely, to appear higher up in the search results?
- How do you feel about writing a review in exchange for products? When is it acceptable or unacceptable?

CASE EXAMPLE 3.1   Amazon's fake reviews

Fake reviews continue to appear across online platforms and have been recognised as unfair practices by government and legislators (Competition and Markets Authority, 2016, 2021; European Commission, 2018). This is an illegal practice in the UK, EU and USA.

Although there are detection systems in place to identify fake reviews and the consequences for brands include significant fines, the unethical business of fake review creation continues to thrive, according to He et al. (2022). This practice misleads consumers, nurtures dishonest competition and damages business reputations.

Reputation is a valuable business asset. Organisations invest in their brand identity by promoting their product and sharing customer feedback online. While verified 2-way review platforms (where buyer and seller rate each other) ensure the authenticity of buyers, unverified systems enable anonymous unprompted reviews. These can damage businesses as they can be malicious and impact future sales.

As the importance of reviews has been recognised, the market for fake reviews has developed. According to researchers He et al. (2022), reputation systems are being manipulated by fake reviews. Even though this is illegal, there are people in all marketplaces, from Amazon to Wayfair, offering their services to post positive reviews. This weak practice occurs in many countries including the United States, Canada, United Kingdom, Germany, France, Italy, Spain, Japan, Hong Kong and China. It is a global problem.

As He and colleagues note,

> sellers create private Facebook groups where they promote their products by soliciting users to purchase their products and leave a five-star review in exchange for their products by soliciting users to purchase their products and leave a five-star review in exchange for a full refund (and in some cases an additional payment). (2022: 898)

In addition to refunding the purchase cost, many reviewers are offered a commission that is an average of $6 and as high as $15. Reviewers benefit from gaining free products as well as a small income per item, but this is an illegal activity with consequences.

Although Facebook deletes these groups as soon as they are aware of them, they keep reappearing. Amazon has taken legal action against the admins of over 10,000 of these Facebook groups. In Italy, Amazon has taken legal action against a company trading as AgenciaReviews, which it claimed was using the private messaging app Telegram to organise payments to fake reviewers. With over 8,000 staff working on countering fake content, Amazon has deleted millions of fake reviews. The retail giant spends millions of dollars to reduce fraud, but there is a time lag between the reviews appearing and being deleted. This means that the sellers get a benefit before they are caught.

Fake reviews are damaging for consumers who may buy products they believe are genuine, only to discover the products fail to match the description. They are also damaging for genuine competitors who lose out due to fewer reviews.

Case questions

- What do you think about fake reviews: is it just part of e-commerce or a more serious issue?

(Continued)

- How can honest organisations counter fake reviews by competitors?
- Have you ever purchased goods based on a review, only to be disappointed when the items arrived? What action did you take?

DIGITAL TOOL   Fakespot

As reviews have become such an important part of e-commerce, we have seen an increase in fake reviews. These are a growing issue for consumers and honest organisations, but they can be detected. Started by a customer who felt he had been tricked by poor reviews, Fakespot is a tool that allows you to assess the quality of reviews (and sellers) across the major marketplaces. The tool is a guide rather than 100% accurate as reviewers are becoming more sophisticated.

- You can explore Fakespot here: fakespot.com

3.4.2 COUNTERFEIT WEBSITES

As well as fake reviews there are fake websites. Counterfeit or bogus websites seem authentic because they appear to be a direct copy of the genuine website, they contain detailed product information and high-quality imagery (S. W. Chen et al., 2022). In some cases, the counterfeit website owners advertise on social media and in search engines to direct traffic to their websites, which also appears to add a sign of approval that it is a genuine website.

When consumers visit counterfeit websites there are several levels of damage which can occur:

- Consumers might receive counterfeit goods which are inferior or do not function
- The payment may be taken with no goods provided
- Consumers' financial details (e.g. name, address, credit card data) are used fraudulently with small payments being made to the fraudsters
- Consumers' financial details may be sold on the dark web for a payment

Counterfeit websites are removed when identified by search engines, but as one is removed, another may appear.

While there are technical characteristics of fake websites such as very long URLs (web address) and hyphens in the company name, e.g. The-Purple-Company.com instead of thepurplecompany.com, most consumers are not expecting to arrive at a fake website so may not see the signs.

3.4.3 DESHOPPING

As consumers become more comfortable with online shopping a new behaviour has emerged: **deshopping** (see Key Term). This has existed in store for many years, yet online returns are easier for deshoppers as there are no staff asking questions as to why the goods are being returned. But this is changing as several retailers charge for returns; for example, the Spanish fashion retailer Zara charges nearly £2.00 when goods are not returned via their stores.

KEY TERM   DESHOPPING

Deshopping is 'the return of products after they have fulfilled the purpose for which they were borrowed'. It is a fraudulent returns behaviour, but although it is a form of theft deshoppers are said to consider it as simply being naughty. Examples of deshopping include buying a dress for a party, wearing it and returning it, claiming it is unsuitable or faulty. Yet in some cases, shoppers purposefully damage the clothing, for example unpicking the seams or cutting a hole in the garment.

While it seems like deshopping only impacts on the large online retailers, everyone ends up paying more as retailers add the costs to the price of all goods. Many of the goods returned cannot be resold and are added to trade waste. With clothing being worn only once and destroyed, this is an anti-environmental and unsustainable practice.

It's not only clothing. According to Dr Tamira King, deshopping behaviour occurs with homewares too. A family holding a party might buy extra tables and chairs. After the event, they return the goods and say they're unsuitable, although they've been used.

DISCOVER MORE ON DESHOPPING

Read 'Unethical consumers: Deshopping behaviour using the qualitative analysis of theory of planned behaviour and accompanied (de)shopping' published in *Qualitative Market Research*, by King & Dennis. Although this was written in 2006, it provides examples of deshopping behaviour as well as the ethical and legal issues to consider.

Smartphone Sixty Seconds® – Explore counterfeit websites

- Major corporations as well as smaller businesses have fallen victim to counterfeit websites. To understand who this has impacted, take out your mobile phone and search for 'examples of counterfeit websites'.
- What did you discover?
- Were there any surprises?
- How do you feel about counterfeit websites?

Activity 3.3   Create a presentation to restore consumer confidence

Imagine you are working for an organisation that has suffered from counterfeit websites. Apply your knowledge of counterfeit websites and in groups discuss ideas that will restore consumer confidence. Prioritise the top 3 actions and create a presentation for the senior management team.

3.5 FUTURE OPPORTUNITIES IN E-COMMERCE

E-commerce opportunities are less about new products, and more about how they are promoted to consumers using techniques such as live-streaming. The future also presents an opportunity for a better understanding of sustainability within e-commerce, which is discussed in this section.

3.5.1 LIVESTREAMING

Livestreaming is *synchronously* sharing video content, often by amateurs known as streamers, where audiences interact in real time. The interaction can be with the streamer or other members of the audience through chat or messaging (Ang et al., 2018).

Vloggers, knowns as YouTubers, creators or uploaders (Törhönen et al., 2021), also share video content but this is *asynchronous* or pre-recorded where the finished video is shared. Vloggers may edit the content, and depending on where it is posted the audience may or may not be able to add comments.

Livestreaming is seen to have greater credibility (Dwivedi et al., 2020) as it conveys social presence (Short et al., 1976); it is in real time and possesses immediacy – the feeling of being in the same place, as well as providing intimacy as many people feel the streamer is speaking directly to them. Social presence is a key concept in social media marketing, and as researchers Professor Ang and colleagues noted (2018: 2079), this is why 'a livestreaming social viewing strategy will incorporate cues such as "Live" and "Number of People Watching Now" to highlight real-time shared viewership'.

Streamers operate on channels including YouTube, TikTok and Twitch as well as through traditional social media, for example Facebook Live and Instagram Live. E-commerce channels also offer livestreaming which is often managed by the giant marketplaces such as Amazon and Alibaba.

You may think that livestreaming only applies to gamers using Twitch, or influencers sharing new products, but it's much bigger, as Table 3.3 demonstrates.

The growth in livestreaming is not surprising. Influencers use it to build their personal brands and gain income. Gamers enjoy playing with an audience; as researchers Maria Törhönen and colleagues noted (2021), this becomes a mixture of work and play. Tourism destinations gain more interest when individuals share and stream from their destination. From an e-commerce perspective, there are serious benefits

Table 3.3   Sectors using livestreaming with examples and income models

Sector	Examples of how livestreaming is used	Examples of platforms	Income model
e-commerce – retailers	To showcase products	Amazon Live, Taobao Live	Retailers taking orders for products while live
e-commerce – influencers, brand spokespeople	Product unboxing where an influencer reveals the contents of a specific product, from laptops to lipsticks	Instagram Live	Influencer paid a commission or a fee for the project
Gaming	Gamers playing video games and audiences watches their performance	Twitch, PlayStation, Xbox	Partnership and affiliate programmes
Tourism	Friends sharing holidays	Social media	None
Health and fitness	Fitness videos where viewers can follow along to the workout	YouTube Live	Advertising revenue
Education	Students doing their homework together	StreamWork	Subscription based or advertising revenue
Medicine	In surgical education	Smart glasses, GoPro	None

to livestreaming. When consumers have a more authentic viewing experience, they are more likely to subscribe to the content and search for more details – both these actions increase the intention to purchase (Ang et al., 2018).

However, if the amateur is paid or sponsored with free goods, they must declare this. This is a legal requirement in several countries. This is often done using a hashtag such as #ad or #sponsored. Plus, if they are being paid they've turned professional and are no longer amateurs!

DISCOVER MORE ON LIVESTREAMING

Read 'Streamers: The new wave of digital entrepreneurship? Extant corpus and future research agenda' published in *Electronic Commerce Research and Applications* by Maria Törhönen and colleagues. This article explores the literature and the terminology around livestreaming.

3.5.2 SUSTAINABILITY IN E-COMMERCE

There is greater awareness of sustainability and our environment, yet this does not appear to reduce our online shopping activity. Retail e-commerce sales have increased every year and by 2026 are expected to reach $8.1 trillion worldwide (Chevalier, 2022).

Yet there are concerns about the environment, the social issues it creates and economic factors within e-commerce. The environmental impact of e-commerce often relates to the packaging and delivering of goods (Rita & Ramos, 2022). For example, one of the challenges is known as 'the last-mile distribution' which researchers have recognised as the 'most expensive and time-consuming portion of delivery, accounting for up to 53% of the overall shipment cost' (Rita & Ramos, 2022: 15). This is why

Amazon and other retailers have introduced collection lockers – one delivery to many people, which aims to 'reduce greenhouse gas emissions, noise, and air pollution'. (Rita & Ramos, 2022: 3).

There are concerns as to whether the amount of shopping is sustainable. This has led to the circular economy (see Chapter 12) so that we reuse rather than dispose. Some e-commerce stores are declining to participate in Black Friday and encouraging customers to reuse or repair rather than buy new every time (Armstrong Soule & Sekhon, 2022). The challenge is trying to balance the needs of the environment with those of consumers, and also with retailers, at the same time.

CASE EXAMPLE 3.2   Wastezon

Championing the circular economy, Wastezon has designed an app to recycle e-waste, from old computers and phones to fridges to fans. Their vision is 'From trash to cash, Leveraging technology to create a waste-free world'.

The story behind the business is described by Africa ClimAccelerator (2022: 1).

A near fatal accident at a landfill birthed a passion to reduce waste for Wastezon founders Ghislain Irakoze and Jacqueline Mukarukundo. Mr Irakoze and his best friend were carrying out an environmental assessment for a school project when a heap of garbage tipped over and almost killed his friend.

Starting out as a 'recycle for the environment' project, a business idea was developed. With 'less than 20 per cent of waste recycled every year' (Statista, 2022: 1), e-waste is a problem worldwide as we buy more and more and newer and newer electronic goods online.

The Republic of Rwanda has a National E-waste Policy. The government defines e-waste as:

> E-waste encompasses all discarded and disposed electrical and electronic equipment (EEE), which is defined as equipment dependent on electric currents or electromagnetic fields in order to work properly, but also any for the generation, transfer and measurement of such currents and fields. (Republic of Rwanda, 2016: 4)

Within a country where e-waste is understood, the friends decided to take action to reduce the growing amounts of waste and created an app to recycle household electronics.

Based in Rwanda's capital city Kigali, Wastezon has so far reused or recycled over 400 tons of e-waste, diverting over 2,600 carbon emissions. Their work has been recognised as they are winners of a large project to mitigate global warming. Wastezon has won many international awards, including mHUB Climate and Energy Tech Startup Pitch Competition, Young Champions of the Earth and The Resolution Project.

The app has been extended and 'Wastezon 2.0 provides users with security and quality vetted second-hand electronics' (Wastezon, 2022: 1). Plus the organisation has gone further, with a desktop portal: 'developed for Manufacturers and Recyclers, WastezonX provides traceability and tracking infrastructures for efficient materials returnability and reverse supply chain management' (Wastezon, 2022).

These developments cleverly link both the consumers and manufacturers to developing an environment with reduced waste.

Wastezon has also created many jobs, from project and operations managers to associates in materials science, to better understand the raw materials.

Case questions

- What do you notice about Wastezon's approach to a challenging problem?
- What other examples can you find of online businesses starting as a result of a potential disaster or real need?
- How can consumers be convinced to buy less or keep older products for longer?

JOURNAL OF NOTE

Electronic Commerce Research has focused on e-commerce for over 20 years. It considers the technologies and how they impact on our society, individuals and businesses.

CASE STUDY

PAYPAL AND E-COMMERCE

PayPal employs over 30,000 people, representing around 150 nationalities, in 30 countries. Just over 40% of staff are based in the USA with the remaining 60% located across the world.

PayPal was born in e-commerce. It was a disrupter, changing how payments were made online. It 'simplifies commerce experiences on behalf of merchants and consumers worldwide' (PayPal, 2021: 4).

Originally known as Confinity, it was established by Peter Thiel (who invested in Facebook) and Max Levchin (who founded Yelp.com). Confinity later merged with Elon Musk's company X.com. The public didn't understand what Confinity or X represented, and as one of the brand names was PayPal this became the company name.

PayPal recognises the growth of different channels, such as social commerce and marketplaces. One of its major marketplaces is eBay which has extended its payment options, so PayPal is no longer the primary method of payment.

Figure 3.3   PayPal's 2-sided system

Source: With permission from PayPal (2022a: 2)

(Continued)

The PayPal system is 2-sided, working for both merchants (sellers) and consumers (buyers). Merchants can build PayPal into their e-commerce system as a trusted brand and consumers can use PayPal as a payment system. The benefit for merchants is that they can use the PayPal brand and it's easier for consumers who don't need to resubmit their credit card details for every website they visit, but simply log in to pay, regardless of whether it's a local or international website. Figure 3.3 shows PayPal's 2-sided system.

While the firm is trusted by thousands of brands, such as Netflix, Spotify and Nike, PayPal is still growing its business. One example is encouraging greater adoption of PayPal in e-commerce settings. To achieve this the firm offers additional benefits to merchants, including:

- PayPal-branded checkout – so consumers see PayPal across every touchpoint from the shopping cart to the final purchase confirmation
- A software development kit (SDK) for developers – this makes adding PayPal to a shopping cart much easier as the elements required are ready made

As a 2-sided system PayPal is also working on greater engagement with consumers. Examples include:

- Providing passkeys for Apple devices – so Apple customers don't need a password and have a faster login to their account
- Enabling faster login using biometrics – so customers can use their face as their password
- Launching a rewards programme for consumers in the USA. This provides one place where the rewards are managed as well as the option to receive personalised shopping deals and use the reward points as part payment

It's not only large businesses and enterprises using PayPal, there are solutions for small and pop-up businesses too. Payments can be made by:

- Scanning a single QR code assigned to the business and paying the amount required
- Selling on social media
- Using the PayPal.me link in chat or via messenger
- Sending invoices with clickable links

In addition to supporting many e-commerce models, PayPal engages in crowdsourcing within its own business. As Tsoukalas (2022: 2) explains:

> Participants in the company's annual Global Innovation Tournament submit their ideas, as in conventional contests. But in a subsequent round, they act as investors, placing wagers on what they think are the best ideas, regardless of the source. In addition, the investment round is open to all of the company's approximately 30,000 full-time employees.

The investment is made in the form of internal tokens called WoWs. All employees are given WoW and those that invest in the top 3 ideas are rewarded with more tokens which can be used for special experiences, from getting the chief technology officer (CTO) to set up your home Wi-Fi or learning a skill from one of the other chief company officers. In a company with over 30,000 people, a one to one with one of the senior team is an extraordinary event.

CASE QUESTIONS

PayPal is maintaining its e-commerce momentum by supporting its merchants and consumers, as well as generating new business ideas. Yet this is a competitive market with more businesses offering digital payment solutions.

- Should PayPal diversify and consider other business ideas, or stick to digital payment solutions?
- PayPal's business is directly linked to how much consumers spend. Is this encouraging the growth of unsustainable spending? How can this be managed?
- Have you used PayPal or similar systems? What worked well and which elements would you improve?

FURTHER EXERCISES

1. For an organisation of your choice, prepare a brief for a new or enhanced website to present to an agency. Include areas to be addressed and highlight the essential features.

2. For an e-commerce retailer of your choice evaluate the options for disintermediation or intermediation, justifying your arguments.

3. Social commerce may be led by social interaction, participation or transactions. Assess a social commerce example of your choice and discuss the focus of its activity.

4. Dropshipping is a weak way to build an online business. Discuss.

SUMMARY

This chapter has explored:

- Types of e-commerce business models
- Branding issues in the era of disintermediation
- The breadth of social commerce activity
- Challenges and opportunities with e-commerce

PART 2

DIGITAL PLATFORMS AND TECHNOLOGIES

CONTENTS

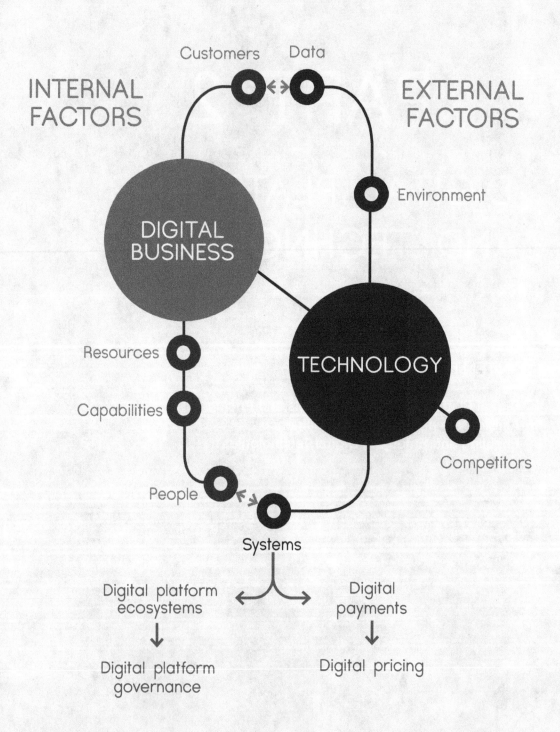

INTERNAL FACTORS

EXTERNAL FACTORS

Customers

Data

Environment

DIGITAL BUSINESS

TECHNOLOGY

Resources

Capabilities

Competitors

People

Systems

Digital platform ecosystems

Digital payments

Digital platform governance

Digital pricing

4

DIGITAL PLATFORMS, PAYMENT MODELS AND PRICING

LEARNING OUTCOMES

When you have read this chapter, you will be able to:

Understand digital platforms, payment models and pricing

Apply the concept of network effects

Analyse digital payment systems

Evaluate digital platform ecosystems

Create a plan to launch a new product by subscription

PROFESSIONAL SKILLS

When you have worked through this chapter, you should be able to:

- Research and critically analyse pricing models
- Create a proposal for a subscription service

4.1 BACKGROUND TO DIGITAL PLATFORMS AND PAYMENT MODELS

Our lives are dominated by digital platforms, from social media to apps. According to Mishra & Tripathi (1: 2020): 'Digital platforms are connected businesses that enable commercial interfaces between at least two different assemblies—with one normally being suppliers and the other consumers.' A definition from L. Chen and colleagues (2022: 151) focuses on the technology: 'Digital platforms refer to a type of platform that serves as a standardized digital interface and utilizes digital technologies to facilitate interactions between different parties.' The key is that technology has enabled the development and growth of digital businesses building platforms such as Amazon, eBay, Meta and Uber.

This chapter explores the key elements of digital platform ecosystems and how they operate with different players. It examines the importance of network effects and why some platforms fail, as well as types of digital payments and digital pricing strategies. It concludes with a review of digital platform governance.

4.2 DIGITAL PLATFORM ECOSYSTEMS

4.2.1 THE KEY ELEMENTS OF DIGITAL PLATFORM ECOSYSTEMS

Traditional non-digital networks operated in a step-by-step system from seller to buyer, with a binary and linear approach. With technology and digital platforms, this traditional 2-way network has changed and has become a more complex multi-sided network, often described as an ecosystem.

Researcher Andreas Hein and colleagues (2020: 90) suggested there are 3 elements to digital platform ecosystems. The first is *platform ownership* and if it is centralised or decentralised. Centralised platform ownership is controlled by a single owner which decides how it operates, such as Meta and Apple. While Meta operates a centralised ownership model, as a concession towards openness, it shares the details of its advertisers (see Digital Tool).

DIGITAL TOOL   Meta ad library

According to Meta, its 'Ad Library provides advertising transparency by offering a comprehensive, searchable collection of all ads currently running from across Meta technologies'.

- You can explore it here to see the top advertisers in your country and their advertising budgets: facebook.com/ads/library

With decentralised platforms, the ownership is managed by a consortium or a community. Examples of decentralised platforms include the WordPress web software system which is used by 43% of all websites worldwide (W3Techs, 2022) and blockchain systems which are shared platforms not owned by a single individual, with transparent record management. The second factor is that the platforms are *value-creating mechanisms* (Hein et al., 2020). They act as an intermediary helping sellers (producers) find buyers (consumers). For example, Uber matches (1) riders with (2) drivers in their (3) location – this is a 3-sided network. The Apple app store (platform owner) matches consumers with apps. This is also a 3-sided network as the app store invites producers to create valuable apps for consumers. WordPress enables producers of website tools to create plugins for its websites, such as forms (e.g. WPForms), search engine optimisation checklists (e.g. Yoast SEO) and e-commerce functionality (e.g. WooCommerce). This is a multi-sided network with many groups involved in the creation, promotion, delivery and consumption of additional content. The value is created within the platform ecosystem which contributes to the entire system.

The third element is what Hein and colleagues (2020: 92) describe as *complementor autonomy,* the freedom that the producers have to create complementary products that are relevant to the ecosystem. Having autonomy provides independence and means that the producers (complementors) can innovate to create products and services. This innovation enriches the ecosystem. The role of complementors is different from a traditional seller situation, which can be determined by the buyers because complementors can decide which products they do – or don't – wish to make. Plus, complementors can work with other complementors. For example, the WordPress e-commerce system WooCommerce works with many payment providers, including Apple Pay and Google Pay. The platform owners make it easy for producers to build complementary products and often offer **software development kits** (see Key Term) to encourage more producers to create more content.

> ## KEY TERM SOFTWARE DEVELOPMENT KITS
>
> Software development kits (SDKs) are ready-made tools or software templates, provided by the platform owner, that can be used to build a piece of software for a specific digital platform. SDKs make the process of creating software or apps much faster and they are easier to add to the connected ecosystem, as they already follow their format.
>
> For example, Apple has SDKs for mobile developers to create apps for the app store such as Apple store. Google provides SDKs for developers to integrate Google products such as maps, automatic sign-ins and analytics.

Earlier research (Alstyne et al., 2016) suggested there were 4 players in the digital platform ecosystem; the platform owner, the technology providers, the producers and the consumers. Whoever controls the platform controls the intellectual property (IP) which may include the name (e.g. Meta), how the platform works and what's included and removed, as well as who can join and who's excluded. The controller is the arbiter – the person or organisation with the final say as to what happens or not.

For example, Apple decides which apps are permitted to join the App store. Providing feedback on its activities in 2020, Apple rejected over 413,000 apps and terminated 470,000 developer accounts (2021). The issue of control of the platform ownership and the value created by the producers is a constant theme that Alstyne and colleagues (2016) recognised. But they also noted the role of the technology tools (interfaces) provided by the providers of the interfaces, whether that's a mobile phone, gaming devices or laptop. Without the providers, the platform cannot exist as they are the connection between the platform owner and the producers. Consumers also play a role and if you have ever shared negative feedback about an app that didn't work well, you are a player in the platform ecosystem, offering feedback to the producer, and also the platform owner. Figure 4.1 shows the relationship between the players in a platform ecosystem.

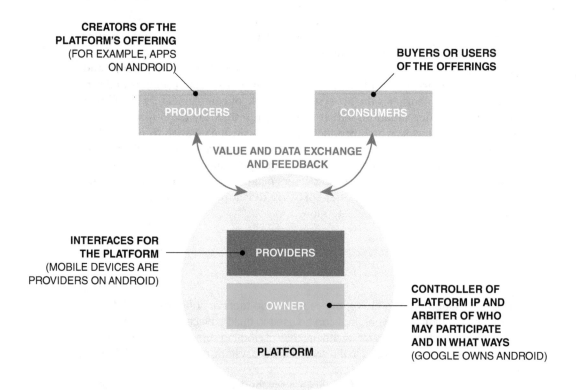

Figure 4.1   The players in a platform ecosystem

Source: Alstyne et al. (2016: 58). Printed with permission of Harvard Business Review

Figure 4.1 is based on earlier research and separates the producers and consumers, yet the researchers recognised that this was interchangeable and that some producers might be consumers and some consumers may also be producers, within a multi-sided network. For example, an Uber driver may also be a rider and the other way around.

4.2.2 NETWORK EFFECTS AND DIGITAL PLATFORM ECOSYSTEMS

The platforms may seem like a successful model that always works. But to function they need larger numbers of users (consumers) with sufficient offers (producers or buyers) to make the platform worth visiting. This is known as network externalities or **network effects** (Katz & Shapiro, 1985). To sum up, 'online marketplaces like Amazon or Alibaba are only attractive to consumers when enough complementors offer their products. Complementors, in turn, participate only if they can reach enough consumers' (Poniatowski et al., 2021: 268).

DISCOVER MORE ABOUT NETWORK EFFECTS

The original article by the creators of network effects, Michael L. Katz & Carl Shapiro's, 'Systems Competition and Network Effects' (1994), considers how network effects occur and the challenges of launching new systems.

Platforms that failed did not gain sufficient users. Do you remember YikYak, Google+ or Whisper? YikYak was an anonymous feedback site that was student focused and a space for negative comments about teachers. Students were unlikely to pay to use the app and advertisers were not keen on being in a toxic space, so it was difficult to gain consumers and producers. Google+ was intended to be an online community app but was difficult to use. As a later entrant to online networking, it was difficult to see why it would benefit users – there was no added value. Whisper was an anonymous app to share secrets and gossip. But its poor data management infringed data protection legislation, so it was removed from the Apple store. The failure of such platforms can be due to factors such as pricing, promotion and usability, but it's often about value. Successful platforms offer value for buyers and sellers and continue to evolve. This is why the main social media platforms continue to add (and remove) features they believe will benefit the users – and the advertisers. As soon as user numbers drop, the platforms panic and find ways to bring in more users.

On the other hand, the mega platforms such as Amazon and Alibaba continue to add more and more products to the store, so their platforms become the easiest places to shop. They constantly add consumers and producers, benefiting from a large and growing network.

Smartphone Sixty Seconds© – Find failed digital platforms

- Take out your mobile phone and search for 'failed digital platforms'.
- Did you find articles about this subject? Delve in to see how many platforms have failed.
- Have you ever subscribed to a platform that was later closed? How did you feel about this?
- Or explore other platforms that have closed. Why did they fail? What could they learn if re-launching?

Activity 4.1   Evaluate a digital platform ecosystem

Consider a digital platform that you use. This could be a social media platform or a shopping platform. Assess the advantages and disadvantages for the different parties involved, and how the ecosystem benefits from the wider network of both buyers and sellers. Consider reasons why the platform might fail in the future or become more successful.

4.3 DIGITAL PAYMENTS

Digital payments take many forms, from online payments to mobile wallets. Mobile devices have enabled easier access to digital payments with access to a digital wallet, removing the need for cash. Digital payment types include those shown in Table 4.1.

Table 4.1   Digital payment types

Payment type	What this means	Example systems
Mobile peer-to-peer payment systems	Paying friends, family or other people via your mobile phone	Venmo, Facebook Messenger, Paym
Pre-loaded credit cards into an app	Payment made to a credit card and monies are drawn down as needed	Typically used for convenience apps such as parking apps (PayByPhone, DashPark, RingGo) and shopping apps (Amazon)
MPOS technology (mobile point-of-sale wireless technology)	Portable point of sale device	Apple stores use MPOS systems so each sales assistant provides a checkout function
Biometric payments	Payment systems controlled by facial recognition from a credit card stored in a mobile phone	Apple Pay, Google Pay
Mobile phone text to pay	Funds are debited to the mobile phone account	Used for fundraising and competitions
Debit card online	Pay now using a card that takes funds from a bank account	Debit cards from high street banks
Credit card online	Pay later using the credit card facility or using Buy Now Pay Later (BNPL) systems	Credit cards (e.g. VISA, Mastercard) or BNPL systems such as Klarna
Cryptocurrencies	Online virtual currency stored in virtual wallets	Bitcoin, Ethereum

Adapted from Hanlon (2022) and Stocchi (2022)

The digital payment types are mainly dependent on money being placed into a credit card or online bank. Technology means that the payments are international and can be used in different channels, including in store, online, via mobile and apps. Regardless of channel, when the credit request is made, the seller makes an instant application to the credit card issuer. This may sound complicated, but digital payment providers such as VISA processes nearly 1.5 trillion dollars in payments a year (VISA, 2022). For example, Figure 4.2 shows how VISA Direct processes credit card payments. This starts with the payment request (1) which is the Original Credit Transaction (OCT) from the originating institution, which could be an online store or business (2). This is sent to your bank (recipient institution) and credited to your VISA account (3) and the funds are released to confirm a payment in store, online or with cash (4). While this looks like a lengthy process, it takes seconds from start to finish.

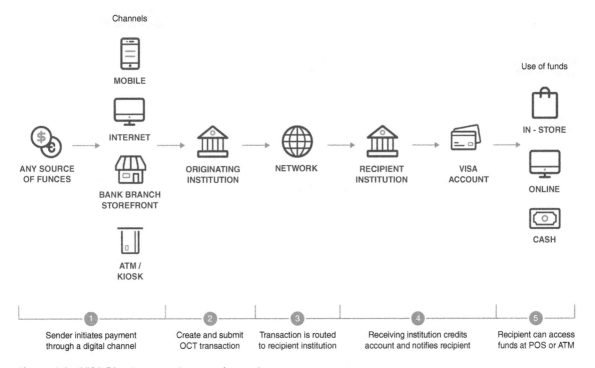

Figure 4.2 VISA Direct payment processing system

Source: VISA Direct (2022: 5). Printed with permission of VISA Direct

4.3.1 ACCESS TO FINANCIAL SERVICES

Having access to a banking service provides financial freedom and less reliance on a cash or shadow economy, which was reduced during the COVID-19 pandemic as more organisations started to accept credit card payments. The World Bank Group (Asli Demirgüç-Kunt et al., 2021) acknowledges that access to making or receiving digital payments is part of financial inclusion. It enables individuals to access regulated loans when needed, rather than relying on more expensive informal systems in the **shadow economy** (see Key Term). It allows individuals to be represented in the workforce, gain access to accommodation, and make and receive money from different sources. Yet to access digital payments individuals often need formal documents, or a device to make the payment, as well as literacy and numeracy skills.

> ## KEY TERM SHADOW ECONOMY
>
> According to advisors at the International Monetary Fund (Schneider & Enste, 2002: 2), 'the underground, informal, or parallel ... or shadow economy includes not only illegal activities but also unreported income from the production of legal goods and services, either from monetary or barter transactions'.

CASE EXAMPLE 4.1 Kudu

Not everyone has access to traditional payment systems, and technology constraints in parts of Africa have resulted in an innovative use of mobile apps to address financial inclusion (David-West et al., 2019). For example, Nigeria, with over 210 million people (Sasu, 2022), represents one of the youngest populations in the world. Access to the internet is mainly via mobile phone (84%), which means that access to finance may be through a mobile phone app. However, affordable access to finance is a challenge (David-West et al., 2019).

The founders, Babs Ogundeyi and Musty Mustapha, were frustrated with bank charges and so launched Kuda Bank (see kuda.com). A neo-bank, expanding across Africa and into the UK, its website explains that the word 'Kuda' means 'love' in Shona, a language spoken in the southern part of Africa. As a challenger bank, Kuda has raised over $90 million in funds from several firms, including Valar Ventures, which was co-founded and backed by Peter Thiel, who is a co-founder of PayPal and was an early investor in Facebook.

With offices in South Africa and the UK, Kuda has big ambitions. Kuda's website states: 'We're a fintech on a mission to make financial services more accessible, affordable and rewarding for every African on the planet.' The Kuda app allows users to save, spend, send and invest money. It has introduced a budget feature so users can see where the money goes and more recently introduced short-term loans to allow app users to borrow small amounts of money before their payday. They are cheaper and more accessible than traditional banks and as their website explains, Kuda is different from other banks because:

> We don't have branches (because you don't need branches). Kuda runs entirely on your phone (with an internet connection) and we'll deliver your debit card to any address in Nigeria.
>
> Because we don't have branches, we save a lot of money. That's why we can afford not to charge you ridiculous fees and pay you more interest than most banks.

They are transparent about how they make money:

> We make money by using collective deposits to make investments and issue credit.
>
> We also make money from commission on airtime purchases and from service fees sellers pay us when people like you shop with their Kuda Card.

To open an account with a traditional bank requires proof of ID (passport, biometric residence permit, full driving licence), 3 years of your address history and a mobile phone number, plus you must be at least 18 years old to access the app. Kuda only needs an email address and a phone number, and you need to be at least 16 years old. This is how digital financial inclusion works, removing traditional barriers.

Case questions

- What do you think about Kuda or other neo-banks? There are many benefits, but are there any risks?
- Do banks or financial institutions need to have branches for customers to visit? Why is this?
- Mobile money is changing how banking works, but what are the downsides?

According to the World Bank's research (Asli Demirgüç-Kunt et al., 2021) there are concerns about using digital banking in several countries, due to the lack of transparency and the potential for data or identity theft and fraud. Also, in some locations, the nearest bank may be some distance, which is where mobile phone banking systems can provide an alternative solution.

DIGITAL TOOL   Global Findex Database

The World Bank reports on access to finance worldwide, highlighting financial inclusion and digital payments.

- You can explore it here: worldbank.org/en/publication/globalfindex

4.3.2 CRYPTOCURRENCIES

According to Hanlon (2022: 18), 'in 2009 a new form of digital currency was introduced to the world, a cryptocurrency called Bitcoin. Created anonymously, it works on the basis of peer-to-peer financing. There are no banks, no third parties, no bank vaults, no cash machines involved with Bitcoin'.

Bitcoins are created by mining, and an industry of Bitcoin miners has developed but this consumes significant energy (see section 6.4.1). This has not stopped the development of over 10,000 cryptocurrencies. PayPal is making it easier for ordinary citizens to store and access their cryptocurrency and other payment systems may follow their lead.

Activity 4.2   Analyse digital payment systems

In groups consider the different types of digital payment systems available to you as students.

- Which digital payment systems do most of the group use? Why is this?
- What are the greatest challenges of managing digital payments for individuals?
- How do you feel about credit systems such as *buy now pay later*? Are these helpful or dangerous systems? Why is this?
- What are the greatest challenges of managing digital payments for organisations?
- How could future payment systems improve for individuals and organisations?

4.4 DIGITAL PRICING

Traditional pricing is less dynamic than digital pricing. In stores, the prices are printed onto labels which are usually attached to the goods or on the shelves. Making changes requires significant effort, removing and replacing prices. A short-term solution is to offer flash sales – time-limited discounts off specific goods. Digital pricing allows greater flexibility for merchants as well as pricing strategies which can involve free services, freemium, subscription, tiered or dynamic pricing. Let's explore each of these options.

4.4.1 FREE DIGITAL SERVICES

Many digital services appear to be free although they are funded through the sale of other services. For example, services from many tech companies are paid for by advertising, including:

- Alphabet products (Google Chrome, search results, YouTube)
- Meta products (Facebook, Instagram, Messenger, WhatsApp)

But the challenge is if the service is free, you are the product. Your online behaviour, your profile and your data are shared with advertisers through the use of code known as cookies. Yet, as data protection legislation was enforced across many countries, tech companies changed their behaviour towards third-party cookies. For example, Apple introduced *Web and App Tracking Transparency*, so allowed users to decide whether or not an app or website could track their online behaviour. Google also plans to remove third-party cookies. Table 4.2 shows different types of cookies, their advantages and their disadvantages.

As Table 4.2 shows the different types of cookies where their purpose is to collect data, yet the United Nations Conference on Trade and Development (2021) explains that data protection legislation exists in 71% of countries. Some (9%) have draft legislation. There are issues with the remaining 20% because 15% have no legislation and 5% appear to have no data.

Table 4.2   Types of cookies

Cookie type	What this means	Advantages	Disadvantages
First-party cookies (also known as persistent cookies)	Cookies embedded into websites	• Allows web visitors to navigate a website in a personalised way, e.g. to log in and view previous orders • Not shared with other websites • Often used for shopping websites and places where you log in and save the website to save the data	• Only relates to a single website, does not provide details about subsequent websites the user visited
Third-party cookies	Cookies placed on your device (e.g. mobile or laptop) after visiting a website and the data (websites visited, time spent on site, etc.) is sent to a third party, typically an advertiser	• Provides data for marketers, e.g. identifying users with interests in specific topics • Shows where users are in the customer journey and if searching or ready to buy the goods • Can track users across multiple websites	• Seen as intrusive and governed by legislation in many countries • Unlikely to exist in the future
Session cookies	Temporary cookies	• Convenient when shopping online as they remember the pages visited on a website • Only retain your data while you're on the site	• When you close the website, the cookie expires and you may need to start the process again

DIGITAL TOOL   Data Protection and Privacy Legislation Worldwide

The United Nations Conference on Trade and Development tracks data protection and privacy legislation worldwide.

• You can see the data protection and privacy legislation in your country here: unctad.org/page/data-protection-and-privacy-legislation-worldwide

Smartphone Sixty Seconds© – Check cookie policies

• Take out your mobile phone and log in to a social network platform you use.
• Find the privacy policy (you may need to search for this) and spend only 5 minutes reviewing this.
• How much of the policy did you review? How many pages? Did you discover more about how your data is used?
• How much time do you think you would need to review the whole policy? How do you feel about this?

4.4.2 FREEMIUM

Moving beyond free digital services, another pricing strategy is freemium, which 'involves selling a base version of the product for free, and making premium product features available to users only on payment' (Runge et al., 2022: 102). This is also known as free to fee where the products aim to convince users to move towards the fee-paying version. According to Runge and colleagues (2022), there is complementarity between the free goods and the paid-for options, as typically the paid-for options enhance the basic or downgraded version. Premium features involve additional features or advertising-free versions. They are available in different apps and platforms, such as:

- Games where users pay for in-game currency to enhance the gameplay
- Professional social media, to access additional features, such as sending in-mails on LinkedIn
- Lifestyle, to access additional features, such as greater statistics with Strava or to access an ad-free version, such as Duolingo or Spotify
- Productivity, to access greater storage, such as Apple's iCloud or Dropbox

Researchers Deng and colleagues (2022: 1) recognise that 'Freemium is a prevalent pricing model for mobile apps'. They also suggest that it is a useful way for users to sample a product before committing to pay for the service. However, the more that users consume the base product, the more likely they are to pay for premium alternatives (Runge et al., 2022).

Freemium is also used as a referral system. For example, Dropbox, the online storage system, rewarded users for recommending other users. Another example is the language-learning app Duolingo, which rewards users with additional benefits when they share their results with friends. Researchers Belo & Li (2022: 8933) suggest that as a business model freemium 'can be an effective growth and monetization strategy for platforms'. However, it can be challenging to encourage free users to pay for additional features (Belo & Li, 2022). Plus, free versions can cannibalise paid-for apps (Deng et al., 2022).

4.4.3 DIGITAL SUBSCRIPTIONS

Subscriptions started over 500 years ago with payment for regular access to publications. Gartner researcher Mark Lewis (2022: 2) provides a helpful definition of a subscription as 'a contract between a supplier and a customer for the supply of a product or service over an extended period of time'. Subscriptions are available as fixed or variable recurring payments:

- Fixed recurring payments are where a regular amount is paid each month, for example $0.99 per month for access to Apple iCloud
- Variable recurring payments are often based on usage; for example your mobile phone bill may increase if you use too much data or minutes. Energy

bills are usually variable based on the amount of electricity, gas or other source used

According to Coppola (2022b: 1), 'The market size of the digital subscription economy worldwide amounted to 650 billion U.S. dollars in 2020'. This means that it is an attractive market for investors and many organisations are moving from one-off costs to regular monthly payments. The largest areas for subscriptions are IT, then media and communications (Coppola, 2022a). A leading player in IT services subscriptions is Microsoft, selling Software-as-a-Service (SaaS) with a monthly fee per user. You may be more familiar with media and communications subscriptions such as Netflix, Spotify, Dropbox and iCloud, yet subscriptions surround our daily lives, as Figure 4.3 illustrates.

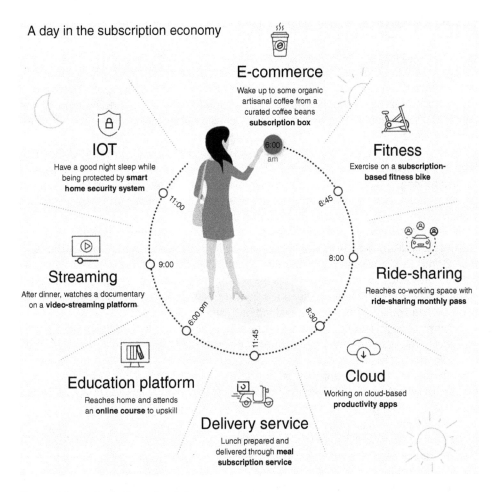

Figure 4.3   A day in the subscription economy

Source: UBS Editorial Team (2021). Printed with permission of UBS

Activity 4.3   Create a proposal for a subscription service

In groups prepare a proposal for a subscription service for an existing product. This could be a food or entertainment service that you have experienced. The proposal should include the rationale as to why this is a good idea, as well as identifying potential challenges and the amount to be charged.

Another growing area for subscriptions are podcasts, as Case Example 4.2 'Podimo' explains.

CASE EXAMPLE 4.2   Podimo

Podimo is a digital podcast company that was founded in Copenhagen in 2019 by entrepreneur Morten Strunge. It has developed a subscription-based audio service, offering podcasts and audiobooks in European countries, including Denmark, Germany, Spain, Norway and across Latin America. Through a range of partnerships with Disney and Paramount, the service is also available in the USA. There are expansion plans to take the service into many more locations.

Its content includes Podimo-exclusive material as well as regular podcasts. Its audiobooks feature best-sellers, classic books and a children's section. The firm has in-house product studios managed by engineers and product managers. The engineers and tech support are expected to have knowledge of several SDKs and have options for remote or hybrid working from countries such as Lithuania and Denmark.

When the podcast app is downloaded and topics are selected, the app suggests similar content that is likely to be of interest. Podcasts are long-form and short-form, which is less than 20 minutes, and are said to be more popular with listeners. As listeners explore the different material, podcast suggestions become more personalised; this is called 'smart curation'. Other product features comprise in-app video, updates when new episodes are available, and offline listening to download and listen later.

In terms of pricing and payments, the app is free for a 7-day trial and then priced at €5 per month. This premium service is free from advertisements. This contrasts with firms such as Apple which offers a freemium service with the basic version paid-for by advertisements. What makes Podimo different from other podcast platforms is that it shares a portion of its revenue with the podcast creators, not the way Spotify shares with the top creators, but specifically with the podcasters whose material is consumed.

The Podcaster Studio page enables creators to upload their audio material and add descriptive content so it's easy for listeners to find in the podcast library. The Podcaster Studio includes a dashboard with access to ratings, follower numbers and the amount of content that listeners consume.

Recognised as a rising star, the platform has attracted funding of over $170 million from different investors. The money has been used to build the team which comprises over 220 employees in over 20 different countries. Plus, the firm has made some big hires, including the former VP of Content at Spotify Sachin Doshi and former Apple Music executive Claus Thune.

However, this is a competitive market with a growing number of podcast platforms such as Buzzsprout, Podbean and SoundCloud. Trying to stand out as a new platform is a challenge. Yet the numbers of podcast listeners continue to increase and users may be seeking alternatives. Podimo is well placed with a different approach to revenue sharing which makes it an interesting firm to watch.

Case questions

- What do you think about Podimo's approach of revenue sharing with creators?
- Podimo aims to provide advertising-free podcasts in exchange for a regular subscription. Is this a good idea or would listeners find advertisements more acceptable than payments?
- How can subscription services such as Podimo keep their subscribers? What are the challenges they face in subscriber retention?

4.4.4 DYNAMIC AND PERSONALISED DIGITAL PRICING

Another advance in technology is automation, which directly impacts on pricing. According to Scully (2022), marketing automation offers dynamic pricing based on customer profile and customer behaviour which is driven by code and recognised as a form of **algorithmic pricing** (see Key Term).

KEY TERM ALGORITHMIC PRICING

According to Seele and colleagues (2021: 702), algorithmic pricing 'is a pricing strategy that builds on computer algorithms, which set prices for goods and services dynamically at either the aggregate or individual level'. The algorithms gather data on competitors' prices, market conditions and the searcher characteristics and adjust the online price.

Dynamic algorithmic pricing based on customer profiles may offer personalised content with more expensive holidays (Scully, 2022) being shown to customers characterised as having greater income levels based on previous searches, their likes and dislikes and their location. Equally, if a website recognises a visitor has landed on the web page previously, they may offer voucher codes for new or returning customers, based on cookie data (see Table 4.2). Dynamic algorithmic pricing based on customer behaviour can change depending on where the web visitor is in their customer journey (Scully, 2022). Those at the start of the customer journey may be conducting research and exploring many websites. As the knowledge is gained and the customer refines their search, they may be ready to purchase. For example, holiday offers may vary depending on the frequency of visits to the website and the search terms used. Someone starting to explore the idea of a visit to Norway may seek 'holidays to Norway' in a search engine, which is a broad search indicating initial research, rather than a specific request. Compare that to the search terms 'guesthouses in Bergen, Norway, fjords in July', which is a refined search that indicates the web visitor has decided the location and has started planning the trip (see Chapter 11 'Digital Customer Experience Management' for more on customer journeys) and may be ready to purchase, and in this case, a time-limited offer may appear. But there's a dark side too, as shown in Ethical Insights **Discriminatory personalised pricing**.

ETHICAL INSIGHTS   Discriminatory personalised pricing

It is recognised that algorithms adapt prices based on customer profiles and this can lead to bias where some customers are charged much more than others based on age, gender, ethnicity or other factors.

Earlier in its store development, Amazon used discriminatory personalised pricing, but this was soon ended due to a backlash (Hufnagel et al., 2022). Yet dynamic pricing can be a useful way to sell off goods that may be expiring, such as aeroplane seats or theatre tickets. But there are risks in using dynamic personalised pricing as consumers can more easily share variations in social media, so the practice is less likely to remain hidden.

Using artificial intelligence (AI), the company QuickLizard helps businesses to automate dynamic pricing, but is acutely aware of the potential for bias. They note 'Artificial intelligence may be capable of parsing through data, recognizing patterns, and drawing conclusions, but it begins with a team of human programmers. These programmers enter any engagement with a set of personal biases' (QuickLizard, 2023: 6). They recommend that biases should be recognised and addressed before being called out by shareholders. See Chapter 5 for more on AI.

- Have you and your classmates experienced different prices for the same goods and how do you feel about this?
- What factors lead organisations to dynamically alter pricing?
- Is it a benefit if different prices for different people mean that some gain lower prices than others?

DISCOVER MORE ON DYNAMIC AND DIGITAL PRICING

Read 'Mapping the ethicality of algorithmic pricing: A review of dynamic and personalized pricing' by Seele and colleagues (2021). This article reviews the literature in this area and discusses ethical issues relating to dynamic pricing.

4.4.5 PRICE COMPARISON WEBSITES

In a digital context, a helpful mechanism for consumers is price comparison websites which are considered specialised search engines (Laffey, 2022: 199), also known as aggregators as they crawl through websites and combine information, presenting collections of data in one place. Price comparison websites enable consumers to review the best prices before making a purchase, making prices more transparent. Price comparison websites are used in many sectors, such as:

- Car and travel insurance, e.g. CompareTheMarket
- Hotels, e.g. Kayak, Trivago
- General goods, e.g. Pricerunner

There are downsides to price comparison websites as the focus is purely on price, not the service or added value. Research has discovered that because the price comparison websites charge firms to appear on their sites, the costs increase for everyone (Ronayne, 2021).

DISCOVER MORE ON PRICE COMPARISON WEBSITES

Read 'Price comparison websites' by Des Laffey (2022). This chapter explains the different types of price comparison websites and how they collect data and generate revenue, as well as the challenges with this process.

4.5 DIGITAL PLATFORM GOVERNANCE

As digital platforms continue to increase in size and power, a frequent concern is the **governance** (see Key Term) of the platforms. The greatest issues are about the amount of data collected and the 'level of control over how the information is collected' (Unni, 2022: 338). According to Flew (2021), these issues are summarised in 7 main areas of public concern with digital platforms. These are:

- Online privacy and security
- Data concerns
- Algorithmic sorting
- Disinformation and fake news
- Hate speech and online abuse
- Impact on media and creative industries
- Information monopolies

To manage these concerns, legislation is developing to formally govern the platforms in different geographical areas, as the examples in Table 4.3 show. These are in addition to the General Data Protection Regulation in place across Europe and the California Consumer Privacy Act which give individuals more control over the management of their data (Unni, 2022).

Table 4.3   Legislation of digital platforms

Area	Legislation	Purpose of legislation
Africa (some countries)	The African Union (AU) Convention on Cybersecurity and Data Protection (known as the AU Convention)	To protect data
Australia	Online Safety Act	To manage cyberbullying and online content
China	Data Security and Personal Information	To address online privacy and security
European Union	The Digital Services Act and Digital Markets Act	To protect users' rights
		To maintain fairness for businesses
Norway	Marketing Act	To label content which has been enhanced or edited by influencers
Japan	The Act on Improving Transparency and Fairness of Digital Platforms	To ensure the platforms provide transparency and act fairly
UK	The Digital Economy Act	To manage data sharing

> **KEY TERM**   GOVERNANCE
>
> Governance involves establishing and implementing the frameworks or guidelines to manage an entity which may be citizens, organisations or regions. L. Chen and colleagues (2022: 153) suggest that platform governance 'can be seen as consisting of a set of over-arching rules, constraints, and inducements that platform owners develop and utilize'.

Digital platforms, from Twitter (now X) to Meta products such as Facebook, have been subject to multiple fines and misdemeanours due to fake news, hate speech or online abuse (Ounvorawong et al., 2022). This indicates they are unable to govern their own organisations and lawmakers have decided to intervene to manage the platforms which have strongholds or monopolies in certain areas.

The key issues around digital platform governance are incentive and control. Incentive is where material is shared and both parties benefit; for example, sharing customer profile data or sharing financial gains. Apple shares software tools to enable producers to create more apps for its devices. This means that both Apple and the producer benefit from the arrangement. However, in some cases there can be an impact on the creative industries where users are encouraged to create their own content, working for free to help promote the platform.

Control is where the platforms limit access or remove privileges. For example, Twitter decided who was and was not allowed to use their platform when fake news was being shared. Also, Amazon and eBay reduce access to top seller benefits when seller rankings drop.

The future of digital platforms is likely to be surrounded with greater legislation and enforced accountability. As platforms such as X overshadow news media, Alphabet's Google search platform monopolises online search, and Meta products from WhatsApp to Messenger dominate messaging services, the next era of digital platforms will see greater care and control, especially with widespread application of artificial intelligence which we explore further in Chapter 5.

JOURNAL OF NOTE

The Journal of Emerging Market Finance *(JEMF)* is a 'forum for debate and discussion on the theory and practice of finance in emerging markets'. Emerging markets take a different approach and consider financial inclusion, rather than assuming finance is available to all. The journal explores different financial products such as microfinance and the challenges with foreign investment.

CASE STUDY

PAYPAL'S DIGITAL PAYMENT PRODUCTS

PayPal is a digital payment platform that has acquired or partnered with many payment companies to expand its offer to vendors, merchants and consumers. It is not always obvious which brands are owned by PayPal as it is a 'house of brands' and keeps the original brand names. The firm provides peer-to-peer payments (P2P) so friends can pay each other, checkouts for online stores, processing systems for online stores, payout tools to pay people back, in-person payments, business and risk services as well as marketing tools. Figure 4.4 shows the range of payment solutions offered and the different brand names.

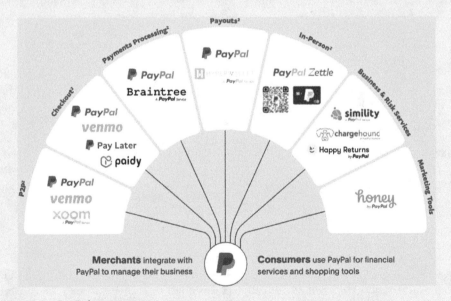

Figure 4.4   PayPal payment systems

Source: PayPal, 2022a with permission from PayPal.com

(Continued)

P2P payments include Venmo, which started 'as a way for founders Andrew Kortina and Iqram Magdon-Ismail to pay each other without having to exchange cash or write a cheque' (Curry, 2023: 1). Venmo is used by nearly 80 million people and became popular with students in the USA as an easy way to pay friends, collect money from friends and pay for takeaway food. Companies taking payments via Venmo include musical artists who sell merchandise at gigs and smaller businesses who need a simple solution to collecting payment. Venmo is considered to be a digital wallet as you can add currency to the account or use with a credit or debit card. Available in the USA, Venmo can also be used at the checkout by firms, including Uber Eats. Additionally, PayPal recognises new digital currencies and are using Venmo to address this. PayPal has:

> [i]ntroduced the ability to buy, sell and hold cryptocurrency through Venmo and launched an education portal within the app to help consumers make informed decisions about purchasing digital currencies. Additionally, we launched Cash Back to Crypto for the Venmo Credit Card, giving card holders the ability to automatically purchase cryptocurrency from their Venmo account using cash back earned from card purchases. (PayPal, 2021: 26)

As well as Venmo, another P2P system is Xoom, which allows users to send money to a bank account, to a debit card, to a mobile phone or send cash to be collected or have cash delivered to your door. Available in over 150 countries, Xoom is a way for family and friends to pay their bills from an app instead of queueing in a bank.

In addition to the P2P systems, Zettle is used for in-person B2C (business-to-consumer payments. As a point-of-sale system Zettle is designed for individual vendors and smaller businesses to take card payments using a less complex device in store and also outdoors. It is a popular payment solution for vendors at pop-up stores, outdoor fairs and exhibitions, as well smaller stores.

Following the COVID-19 pandemic, fewer people carry cash, so paying for goods has moved, in many cases, towards debit or credit cards. One case where this has been successful is *The Big Issue*, which is a magazine sold by those experiencing poverty and homelessness. *The Big Issue* started in the UK and expanded to 41 countries from Australia to Japan. The 'vendors' – *The Big Issue* sellers – sell the magazine for a small profit to help them get back into work. To address the lack of physical cash being carried by people who might buy the magazine, PayPal (2021: 22) noted that the firm 'helped equip vendors with Zettle card readers and PayPal QR codes to offer touch-free digital payments'. It also notes: 'The Big Issue found that vendors who offer cashless payment options earn an average of 30% more than those who do not.'

Venmo and Xoom are designed for P2P payments, so you can more easily pay friends and family. Zettle is a different product that is aimed at small businesses. Hyperwallet is another digital payment system that is designed to transfer money to contract workers or freelancers in different countries. It offers ready-made compliance, so the finance team doesn't need to work out regulations in different countries. For companies working in marketplaces such as Fiverr and Upwork, Hyperwallet can take payments from customers and make payouts to many different people.

CASE QUESTIONS

PayPal has a range of payment solutions and continues to innovate and bring more support to its merchants.

- With so many payment tools, how are digital wallets managed by individuals?
- What are the greatest challenges facing PayPal's range of products?
- What are the downsides of a digital wallet and why is this?

FURTHER EXERCISES

1. Analyse the role of mega digital platforms and their impact on smaller organisations.

2. Create a plan to launch a new food or entertainment product by subscription.

3. For an organisation of your choice, undertake research, and critically analyse their pricing models in comparison to 2 competitors.

4. The future of money is digital and cash will no longer exist in 10 years' time. Discuss.

SUMMARY

This chapter has explored:

- The key elements of digital platform ecosystems and the players involved
- Types of digital payments and the shadow economy
- Digital pricing strategies, including free services, freemium, subscription, dynamic and price comparison websites
- Challenges with digital platform governance

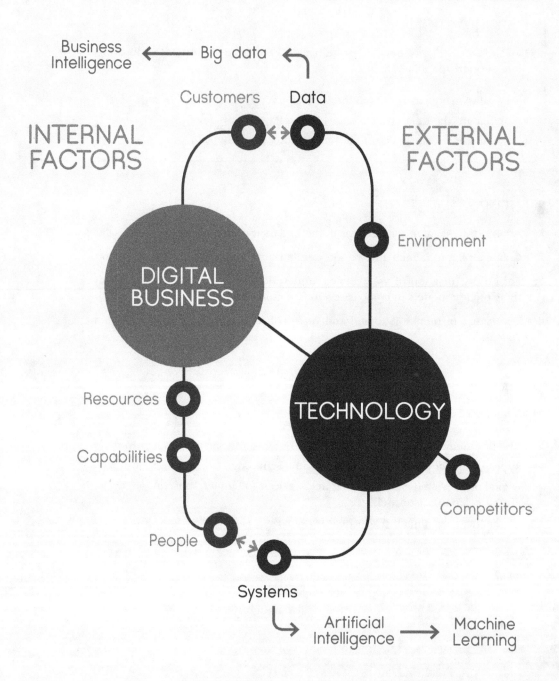

Business
Intelligence ← Big data ←

Customers   Data

INTERNAL
FACTORS

EXTERNAL
FACTORS

Environment

DIGITAL
BUSINESS

TECHNOLOGY

Resources

Capabilities

Competitors

People

Systems

Artificial   →   Machine
Intelligence   Learning

5

AI, BIG DATA AND BUSINESS INTELLIGENCE

LEARNING OUTCOMES

When you have read this chapter, you will be able to:

Understand the concept of big data

Apply big data potential for organisations

Analyse data for business intelligence

Evaluate opportunities for machine learning

Create a plan to harness business intelligence

PROFESSIONAL SKILLS

When you have worked through this chapter, you should be able to:

- Disseminate best practice of AI
- Apply principles relating to governance and regulatory compliance to big data

5.1 BACKGROUND TO AI, BIG DATA AND BUSINESS INTELLIGENCE

Artificial intelligence (AI) is using computers to automate or enhance tasks. For AI to be successful it requires data, and lots of it, which is known as big data. When AI has access to big data it can provide business intelligence.

For example, Microsoft and Google have been using AI for many years. When you start typing an email and predictive text appears, that's powered by AI. Both Google and Microsoft offer conversational speech recognition: you start speaking and your voice is recognised. This works with Siri and Google as well as in documents, so if you can't type, open a Word or Google document and use Dictate or Voice Typing.

This chapter explores the different types of AI, how they are applied and the interconnected elements of big data and business intelligence.

Smartphone Sixty Seconds© – Identify the growth of artificial intelligence

- Take out your mobile phone and search for 'growth of artificial intelligence'.
- What did you discover? Any interesting facts or figures?
- Why is this?

5.2 ARTIFICIAL INTELLIGENCE (AI)

5.2.1 THE EVOLUTION OF AI

Computer scientists have been exploring the concept of artificial intelligence (AI), or using systems to complete tasks and generate material, for decades. Early versions of AI involved computers competing with experts to win games; for example, IBM's Deep Blue computer system which played chess with the world champion Garry Kasparov. Deep Blue and Kasparov played 6 games in 1997 and the computer won 2 games, Kasparaov won 1 and there were 3 draws. Deep Blue was based on machine learning where different scenarios for chess games had been programmed and where the computer learned from the games. After Deep Blue had been launched, researchers in London started programming another computer to play basic games. This resulted in DeepMind, which is notable as it was the first computer to beat a professional player in the board game Go, where 2 players battle to control more of the board with their counters. But in 2023 Kellin Pelrine, an American player, beat Go! He won 14 of 15 games, using a computer system to identify potential weaknesses in the board game. According to the *Financial Times* journalist Richard Waters (2023), they took advantage of a blind spot. This demonstrates that while the computers may be good, they don't think like people – yet.

DeepMind was later acquired by Google after a sale to Facebook fell through. Google started to explore the ethics of AI and were founders of **the partnership on Artificial Intelligence** (see Digital Tool) as this was a concern. The European Commission published the report *Ethics by Design and Ethics of Use Approaches for Artificial Intelligence* (2021a) as they wanted to ensure that those working in AI respected humans, their privacy and data, as well as being accountable and transparent in their procedures. For example, in Chapter 4 we considered Ethical Insights **Discriminatory personalised pricing**, which in part is due to programmers who may introduce their own bias into the code. A key aspect of all elements of AI is for developers to adopt **FATE** – fairness, accountability, transparency and ethics (see Discover More), to reduce bias and to create AI for good.

DIGITAL TOOL   The partnership on artificial intelligence

The partnership on artificial intelligence is a non-profit organisation and its website states that it creates 'tools, recommendations, and other resources by inviting voices from across the AI community and beyond to share insights that can be synthesized into actionable guidance'. Their mission focuses on AI empowering humanity and inclusion. Their partners comprise the major tech firms as well as many well-known organisations that use AI.

- You can explore it here: partnershiponai.org

DISCOVER MORE ON FATE

Read 'FATE in AI: Towards algorithmic inclusivity and accessibility' by Isa Inuwa-Dutse (2023). This article explores ethics in AI and the issues of fairness, accountability, transparency and ethics.

5.2.2 DEFINITIONS AND TYPES OF AI

While AI has been established for many years, there is confusion about what AI is and is not. This is in part due to its evolution from 'narrow to general to super-intelligenced' (Kaplan & Haenlein, 2020: 39). In movies AI is the villain! You or your classmates may have heard of the replicants in *Blade Runner*, or The Supreme Intelligence in *Captain Marvel*, or the evil robots in the *Terminator* film franchise. The movies tell us that AI will be very bad for civilisation.

AI is about computers learning from information provided and can be defined as 'a system's ability to interpret external data correctly, to learn from such data, and to use those learnings to achieve specific goals and tasks through flexible adaptation' (Kaplan & Haenlein, 2019: 15). Kaplan & Haenlein (2019) note that

AI is 'classified into analytical, human-inspired, and humanized AI, which they suggested was a hierarchy of AI types starting with cognitive, then emotional and finally social.

ANALYTICAL AI

Analytical AI is human-inspired where the computer understands human emotions and can offer a response based on learning to recognise facial expressions or other behaviour. Although this is still in development, it is being used in the automotive sector with self-driving cars that recognise if the driver is driving too quickly. This is not too complex as the car's computer will have access to speed limits in the area and measure the difference between the permitted speed and the driver's actions.

HUMAN-INSPIRED AI

Human-inspired AI adds emotional intelligence which is where computers are trained to recognise different emotions, from sadness to happiness. But if a person has a confused expression, the wrong response may be generated.

HUMANISED AI

Humanised AI also recognises emotions and takes this one step further as it can respond with social awareness. This is the AI we have seen in movies where robots think and have feelings, yet this is not fully developed and is predicted to occur in the future. Figure 5.1 summarises the types of AI.

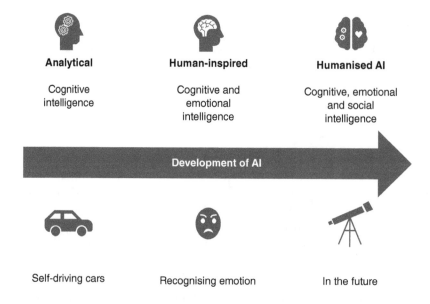

Figure 5.1   Types of AI

The 3 types of AI are all considered generative; that is, they can reproduce or generate material automatically. However, it is important to recognise that AI is not human intelligence (Kaplan & Haenlein, 2020) and is based on a system being fed data to analyse and take algorithmic decisions.

5.2.3 MACHINE LEARNING

A core part of AI is machine learning where the 'learning process is accomplished by machine itself through collecting data, analyzing data and making predictions' (Wang et al., 2019: 2). Figure 5.2 provides a hierarchy of machine learning which at the top level 'can be further sub-divided into 4 categories: supervised, semi-supervised, unsupervised, and reinforcement learning' (Wang et al., 2019: 2).

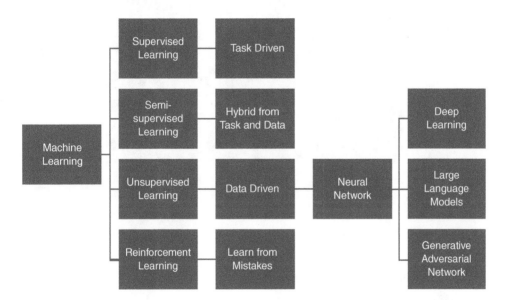

Figure 5.2   Hierarchy of machine learning

SUPERVISED LEARNING

Supervised learning is task driven where the outputs are pre-defined. For example, many websites ask if you are human and you have to click on all the images showing a bridge, boat or bus, as the example in Figure 5.3 shows. The images have been classified using pre-defined sets of data labels where the machine learns the structure of bridges, boats or buses.

SEMI-SUPERVISED LEARNING

Semi-supervised learning is a hybrid between being task and data driven. An example of this is translation where different language dictionaries such as Google Translate (supervised content) are fed into the data set and from this translations are created.

Figure 5.3 CAPTCHA image example

Source: CAPTCHA.net

This means the data is based on the words in the dictionary, but the output may vary. The challenge is the context, as the meaning intended may not be fully delivered, especially where humour or sarcasm are involved and this could result in poor (or embarrassing) translations.

UNSUPERVISED LEARNING

Unsupervised learning is data driven where the system reviews the data to find anomalies or hidden patterns. This is used by Amazon Web Services to detect potential fraud, such as the use of hacked credit cards across the shopping platform. Unsupervised learning can also be used to detect the presence of bots across social media platforms where misinformation is being spread.

Activity 5.1 Evaluate opportunities for machine learning

In groups evaluate opportunities for machine learning for your university.

- Where could machine learning usefully be applied? Discuss several examples where this would save time and money.
- What are the challenges and how could these be mitigated?

Select one opportunity and discuss the would you and your classmates would recommend for the developers.

NEURAL NETWORKS

Another form of machine learning driven by data is that of neural networks. Based on the idea of the brain, which has nearly 100 billion neurons (brain cells), and makes many connections to different items. For example, you can be in class listening to your tutor, taking notes, thinking about what you're doing later and glancing at messages on your mobile phone; these are separate activities taking place at the same time that connect. In AI the neurons simulate the brain (also known as artificial neural networks) and the networks or nets connect the different neurons. Neural networks need data and training to improve over time – in the same way, the more you study, the better your results! Examples of neural nets include:

- Convolutional neural networks – Used for image data, for example facial recognition, biometric authentication and medical imaging
- Recurrent neural networks – Used to assess sequential and temporal data, for example Google and Apple's voice search or speech recognition
- Graph neural networks – Used to assess networks and connections, for example websites that recommend similar products, social media platforms recommending friends or new connections

DEEP LEARNING

Deep learning is a form of neural network at a deeper level. Where neural nets use the data available, deep learning finds hidden layers in the data and makes these connections. This means that where data is captured, the patterns and hidden layers are recognised and based on this, decisions can be made. For example, in online advertising the system can assess the cost per action (click here, download now) in milliseconds, as well as external factors, and buy advertising at better rates than a human. It would be a laborious task to assess such large volumes of data to draw conclusions.

Deep learning is also used in dynamic pricing where there are many different factors. One example is airlines, and according to Koc & Arslan (2021) the variations include: origin airport, destination airport, day of week, week of year, duration, days to departure, the sequence of previously sold seats, the sequence of previous prices, the sequence of price changes, departure time, arrival time, holiday price, available seat capacity, competitor price, cost per available seat kilometre and target revenue – far too many items for a single individual to compute!

LARGE LANGUAGE MODELS

Large language models (LLMs) are massive neural networks that can generate text that appears to be created by humans. LLMs are often used with chatbots where it's not a calculation, but content that's required. A large dataset provides answers to potential questions and may be able to generate content automatically. An example of an LLM is **ChatGPT** (see case example).

CASE EXAMPLE 5.1   ChatGPT

Open AI is a USA-based research company which was founded in 2015 by Elon Musk (owner of Tesla and X – formerly Twitter) and other tech leaders, Sam Altman (Y Combinator, a venture capital firm), Greg Brockman (Stripe payment processing), Dr Ilya Sutskever (Google Brain), Dr John Schulman and Dr Wojciech Zaremba (NVIDIA graphics firm, Google Brain, Facebook AI). Musk left in 2018 to focus on his other businesses. Open AI is funded by private investors, including Microsoft and Reid Hoffman's (LinkedIn) charitable foundation. This means it has a strong tech foundation, it is well connected and their mission is to 'ensure that artificial general intelligence benefits all of humanity'.

One of their products is ChatGPT. A GPT is a Generative Pretrained Transformer which means that the system is trained on large data sets. It acts in a conversational style which means it can respond to questions and answers, as well as admitting mistakes or acknowledging where it lacks data. Effectively you ask a question or make a request and ChatGPT provides a response. When asked 'tell me about ChatGPT' the response is:

> I am ChatGPT, a large language model developed by OpenAI. I am designed to understand natural language and generate human-like responses to text-based prompts.

> I was created using a machine learning technique called deep learning, which involves training a neural network on large amounts of text data. This training allows me to recognize patterns and relationships within text and use that knowledge to generate responses to a wide range of prompts, from answering questions to engaging in conversation.

> As an AI language model, my abilities are not limited to a particular topic or domain, and I can generate responses on a wide range of subjects. I have been trained on a vast corpus of text data, which includes news articles, books, scientific papers, and other sources of information. This training allows me to provide accurate and informative responses to questions and prompts from users.

> My development is ongoing, and I continue to improve as new data and techniques become available. I am available to assist with a variety of tasks, from providing information to engaging in conversation, and I am designed to be easy and intuitive to use.

ChatGPT became famous (or notorious) as students realised they could ask an essay question and the system would provide a response. Some academics have commented that it can provide essay answers, but the standard of scholarly writing is poor (Thorp, 2023).

There are other challenges at this time such as:

- The responses are generic and lack the depth and detail that would be expected at university
- Some of the content is repetitive
- It does not provide responses about individuals at this time
- It is prone to inventing references!

It is likely it will soon improve, but at the same time educators have access to reverse systems which will detect the use of automatic content generation. Plus any work submitted by students as their own that is completed by a third party, whether that's an essay mill or a machine-learning tool, is a criminal offence in parts of Europe and the UK.

Case questions

- Have you or your peers tried ChatGPT or similar GPT systems and, if yes, what were your impressions?
- What do you feel about students who use automatic or other paid-for services to complete their coursework?
- How can systems like ChatGPT be used for good purposes?

GENERATIVE ADVERSARIAL NETWORKS

Generative adversarial networks (GANs) take a different perspective where 2 neural networks – the generator and the discriminator – work against each other. According to Chesney & Citron (2019), the generator uses source data (such as an image dataset of cats) and the discriminator tries to spot fake data (such as dogs) and from this the generator learns what real cats must look like. GANS have been used to identify **deepfakes** (see Key Term) by comparing genuine images of a person to online versions that appear real but are questionable, and from this can recognise deepfakes.

> **KEY TERM**   DEEPFAKE
>
> A deepfake is a digital manipulation of an image, audio or video that is very realistic and credible (Chesney & Citron, 2019). They are difficult to detect and there have been examples of celebrities and politicians who have been victims of deepfakes. They seem to be participating in activities and were considered real when shared online, but were fake and could result in reputational damage or other harm.

DISCOVER MORE ON DEEPFAKES

Read 'Deepfakes and the new disinformation war: The coming age of post-truth geo-politics' by Robert Chesney & Danielle Citron (2019). This article explains the technical background to deepfakes as well as their advantages and disadvantages.

REINFORCEMENT LEARNING

Reinforcement learning is where the system learns by trial and error within a specific environment. When the machine makes mistakes it learns from these and rewards are provided when the right actions are taken. For example, the machine may be part of a production line, assembling goods and placing back on the line. With no errors, the production line continues – this is the reward. If there is an error, the line stops and the machine making the error is identified and will self-correct against repeating the mistake. Reinforcement learning has been used with self-driving cars: when they crash, that's an error, so they learn to avoid obstacles and slow down!

ETHICAL INSIGHTS   Facial recognition systems

A widespread use of AI, specifically convolutional neural networks, is facial recognition software. This started in the 1960s (Pew Research Center, 2022) and has become more sophisticated with improvements in technology, especially better-quality cameras. At a personal level, we use facial recognition systems to enable our smartphones to recognise our faces. This saves us time instead of re-entering passwords and we might not realise that we're using AI.

Facial recognition systems are widely used in government, law enforcement and organisations in countries across Europe, the USA and China. Its advantages in this environment include:

- Smart policing: Finding missing people, detecting drivers under the influence of alcohol or drugs, providing security at airports and large gatherings
- Smart states: Saving time as biometric passports enable faster border crossings
- Smart cities: Saving time for hotel check-ins, access to public buildings and transport

These facial recognition systems detect, analyse and recognise individuals; however, there are many ethical challenges, such as:

- Creating mass surveillance without individual permission
- Fostering bias as the cameras fail to correctly identify so innocent people can be followed or monitored
- Introducing more potential for fraud

Facial recognition software is not without its critics. Supermarkets are using the cameras to identify previous shoplifters and other offenders. Cameras on streets take snapshots as you walk past which are fed into databases to match with suspect lists. The surveillance cameras are being accused of taking 'faceprints' without permission. In the USA, the city of San Francisco has taken a different perspective and has banned the use of facial recognition software. Speaking to *The New York Times* a city representative commented: 'When you have the ability to track people in physical space, in effect everybody becomes subject to the surveillance of the government' (Conger et al., 2019). Other cities are likely to follow this path, although it creates a conflict with law-enforcement agencies who argue that it hinders crime management.

- Do you use facial recognition systems to access your phone or other apps?
- What are the upsides and downsides from your perspective?
- Are there situations where facial recognition systems should be banned? And why?

5.3 BIG DATA

5.3.1 BIG DATA CONCEPTS

For AI to work effectively it needs information and volumes of it, known as **big data** (see Key Term) as it comprises millions of pieces of information. Researchers Caesarius & Hohenthal (2022) identified 4 factors as to why big data developed. While all are due to technology, they state the first was the development of information technology systems within organisations. The data was organised in **relational databases** (see Key Term) to personalise communications. The second factor was the internet as technology moved from being inside a single organisation to being accessible across the World Wide Web. The third factor was social media and Web 3.0 with greater consumer participation which created new types of data. The fourth factor was the Internet of Things, as technology connected computers with other devices that could share data.

Big data refers to 'the increasing complexity and granularity of information' (Caesarius & Hohenthal, 2022: 69) with key characteristics, originally known as the 4Vs, but with greater understanding and application of data this has increased to the 7Vs (Mikalef et al., 2018):

- Volume – the quantity of data
- Velocity – the speed at which data is created
- Variety – the different types of data (see Table 5.1)
- Veracity – the accuracy and trustworthiness of the data
- Variability – how insights vary or change over time as data is reinterpreted
- Visualisation – the patterns and trends that can be seen in the data
- Value – how data generates business value through useful insights

Each time you place an online order you create more data and add to the **volume**. With millions of orders being placed each day the **velocity** of new data creation is impossible to monitor. The key is the **veracity** of the data as sometimes consumers add in their details incorrectly, perhaps forgetting to add the apartment number, getting the zip code, post code or postal number incorrect – this can result in 2 or more records for the same person. The **variety** of big data types are shown in Table 5.1.

Table 5.1   Variety of big data types

Area	Explanation	Examples
Structured	Highly organized data which is easily accessed and is typically stored in a tabular format with common headings in a **relational database**	Names, dates, addresses, credit card numbers, stock information, geolocation
Unstructured	No pre-defined format and is more difficult to capture, process, and analyze which mostly contains text and multimedia material	Emails, blog entries, wikis, and word processing documents, PDF files, audio files, videos, images, presentations, web pages, social media material
Semi-structured	Not stored in a **relational database** but has certain organizational properties that make it easier to analyze	HTML and XML documents
Metadata	Not the normal form of data, but "data about data", metadata describes the relevant data information, giving it more significance for data users	Documents properties such as the author, file size, file type, date generated, keywords

Adapted from Sarker (2021)

KEY TERM   RELATIONAL DATABASE

A relational database organises data in pre-defined columns and rows. For example, the first name is added to the 'first name' column which enables organisations sending messages to customers to personalise the communication and address them by their first name. The data in a relational database is connected to other pieces of data, such as the first name, last name and address.

Data can be combined with other data, which grows or changes over time. For example, in year 1 at university, the system holds basic demographic details about you. In year 2, your grades from year 1 and your attendance may be added to your data record. By year 3 this has changed, showing the **variability** of data. When considering 500 students and their attendance in class or their grade profile it can be easier to see this in a graph. Imagine you are analysing product lines for Carrefour, one of the world's largest supermarkets with 80 million customer households, 93 million loyalty card holders and 18 million fans on social media (Carrefour, 2021) – where do you start to understand which products are popular and which are not, and in which areas? **Visualisation** can help to provide patterns or trends that indicate in certain locations, on certain days, some products are more popular in customer households with 2 people. This is how the data starts to deliver **value** as the insights indicate the actions needed at a local store level. This may be to share promotions to 2-person households, 8 to 12 hours before they typically start shopping. This sounds ideal, yet the challenge with big data is managing it so that it provides value.

5.3.2 MANAGING DATA

For larger organisations operational systems capture data about the daily operations of an organisation in **relational databases**. Operational systems vary depending on the type of organisation and may include the human resource database (who is at work, off work, vacancies), product database (goods in stock, on order), accounting systems (details of the finances), manufacturing systems (orders being processed, raw materials needed), sales data (customers, orders) and logistics (shipping and location of goods). Some organisations may have physical stores and collect more data at the checkout, which might, or might not, be connected to the organisation's sales data system. Rather than having 5 or 6 systems to manage all the data, some organisations store the data in customer relations management systems (this combines the customer and sales data), or enterprise resource planning (which combines the sales, manufacturing and logistics systems). To capture insights at scale, the data comes together in a **data warehouse** (see Key Term).

KEY TERMS   DATA WAREHOUSE, DATA LAKE, DATA FABRIC AND
DATA MESH

A data warehouse is a place where data is stored. According to Nargesian et al. (2019: 1986): 'A data lake is a massive collection of datasets that: may be hosted in different storage systems; may vary in their formats; may not be accompanied by any useful metadata or may use different formats to describe their metadata; and may change autonomously over time.' Data fabric is a design concept which contains data warehouses and data lakes as well as the associated processes such as machine learning, managed by one organisation. Data mesh is similar to data fabric, but can be managed by different entities.

Structured data can be easier to analyse, but another challenge is combining this with unstructured or semi-structured data and assessing its volume. For example, how can customer profiles and comments on social media or other examples in Table 5.1 be connected? Unstructured data may also be added to a data warehouse. There may be some metadata that can be applied to the data, such as name, location, type of comment, but this may not be consistent.

The structured and unstructured **data warehouses** are brought together in a **data lake**. The data can be live with real-time movement, so more comments from social media or operational systems are brought in. The data is sorted and analysed, leading to insights organisations can use which improves with more machine learning. This linking of the **data warehouses** into the **data lake** is contained with a **data fabric** architecture system, as shown in Figure 5.4.

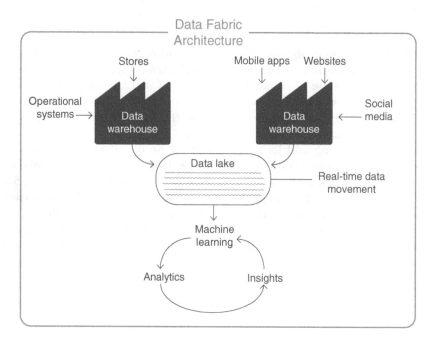

Figure 5.4   Data fabric architecture

DIGITAL TOOL   Dataset Search

Google hosts a dataset search tool which it explains as: 'Dataset Search is a search engine for data sets. Using a simple keyword search, users can discover data sets hosted in thousands of repositories across the web.'

- You can explore it here: datasetsearch.research.google.com

5.3.3 APPLICATION OF BIG DATA

Big data is used by many businesses across many sectors, as the examples in Table 5.2 demonstrate.

Table 5.2 Application of big data

Sector	Example
Airlines	British Airways uses data to analyse flights, including identifying trends and patterns which could improve performance
Financial services	UBS has over 70,000 employees and uses data to support their human resources function
Gaming	PlayStation uses data to improve games by analysing customer behaviour
Toys	LEGO uses data to improve the shopper experience by monitoring online forums and from this feedback to their teams to take action to optimise their website

As a result, jobs for data engineers have increased over the past 5 years. This is likely to continue as organisations discover more ways to create value from their data.

CASE EXAMPLE 5.2 Netflix recommendation system

Netflix is a video-streaming platform and describes itself as 'one of the world's leading entertainment services' (Netflix, 2022: 1) and offers TV series, films and games that are available on large and small screens via its online app. It has more than 200 million paying subscribers in 190 countries and delivers content in many languages. In addition to broadcasting films made by other companies, Netflix has become a production studio and is creating its own movies and TV shows.

This is a lucrative market, and there are forecast to be 3.5 billion digital video viewers worldwide and the market is forecast to reach $235 billion by 2028 (Statista, 2023b). As a result, Netflix has many competitors, including Amazon Prime, Disney+, YouTube TV, Paramount+, HBO Max, Hulu and Apple TV+.

According to its Annual Report (Netflix, 2022), the firm spent 9% or $2.7 billion of its revenue on technology and development. A key aspect to the technology is machine learning (ML). Netflix has a research department which focuses on machine learning for several reasons:

- To improve delivery of the movies and shows, by enhancing video and audio encoding, as well as optimising the production of original movies and TV shows in Netflix's own studio. ML also helps shape Netflix's catalogue of movies and TV shows by learning characteristics that make content successful.
- To better manage advertising placement and budgets as ML automates their advertising spend, channel mix and advertising creative.
- To enhance member experience and power the algorithms in the recommendations system.
- To test different options with prototypes that can be designed, implemented, evaluated and, if they work, go into production. Netflix also conducts offline experiments and online A/B testing with ML.

Netflix has developed a recommendations system which they promote as 'Figuring out how to bring unique joy to each member', which they explain as (Netflix Help Center, 2023: 1):

Our business is a subscription service model that offers personalized recommendations, to help you find shows and movies of interest to you.

(Continued)

Whenever you access the Netflix service, our recommendations system strives to help you find a show or movie to enjoy with minimal effort. We estimate the likelihood that you will watch a particular title in our catalog based on a number of factors including:

- your interactions with our service (such as your viewing history and how you rated other titles),
- other members with similar tastes and preferences on our service, and
- information about the titles, such as their genre, categories, actors, release year, etc.

In addition to knowing what you have watched on Netflix, to best personalize the recommendations we also look at things like:

- the time of day you watch,
- the devices you are watching Netflix on, and
- how long you watch.

There is transparency in how the recommendation system works and they also state that they do not include demographic details in the process. The idea behind the recommendation system is that subscribers will continue to discover new movies and will continue to renew their subscription. The challenge is that as soon as subscribers lose interest in the TV shows and movies available, they might leave or switch to a competitor in this ever-changing market.

Case questions

- What do you notice about the data gathered to power the recommendation system?
- What other examples can you find of data being used in this way? How does this impact on you?
- Although Netflix does not capture demographic data, it has a rich source of material and knows all about your online viewing. How do you feel about this?

Activity 5.2   Apply big data potential for organisations

Imagine you are the new manager of an organisation you know well.

- Define the data they gather about their customers or other stakeholders
- Judge where there is potential to apply big data to gain valuable insights
- Prepare an argument that will explain how the data could be applied and how this will enhance the organisation

5.3.4 CHALLENGES AND OPPORTUNITIES WITH BIG DATA

Big data presents many challenges. There is a large amount of personal data being collected and it could be abused. While some of the data may not be secret, it may be private and personal. Plus when all the different pieces of data are joined together they paint a rich picture which not everyone may want to share. A key factor within data protection legislation is that personal data belongs to the individual and must be processed using the relevant legislation, so it's important that proper governance – management of the data – is in place.

Other challenges include the assessment of unstructured data (e.g. from social media posts) and trying to add relevant metadata (e.g. demographics, product feedback) so that it makes sense. This can reduce the ability to deeply analyse the data, providing a superficial overview. Plus, data lakes may contain duplicate data and may need 'cleaning' (Nargesian et al., 2019).

Big data creates opportunities for organisations to better connect the data and learn more. For example, logistics firms can use data to optimise their delivery routes, which means they use less energy to deliver online orders. Other opportunities using AI, specifically machine learning, are with language tools. For example, Grammarly, the plug-in writing checker, is based on AI as a large language model and gains big data from its 30 million users, which means it is constantly learning and updating options to improve grammar, punctuation and spelling.

Smartphone Sixty Seconds© – Explore AI grammar checkers

- Take out your mobile phone and search for 'AI grammar checker'.
- Select one of the AI grammar checkers and explore further.
- Who created the firm? How does the grammar checker use AI?
- What do you think of educational AI tools? Do they make students dependent upon them and, if yes, is this a good thing?

DISCOVER MORE ON DATA WITHIN DIGITAL PLATFORMS

Read *Digital Economy Report 2021 – Cross-border data flows and development: For who the data flow* by the United Nations (2022). This report provides insights into the operations of the digital platforms, as well as giving examples of the major worldwide platforms and the challenges they present.

5.4 BUSINESS INTELLIGENCE

Business intelligence is defined by Niu et al. (2021: 1) as 'a firm's potential to effectively use the information gathered during day-to-day activities'. These day-to-day activities can include providing customer service, researching the market and managing operations. The information gathered may involve:

- Structured data: Market data such as market share, number of competitors and variety of products available in the sector
- Semi-structured data: Operational feedback such as the time from order being received to being processed, any issues with quality of goods and issues within the supply chain
- Unstructured data: Customer feedback or other online conversations

The types of intelligence which can be gathered include competitor, consumer, industry, commodity intelligence and operational. Business intelligence is making sense of the data, and according to Niu et al. (2021) the data can be current or historical and can be used to:

- Understand customers better
- Improve marketing technology
- Make personalisation possible
- Identify real-time problems and opportunities

Activity 5.3.   Analyse data for business intelligence

In groups identify what types of data you have shared with organisations when making an online purchase. Analyse how the data could be used by the organisation for business intelligence.

5.5 GOVERNANCE AND ETHICAL ISSUES

Careful management and governance of data is a legal requirement in most countries (see Digital Tool: **Data Protection and Privacy Legislation Worldwide**). While many organisations follow the law, the practices may raise ethical concerns and there are many concerns about the use of artificial intelligence.

There are questions about how AI impacts on business and society. Researchers Christelle Aubert-Hassouni and Julien Cloarec raise the concept of technological social responsibility. Managing technological social responsibility in organisations needs further investigation and Aubert-Hassouni & Cloarec (2022) suggested one solution for managers is to 'ask themselves what they would have done if the breaches involved their own data' (Aubert-Hassouni & Cloarec, 2022: 552). This approach to data governance makes it personal and perhaps shines a light onto how people feel when their data is shared without permission.

There are calls to ensure that 'AI applications have been developed based on ethical principles and do not embed within them unknown biases' (Enholm et al., 2022: 1719) as these impact on society. According to Enholm et al. (2022: 1723), 'in the absence of appropriate AI governance practices, negative and unintended consequences can occur'. They add that bias 'can result in discrimination or unfavourable outcomes to particular ethnic groups, genders, or population clusters' (1724). Organisations from IBM (see Digital Tool: **AI Fairness**) to the European Commission are supporting trustworthy AI which is created based on ethical principles, and adopting the concept of FATE – fairness, accountability, transparency and ethics.

DIGITAL TOOL   AI fairness

IBM hosts a portal about AI fairness which it describes as an 'open source toolkit can help you examine, report, and mitigate discrimination and bias in machine learning models throughout the AI application lifecycle'. The portal includes videos, links to journal articles and tutorials to explain bias and provide guidance on bringing fairness into AI.

• You can explore it here: aif360.mybluemix.net

Another approach is for AI to be human-centred AI (HCAI), where 'the user rather than technology [is placed at] the center of AI development' (Bingley et al., 2023: 1). HCAI would then enhance mundane tasks. The challenge is ensuring organisations adopt this way of working.

JOURNAL OF NOTE

Journal of Business Ethics addresses ethical issues related to business including new technologies, such as the positive and negative impact of AI. All aspects of businesses such as 'systems of production, consumption, marketing, advertising, social and economic accounting, labour relations, public relations and organisational behaviour are analysed from a moral viewpoint'.

CASE STUDY

PAYPAL'S MANAGEMENT OF DATA TO GENERATE INSIGHTS

Data drives PayPal. The firm knows which businesses are successful and which are struggling. It also knows who sends money and on what day of the week and to whom. With over 425 million active accounts it has a lot of data which comes into 13 data centres. The data needs to be governed carefully. Data protection legislation requires organisations to place privacy at the heart of their business, which PayPal recognises and has a data officer on its board of directors. PayPal shares that:

(Continued)

> We embody a privacy-first culture that prioritizes responsible use of data and customer empowerment through transparency, education, platform enhancements and product innovations. We remain committed to providing our customers with a trusted, value-driven experience, which incorporates a proactive approach to data protection and cybersecurity management. (PayPal, 2021: 37)

The data PayPal captures includes personal and online identifiers: your name, date of birth, address, credit card details, income and expenses. While some of this may not be secret, it is personal and this means PayPal has a strong duty of care to safeguard your data. Your individual data may tell a personal story, but when your purchases are combined with purchases from other people this starts to build a richer picture about locations, store preferences and spending habits. Like other payment systems PayPal can identify which locations are on trend, which stores are popular with people aged 25 and which days of the week spending goes up or down.

PayPal acknowledges that their 'payments platform connecting merchants and consumers enables PayPal to offer unique end-to-end product experiences while gaining valuable insights into how customers use our platform' (PayPal, 2022a: 4). This richer data provides business intelligence and enables PayPal to 'offer tools and insights for utilizing data analytics to attract new customers and improve sales conversion' (PayPal, 2022a: 5).

For example, one of the pieces of data available is as follows:

> Number of payment transactions per active account reflects the total number of payment transactions within the previous 12-month period, divided by active accounts at the end of the period. The number of payment transactions per active account provides management with insight into the average number of times a customer account engages in payments activity on our payments platform in a given period. (PayPal, 2022a: 31)

This data can be translated into insights so that stores can send offers to regular customers. PayPal data scientists generate insights by mining PayPal's rich data to develop a deep understanding of the consumer experience. However, consumers' attitudes towards data sharing may be changing. PayPal explored how customers feel about data privacy and protection in the US and India, and from this they found that:

> As digital applications and services grow in availability and complexity, it is increasingly important to mitigate vulnerabilities that can result from data sharing — particularly for underresourced populations. PayPal sponsored research conducted by Decodis, a social research company, to better understand the experiences, attitudes and behaviors that low- to middle-income internet users exhibit as a result of the rapid, global adaptation and expansion of digital services. This early work concluded that consumers can articulate thoughtful and nuanced opinions about their data sharing, and that they have the desire and capacity to increase their knowledge and confidence in participating in the digital world. Future research is expected to uncover deeper insights into potential consumer behavioral change. (PayPal, 2021: 37).

While PayPal uses data to provide insights, improve product offers and increase sales, consumers are gaining greater awareness of the data that is being used and how. In the future the availability of such rich data may decline.

CASE QUESTIONS

PayPal has suffered data breaches and employs many security engineers who work on PayPal's Enterprise Cyber Security (ECS) standards, to minimise the impact of data incidents. As protecting data has become a responsibility for individuals, 2-factor authentication is growing, requiring 2 forms of identification to confirm a payment which is made easier with mobile phones.

- Have you or your classmates ever had your financial details misused? What happened and why? What steps were needed to resolve the situation?
- How can individuals be educated about the security risks with data and take this seriously? Create a plan to educate individuals about the dangers of big data.
- What is the future of PayPal's data? It provides incredible insights, but is based on big data from any consumers – is this acceptable?

FURTHER EXERCISES

1. Evaluate the risks in using large language models for organisations. They appear to bring only benefits; consider the risks to reputation and the potential damage.

2. Deepfakes are seen as negative and intrusive when used on living people. Prepare a presentation on how they could be used to bring history to life.

3. For an organisation of your choice, create a plan to harness business intelligence within the legal framework of your location.

4. Artificial intelligence is the future. It will replace mundane tasks and emancipate workers. Discuss.

SUMMARY

This chapter has explored:

- Types of AI and the hierarchy of machine learning
- Big data concepts and its challenges and opportunities
- Types of business intelligence
- Governance and ethical issues in big data and AI

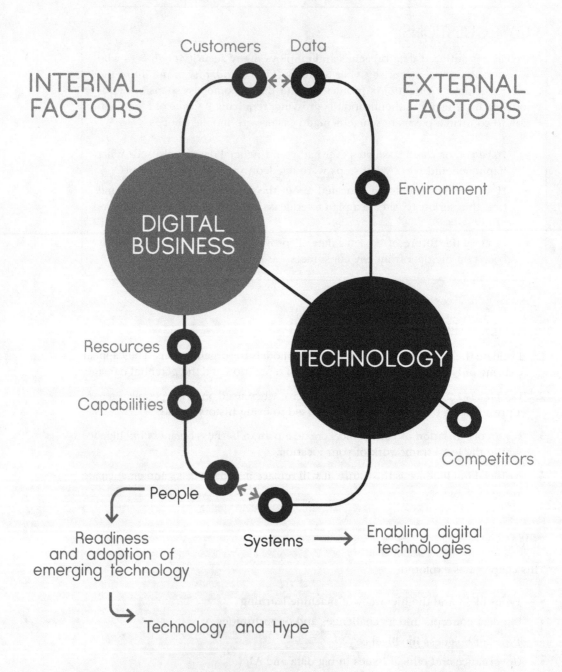

INTERNAL
FACTORS

EXTERNAL
FACTORS

Customers   Data

DIGITAL
BUSINESS

Environment

Resources

Capabilities

TECHNOLOGY

Competitors

People

Systems

Readiness
and adoption of
emerging technology

Enabling digital
technologies

Technology and Hype

6

ENABLING AND EMERGING DIGITAL TECHNOLOGIES

LEARNING OUTCOMES

When you have read this chapter, you will be able to:

Understand enabling technologies

Apply the hype cycle

Analyse challenges with enabling or emerging technologies

Evaluate technology readiness

Create a proposal for the Internet of Everything

PROFESSIONAL SKILLS

When you have worked through this chapter, you should be able to:

- Disseminate data science practices promoting professional development and use of best practice
- Identify the strategic importance of technology-enabled business processes

6.1 BACKGROUND TO ENABLING DIGITAL TECHNOLOGIES

Technology is at the core of the digital business framework and has enabled big data and artificial intelligence. The growth of technology was identified around 60 years ago by Gordon Moore, the Director of Research and Development at Fairchild Semiconductors (a component needed in electronic chips that power your devices), who predicted that the number of components would double every year as the costs decreased, making more powerful computers (Moore, 1965). Moore envisioned the future of technology with home computers, automated controls for cars and 'personal transportable electronic equipment' (Moore, 1965: 33) which we would call wearables and mobile phones. This was at a time when fewer than 62% of US and fewer than 35% of UK households had 1 landline phone at home (to share with the whole family). This became known as Moore's Law and was the foundation for developing electronics in Silicon Valley. Writing in *MIT Technology Review*, David Rotman (2020: 1) called this 'the greatest technological prediction of the last half-century'. Moore's Law is considered to be at an end by some, but still continuing by others. It continues to make contributions; as Rotman added: 'it has also fueled today's breakthroughs in artificial intelligence and genetic medicine, by giving machine-learning techniques the ability to chew through massive amounts of data to find answers'. These technological breakthroughs often occur due to **enabling technology** (see Key Term).

> **KEY TERM**   ENABLING TECHNOLOGY
>
> Enabling technology is a product or service that makes significant change within an organisation possible. For example, Global Positioning System (GPS) trackers in delivery vans enable customers to see what time their goods are arriving, reducing inbound communications (e.g. social media messages, telephone calls and emails) to the organisation.

In this chapter we will explore technology and hype, the readiness of technology products, organisations and society to adopt new technology. We will then explore technology enablers which shape business practice, many of which are still emerging, and the ethical dilemmas surrounding new technology.

6.2 TECHNOLOGY AND HYPE

Technology gains attention with the possibility of innovations that make life easier, change how we work and disrupt business. This is the notion of hype (an abbreviation of *hyperbole*, meaning to exaggerate) in technology which was discussed by Professors Theoharakis and Wong who explored 4 types of stories about technology that created the hype:

- Technical stories where the primary topic is the technical aspects and capabilities of the technology (e.g., standards setting activities, technology features)

- Product Availability stories where the primary topic is about new products supporting the specific technology (e.g., product launch announcements)
- Product Adoption stories where the primary topic is about the adoption of products based on the particular technology (e.g., adoption case studies)
- Product Discontinuation stories where the primary topic is about the discontinued use/adoption of products based on the particular technology and their re-placement by products that support a competing technology (2002: 402)

While the stories support the hype, the consulting firm Gartner developed the Hype Cycle which identifies the life cycle of different technologies. The Hype Cycles are similar to a product life cycle graph and identify different phases (Gartner, 2023) which are all linked to the types of stories identified by Theoharakis and Wong (2002).

- Innovation Trigger – When a possible new technology gains attention. At this stage it is a concept rather than a ready-to-launch product. This can include *technical stories* that promise new capabilities.
- Peak of Inflated Expectations – There is enthusiasm about the new development and this includes the *product adoption stories.*
- Trough of Disillusionment – This is where technical stories may report failures and the product does not deliver its promises. *Product discontinuation stories* also occur and this is when most tech companies improve or abandon the product.

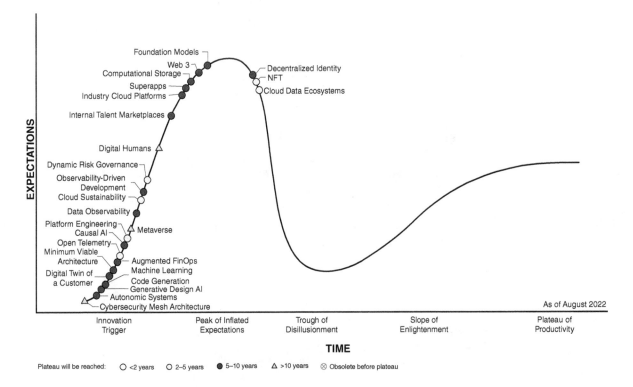

Figure 6.1   Gartner Hype Cycle for Emerging Technologies, 2022

Source: Gartner (2022b). Printed with permission of Gartner

- Slope of Enlightenment – This can be a mix of *technical stories* where the benefits of the technology are shared and supported by positive *product adoption stories*.
- Plateau of Productivity – The technology gains wider *product adoption* and these stories are shared.

The purpose of the Hype Cycle is to draw a distinction between the hype and the technology which may benefit an organisation. Figure 6.1 shows the 2022 Gartner Hype Cycle for Emerging Technologies which Gartner (2022b: 1) notes focuses on 3 areas: expanding immersive experiences, accelerating artificial intelligence (AI) automation and optimising technologist delivery.

Expanding immersive experiences include the metaverse (see Chapter 2) where individuals are moved into virtual or augmented worlds. The speed of AI automation was discussed in Chapter 5. We will look at optimising technologist delivery in Chapter 7.

Smartphone Sixty Seconds© – Find hype cycles

- Take out your mobile phone and search for 'Hype cycle for emerging tech, 2022'.
- Select one of the technologies of interest and read more.
- Were you aware of this technology?
- How will this technology impact on your daily life?
- Which technologies do you believe are hype and won't survive?

While some technology is exaggerated and promises everything and delivers nothing, organisations need to be prepared to work with key technologies across their business operations, which we will explore next.

Activity 6.1   Apply the hype cycle

In groups, consider 2 technologies that are gaining attention and apply to the hype cycle. Which stages are the technologies at? Why is this? Discuss whether they will gain wider product adoption or are likely to fail and justify why this may be.

DIGITAL TOOL   World Economic Forum

The World Economic Forum is 'the International Organization for Public–Private Cooperation'. It meets annually in Davos, Switzerland with politicians, activists and pop stars discussing major issues. It has recognised emerging technologies as a key topic for discussion.

- You can explore more here: weforum.org/topics/emerging-technologies

6.3 READINESS AND ADOPTION OF EMERGING TECHNOLOGY

Before investing in new technology, organisations need to consider many factors: why the technology is needed, what it will contribute, who will manage it, how it will connect with other systems, and when it will be introduced and how. Millions of dollars and euros are spent on technology projects that fail. Sometimes it's the technology which wasn't fully tested – it was living on its hype – yet more often it's the organisation that wasn't ready to introduce the technology or had unrealistic goals.

Smartphone Sixty Seconds© – Explore failed technology projects

- Take out your mobile phone and search for 'failed technology projects'.
- What did you discover? Were there any surprises?
- Why did these projects fail and what lessons were learned?

6.3.1 TECHNOLOGY, SOCIETY AND ORGANISATIONAL READINESS

To assess technology, the technology readiness level (TRL) scale was created by NASA (2012) to assess when a technology was mature enough to be used. The TRL is used to assess public funding projects in Europe (Bruno et al., 2020). While this is a well-accepted process for testing whether the technology is ready, it fails to consider whether the organisation or society is ready for the technology. Researchers Ilenia Bruno and colleagues (2020) recognised this and adapted a society readiness model (SRL) from Innovation Fund Denmark (2018). Bruno et al. (2020) expanded the concept of readiness and considered organisational readiness levels which they developed using the same format. Table 6.1 shows the scales for the technology, society and organisational readiness levels.

Table 6.1   Technology, society and organisational readiness level scales

Technology readiness level		Society readiness level		Organisational readiness level	
Maturity level	Description	Maturity level	Description	Maturity level	Description
TRL1	Basic principles observed	SRL1	Identification of the generic societal need and associated readiness aspects	ORL1	Identification of the organisational need (infrastructures, capabilities, skills) and associated organisational readiness aspects
TRL2	Technology concept formulated	SRL2	Formulation of proposed solution concept and potential impacts; appraisal of societal readiness issues; identification of relevant stakeholders for the development of the solution	ORL2	Formulation of proposed solution concept and potential impacts; appraisal of organisational readiness issues; identification of relevant roles, processes, functions and structures for the solution

(Continued)

Table 6.1   (Continued)

Technology readiness level		Society readiness level		Organisational readiness level	
Maturity level	Description	Maturity level	Description	Maturity level	Description
TRL3	Experimental proof of concept	SRL3	Initial sharing of the proposed solution with relevant stakeholders (e.g. through visual mock-ups): a limited group of the society knows the solution or similar initiatives	ORL3	Comprehensive description of proposed solution's impacts within the organisation in terms of roles, competences and skills, physical infrastructures required
TRL4	Technology validated in lab	SRL4	Solution validated through pilot testing in controlled environments to substantiate proposed impacts and societal readiness: a limited group of the society tests the solution or similar initiatives	ORL4	Solution validated through simulation of major induced changes to substantiate proposed impacts and organisational readiness: the organisation which is developing the solution starts to acquire roles, competences and skills, physical infrastructures required
TRL5	Technology validated in relevant environment	SRL5	Solution validated through pilot testing in real or realistic environments and by relevant stakeholders: the society knows the solution or similar initiatives but is not aware of their benefits	ORL5	Proposed solution validated through pilot testing in real or realistic organisational environments: the organisation which is developing the solution achieves roles, competences and skills, physical infrastructures required
TRL6	Technology demonstrated in relevant environment	SRL6	Solution demonstrated in real world environments and in co-operation with relevant stakeholders to gain feedback on potential impacts: the society knows the solution or similar initiatives and awareness of their benefits increases	ORL6	Solution demonstrated in real world environments and in co-operation with relevant stakeholders to gain feedback in order to improve roles, processes, functions and infrastructures required
TRL7	System prototype demonstration in operational environment	SRL7	Refinement of the solution and, if needed, retesting in real world environments with relevant stakeholders: the society is completely aware of the solution's benefits, a part of the society starts to adopt similar solutions	ORL7	Refinement of the roles, processes, functions and infrastructures required and retesting of the solution in relevant organisational environments

Technology readiness level		Society readiness level		Organisational readiness level	
Maturity level	Description	Maturity level	Description	Maturity level	Description
TRL8	System complete and qualified	SRL8	Targeted solution, as well as a plan for societal adaptation, complete and qualified; society is ready to adopt the solution and have used similar solutions on the market	ORL8	Targeted solution, as well as a plan for organisational embedment, complete and qualified: roles, processes, functions and infrastructures are available
TRL9	Actual system proven in operational environment	SRL9	Actual solution proven in relevant societal environments after launch on the market; the society is using the solution available on the market	ORL9	Actual solution proven in relevant organisational environments: roles, processes, functions and infrastructures are correctly used for the solution on the market

While these readiness level scales may look similar, there are differences. The TRL focuses solely on the technology whereas the SRL considers the societal need and engages with stakeholders from the start. Research has found that 'for innovations to become adopted and to realize their full potential, social needs and behaviors are often more important than merely economic, political or technological aspects' (Schraudner et al., 2018: 3).

The ORL looks at whether the organisation has the infrastructure, capabilities and skills to take on the technology. To successfully implement new technology, organisations need to be prepared and that includes employing or training staff with the relevant competencies and skills.

Activity 6.2   Evaluate technology, society and organisational readiness

In groups, using Table 6.1, select an emerging technology and evaluate which readiness level the technology has reached. Contrast with societal and organisational readiness and compare the differences. Consider why this may be and the challenges that may arise. Reflect on whether your groups have any concerns about the technology either in society or in an organisation.

6.3.2 TECHNOLOGY ADOPTION

Organisations and society can be prepared for new technology to be introduced, whether that's healthcare using AI to scan medical tests, businesses responding to web queries with chatbots, or governments using virtual assistants to answer complex questions. However, are the patients, customers and citizens ready to use the technology?

A theoretical model was developed to assess whether individuals would adopt a technology from a psychological perspective. This was the technology acceptance model (TAM) which incorporates 4 elements (Davis, 1989):

- Perceived usefulness (PU) – does the technology bring benefits, is it useful?
- Perceived ease of use (PEOU) – how easy or complicated is it to use?
- Attitude towards use (AT) – does the person have a positive attitude towards using the technology?
- Behavioural intention to use (BI) – how likely is the person to adopt or reject the technology?

TAM is considered an older model and has been adapted and extended several times, yet it is still the basis for many current studies. For example, researchers Zhong et al. (2021) explored customers' willingness to use facial recognition payment technology driven by AI. They extended the technology acceptance model and added more items to be tested:

- PE – perceived enjoyment as having fun using new technology was identified by research
- FC – Facilitating conditions which they defined as 'a customer's perception of the availability of essential resources and support in order to perform a particular task' (Zhong et al., 2021: 4)
- PIN – Personal innovativeness as whether an individual is willing to try new technology.

Table 6.2 shows some of the items Zhong et al. (2021) tested on a Likert scale from '1 = strongly disagree' to '5 = strongly agree'.

Table 6.2   Extended technology acceptance model

Item	Question
PE1	I enjoy using facial recognition payment
PE2	The use of facial recognition payment enables me to enjoy shopping
PE3	The use of facial recognition payment will bring me some joy
FC1	I can easily access information to know how to use facial recognition payment
FC2	Facial recognition payment is compatible with other technology I use (WeChat pay, or Alipay, etc.)
FC3	I can obtain guidance and instruction easily if I have difficulties in using facial recognition payment
PIN1	If I have heard of a new technology, I will try to find ways to experiment with it
PIN2	I am always the one who wants to try out new technologies among my friends
PIN3	It is fun to try out different technologies
PEOU1	The use of facial recognition payment is easy for me
PEOU2	The use of facial recognition payment is understandable and clear for me
PEOU3	It won't be hard for me to become skilful at using facial recognition payment
PU1	Facial recognition payment can help me pay quickly
PU2	It is useful to use facial recognition payment

Item	Question
PU3	The use of facial recognition payment is beneficial to me
AT1	The use of facial recognition payment is a good idea
AT2	The use of facial recognition payment is a wise idea
AT3	I like to make purchases using facial recognition payment
IU1	I intend to use facial recognition payment in the next few months
IU2	I will continuously purchase things using facial recognition payment
IU3	Overall, I am willing to use facial recognition payment when I purchase things

Notes: PEOU = perceived ease of use; PU = perceived usefulness; AT = attitude; IU = intention to use; PE = perceived enjoyment; FC = facilitating conditions; PIN = personal innovativeness

Source: Adapted from Zhong et al. (2021)

The technology acceptance model and its variations are a helpful way to assess whether a technology is likely to be used. While a technology may be perceived as useful (PU), the intention to use (IU) may be low which means that it is more likely to move into the 'trough of disillusionment' in the hype cycle.

DISCOVER MORE ON THE TECHNOLOGY ACCEPTANCE MODEL (TAM)

Read the original article that introduced TAM: 'Perceived usefulness, perceived ease of use, and user acceptance of information technology' by Fred Davis (1989). This article provides the background and shows the scale questions that were used to build the model.

6.4 TECHNOLOGY ENABLERS THAT SHAPE BUSINESS PRACTICE

Having considered how organisations and society need to be ready to adopt a new technology, there are systems that improve and enhance business performance, known as technology enablers. Technology needs infrastructure which includes energy supply, wireless networks and the **Internet of Everything** (IoE) (see Key Term).

KEY TERM   INTERNET OF EVERYTHING (IOE)

According to Avula et al. (2021: 72), the 'Internet of Things (IoT) is a powerful data network comprising of various objects such as sensors, radio frequency components, smart appliances and computers that can be connected via the Internet. The Internet of Everything (IoE) is an evolution of IoT, and it is considered as a combination of data, people, process, and physical devices'.

6.4.1 ENERGY CONSUMPTION

We keep photos, music and messages on our devices, which store them in the cloud and cloud energy consumption continues to increase. According to the International Energy Agency (IEA, 2022), digital technologies provide opportunities and challenges for energy use. Energy usage is measured in Terawatt hours (TWh) and 1 TWh is the equivalent of 1 trillion watts for 1 hour. To put this into context, the IEA reports that in 2020, the entire TWh for Greece was 51.9, Norway was 124.8, Ukraine was 130.54, Australia was 254, the UK was 302.8 and the USA was 4109.39. In 2021, global data centre electricity use was 220 to 320 TWh, which is up to 1.3% of global electricity usage – that's similar to the annual usage by the whole of Australia or the UK. Crypto mining energy use was 100 to 140 TWh in 2021. Machine learning will also increase demand for more energy usage although it's too early to understand what this might be.

DIGITAL TOOL   Key energy statistics

The IEA shares data about energy use for most countries. This demonstrates how much energy is produced, the main energy supplies (coal, electricity, gas, nuclear, oil, renewables) and their total CO2 emissions.

- You can explore it here: iea.org/countries

6.4.2 WIRELESS NETWORKS

We started with the first generation of wireless internet (1G) and we're moving towards 5G and 6G, although we are still using 3G which exists in sensors, for example in home security systems and in car services. There is a plan to strengthen 4G and 5G networks, which means that the earlier generations will be phased out. Researchers Saxena et al. (2021) explain that the benefits of 5G include Ultra-Reliable Low Latency Communications (URLLC), which is used for critical tasks such as driverless cars and remote surgery – you don't want the device to freeze, lag or delay just at the point where the vehicle is on a busy high street, or when a surgeon is operating! Saxena et al. (2021) identify additional benefits, including mobile broadband (eMBB) so that we can stream anything from anywhere, which is supported by massive machine-type communications (mMTC) that will connect many devices across the **Internet of Everything**. Figure 6.2 shows a road map of the evolution of cellular technology with examples, from 1G to 6G.

Wireless 6G networks provide opportunities for logistics, telesurgery, entertainment and business communications. But it's a few years before we get there. In the meantime there are projects taking place to explore how 5G can be used, as SecurePax in Case Example 6.1 demonstrates.

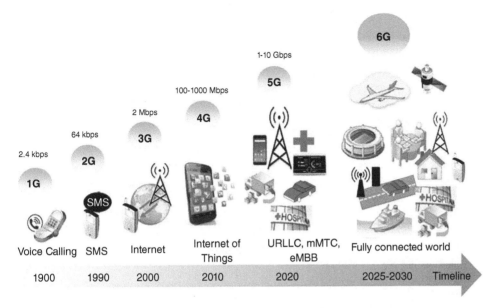

Figure 6.2 Road map of the evolution of cellular technology, highlighting the representative applications, from 1G to 6G

Source: Saxena et al. (2021: 8). Printed with permission of Springer Nature

CASE EXAMPLE 6.1 SecurePax

Shipping ports are busy hubs where passengers join and leave ships and where large containers of goods are transported. Ports have to address many challenges, including the movement of illegal goods and theft of containers. Plus they need to manage large numbers of people disembarking at the same time and ensuring shipping containers are unloaded and loaded with maximum efficiency.

The Port of Turku in Finland takes passengers between Scandinavian, Baltic and German seaports. In January 2023 the port moved over 7,000 containers and over 145,000 passengers. This is a lot of traffic to monitor and manage. The port authorities and their stakeholders have demonstrated that they are enthusiastic about digital technology to speed up operations and enhance customer experiences. As part of this, they have won a technology project to connect information traffic and security; this is known as SecurePax and the successful results will be shared with other ports across Europe.

Funded by the European Union, the aim of SecurePax is to 'develop methods that can be used to identify passengers even better and check that prohibited goods are not brought on board' (Port of Turku, 2023: 1). In partnership with other shipping companies, the system will use the 5G network to map and then identify passengers and containers embarking or disembarking from the ships. Applying the technology readiness scale to SecurePax, they are using 5G which has moved from TR1 to TR6 and is being rolled out in a relevant environment (the port area), which is more challenging than a typical office environment.

Finland has a population of around 5.5 million and globally ranks 9th in technology leadership. For example, organisations in Finland invented SMS messaging, created the first

(Continued)

web browser and released the first smartphone. This means that the society is prepared for new technology. Project SecurePax will enable the Port of Turku to demonstrate, in a real-world environment, how the digital registration and mapping system works. Co-operation with stakeholders such as the port workers, shipping companies and government agencies will be valuable to gain feedback on the potential impact in terms of benefits and any challenges encountered.

The goals of SecurePax are to:

- Identify passengers leaving the passenger terminal from the cruise liners who typically leave the ship and visit for a few hours and return on board, which will save time when they return on board
- Investigate methods to stop unwanted persons from boarding the ship
- Identify dangerous objects carried by passengers, in cars or in luggage, to stop them being brought on board the different ships
- Explore how to 'digitise and harmonise' the security operations throughout the passenger port area of the Port of Turku
- Test a high-speed 5G mobile network in the passenger port area of the Port of Turku

To achieve these objectives, all passengers will need to participate in a digital registration system. Passengers may be delighted with super-fast mobile, but one of the challenges may be that passengers from other countries might not be as technologically ready to adopt the technology.

Case questions

- What do you feel about the idea of all passengers being registered when travelling through an area? There are commercial benefits for tracking people and things, but is this acceptable?
- How can SecurePax protect its data so that it is used for good purposes?
- 5G mobile networks connect people and things, but to work a newer mobile phone may be needed. Are we reaching a time where everyone needs new mobile phones? What is the impact on the environment with a constant need to upgrade?

Activity 6.3   Assess the concept of a fully connected world

In groups, consider your connected world. What devices do you have that are connected and why? What are the advantages? What are the downsides or challenges? How can a fully connected world be governed and what ethical issues may arise?

6.4.3 THE INTERNET OF EVERYTHING

The Internet of Everything (IoE) connects people, things, data and processes so they can collectively perform tasks. For example, smart speakers such as Amazon

Echo, Google Home or Apple HomePod provide informational content (reporting on tomorrow's weather in Berlin, communication services (messaging friends) and home automation (switching on the lights). According to Tuzovic (2022: 529), 'voice interfaces are not just devices of voice recognition, but rather the intersection of a variety of powerful computing and AI capabilities'. The smart speaker is always on and connects to other cloud-based systems to retrieve the data and provide a response.

Within a business environment, the IoE can:

- Improve customer experience with better understanding of shopping habits and preferences
- Enhance innovation by reducing the time to test markets and create prototypes
- Increase efficiency in logistics by improving transportation of goods from different locations and identifying faster delivery routes

Technology involved in the IoE are shown in Table 6.3. Let's explore these technologies further.

Table 6.3   Technology enabling the Internet of Everything

Technology	Description	Key advantage	Key challenge	Example
Blockchain	A decentralised, immutable peer-to-peer network where information on transactions is stored on digital data blocks and distributed to various identical and accessible ledgers	Facilitate better product management with shared databases	Complex to establish	Uber uses blockchain to connect drivers to riders
Cloud Systems	Decentralised and permanently available digital resources such as infrastructure, platforms, and software	Enables fast and simple collection, storage, processing, and exchange of data within and among organisations	Starting to use more energy as storage requirements increases	Universities use cloud systems such as OneDrive or Google Drive to store documents
Cyber-Physical Systems	The integration of various physical systems (e.g. different production machines) and a central processing unit	Improved efficiency and reliability	Some systems may not be compatible with others	Medical devices such as pacemakers where physical devices are inside the body and controlled with an external machine or app
Digital Twin	A real-time virtual simulation model of physical products or processes	Monitors performance and improves productivity	Expensive to establish	The aerospace firm Rolls-Royce uses digital twins for its engines to check performance
Augmented Reality (AR)	Ability to adapt virtual 3D objects into real surroundings	Can enhance customer experience	Devices needed to experience AR	Ikea uses AR to show how furniture looks in your home

(Continued)

Table 6.3   (Continued)

Technology	Description	Key advantage	Key challenge	Example
Virtual Reality	Allows users to connect to sensible electronic simulations	Cost effective method to test prototypes before they are fully developed	Requires investment to develop applications	In Australia, the Melbourne Immigration Museum at Home programme allows visitors to discover history from home
Sensors	Things embedded in devices to increase their efficiency, such as proximity, temperature, image and motion sensors	Saves energy, recognising when you're at home or at work and switching off power	Concerns over privacy due to tracking and sharing data with other applications	Google's Nest thermostat uses motion and temperature sensors to adjust the heating
Advanced Robotics	Electrical machinery to support humans and automation processes	Enables uniformity of tasks	Fear of robots replacing workers	Germany's DFKI Industrials' TMV-X (terrestrial scouting vehicle) is designed for mapping difficult outdoor environments
Autonomous Vehicles	Intelligent capable vehicles that motion to any unexpected situation from their environments	Automates mobility and has the potential to reduce road deaths	Adoption of self-driving vehicles is still not widely accepted	Google's self-driving Waymo partnered with taxi firm Lyft and is available in San Francisco and Los Angeles, with a human safety driver
Drones	Micro aerial vehicles for delivery, surveillance, and many more	Cost effective method of monitoring difficult to access areas	Concerns over privacy	Farmers use drones to assess crop health
Additive Manufacturing	Process of manufacturing products by joining materials layer by layer based on 3D models	Enables decentralised manufacturing of parts without acquiring and using specialised tools	It can take days to manufacture some objects	Nike footwear uses additive manufacturing for rapid prototypes of customised shoes

Sources: Adapted from Akbari & Hopkins (2022); Gebhardt et al. (2022); Martynov et al. (2019)

BLOCKCHAIN

Blockchain enables organisations to share data through decentralised systems which are stored in cloud systems. As blockchain is a distributed system, the data sits in several places, rather than a single database, which means it is neither owned nor controlled by a single entity. Blockchain is used in sectors, including energy, government and medical care (Khan et al., 2022), and is often associated with cryptocurrency. Researchers Khan et al. (2022) point out that it is disruptive and is changing the supply chain with data shared across the chain (those involved) and removes dishonest conduct as records cannot be altered.

CYBER-PHYSICAL SYSTEMS

Cyber-physical systems combine physical devices and often store data in the cloud. For example, pacemakers are a medical device that saves lives and are implanted near to the patient's heart. Yet they can be connected, via an app, to an online system to share data on how the device is performing and how soon the battery needs changing. The apps are available for physicians to check the patient history and based on this to make amendments to the pacemaker to improve the patient's life. A less complicated example of cyber-physical systems are smart fridges which allow households to see what's inside the fridge, from anywhere. This can save resources as you can check the fridge when you're in the supermarket.

DIGITAL TWINS

The concept of digital twins started at NASA and are an expensive undertaking – to replicate, in digital form, an entire thing. This could be a city (Singapore has a digital twin) or major machinery. This means this technology is less available for smaller businesses due to the cost of creation. Yet as the cost of technology decreases, they may be available in the future. One strong application outside manufacturing for digital twins is a map of a seriously ill person's immune system. This is already available and treatment is trialled on the twin to see whether it works, before administering to the person to ensure the results are beneficial.

> ## DISCOVER MORE ON DIGITAL TWINS
>
> Read the article 'Digital twins: An analysis framework and open issues' by Boyes & Watson (2022) which provides definitions of digital twins and explains how they are constructed.

AUGMENTED REALITY

Augmented reality is accessed with a mobile phone that adds a layer to provide more information. We remain in the real world, but add greater richness through different apps. Retail stores might add filters to help us decide whether to buy something or not, for example Nike providing an app so you can visit a store and try on new trainers without taking the old ones off. Yet it is widely used in organisations such as BMW, who apply AR in their health and safety training, highlighting areas of danger to be avoided.

VIRTUAL REALITY

Virtual reality is accessed via a headset, although Mark Zuckerberg is keen that we may be able to access via screens or mobile phones in the future. The metaverse (see Chapter 2) is a form of virtual reality and is being used by organisations selling virtual goods as well as physical goods. While not everyone can afford a Gucci handbag in real life, buying one in virtual reality is more affordable.

SENSORS

According to Avula et al. (2021: 74), sensors can be embedded into many devices and perform different tasks, such as 'proximity sensors, pressure sensors, gas sensors, temperature sensors, IR sensors, image sensors, motion detection sensors, smoke sensors'. Sensors provide a strong health and safety function as well as reducing and managing resources. There are concerns that sensors are tracking us from when we wake up until we sleep. For example, Google's purchase of the NEST home thermostat sensor may not have been a simple investment as it's linked to individuals' Google accounts and provides more data on their day-to-day behaviour.

ETHICAL INSIGHTS   Digital machines

Digital machines, from advanced robotics and autonomous vehicles to drones (also known as unmanned aerial vehicles – UAVs), have raised many ethical concerns.

Robots have evolved from simple gadgets to AI-powered machines. They provide greater efficiency (Tóth et al., 2022) and can perform mundane tasks; for example, in manufacturing where the same task is repeated on a production line. The main concerns are industrial robots taking people's jobs, although researchers have found mixed results, depending on the context (Chung & Lee, 2022). The other ethical dilemma is with care robots where the machines are located in people's homes to monitor and manage situations, such as healthcare rehabilitation or regular administration of medicines (Maddahi et al., 2022). Roboethics as a branch of ethics was first proposed by science-fiction writer Isaac Asimov (Maddahi et al., 2022) and have evolved to ensure no harm is inflicted.

Autonomous vehicles, better known as self-driving cars – but this can include self-driving vans, lorries and buses – are being developed at speed. Already permitted in some locations in the USA, China and Europe, the main issues concern the safety of passengers, other road users and pedestrians. For example, CNN reported that a self-driving Uber killed a pedestrian in the USA and the 'safety driver' was charged with negligent homicide (Riess & Sottile, 2023).

The costs of drones has made them affordable for individuals, not just companies, and the use of these machines is widespread. While drones can be used in rescue missions or to monitor buildings as they can access difficult areas more easily and possibly faster than individuals, there are ethical concerns including:

- Misuse, disrupting commercial flights at airports in London and Dublin for example
- Privacy violations, spying on neighbours, stalking individuals
- Safety, as battery power fails and they fall from the sky

All digital machines bring benefits, but the issues are about privacy, safety and misuse. Legislation is in place for drones and is being developed for other digital machines. For example, the EU is working on new machinery regulations which, according to Margrethe Vestager, Executive Vice-President for a Europe Fit for the Digital Age, 'will make sure that advanced machines, such as autonomous machines or collaborative robots can be safely placed in the EU market' (European Commission, 2022a: 1).

This area is still a work in progress and will change as we see self-driving cars on the road and more robots looking after elderly relatives.

- Have you ever used a digital machine? If yes, what was this for?
- How do you feel about being driven in an autonomous vehicle? What concerns would you have and why?
- Are there situations where digital machines should not be permitted? Why is this?

CASE EXAMPLE 6.2   Wingcopter

Wingcopter manufactures 'high-performance drones that are operated all over the world in commercial and humanitarian operations'. They claim that their 'drone technology saves and improves lives every day' as they supply medicines, help in disaster relief or provide supplies or services in hard to access areas.

Founded in 2017 south of Frankfurt, in Weiterstadt in Germany, Wingcopter was named a Technology Pioneer by the World Economic Forum just 3 years later. Its drones can deliver up to 3 parcels at a time and travel between 75 and 95 kilometres. Their technology is different as they combine a patented tilt-rotor mechanism which makes the drones stronger and more efficient. The firm is exploring using hydrogen power to reduce emissions and to fly longer distances.

Drones are considered to invade privacy yet Wingcopter has created a different purpose for its drones. For example, it delivers medical supplies within Ireland, Scotland, the islands of Vanuatu and Malawi. In Italy its drones are used to map the topology of volcanos, which is too dangerous for people to do. In Canada the Wingcopter drones are used for wildlife research surveying whales in the arctic. In Norway the drones have inspected long-range power lines, which is a less expensive option than using helicopters.

The chief executive officer is Tom Plümmer, who has gained many awards for being a rising star and guards his privacy as we know little about his background, with no information about him online. Wingcopter has secured over $60 million from venture capitalists and is still building the company. It has over 150 employees with an average age of 34.

It uses machine learning and stores its big data in cloud systems. Its staff work on the premises and remotely depending on their roles. Wingcopter is a company to watch with major investors from Germany and the USA.

Case questions
- What do you think about Wingcopter and the services it provides? Are there any downsides?
- How can organisations like Wingcopter ensure they stick to their ethical guidelines of doing good and providing drones for humanitarian and commercial purposes?
- How else can drones be used for positive purposes?

ADDITIVE MANUFACTURING

The last element in the IoE is additive manufacturing, which was initially described as 3D printing, but has developed so that it is no longer a static 3-dimensional model and can be a dynamic movable item. The additives used depend on the application and can include polycarbonates, ceramic materials, stainless steel and precious metals.

DISCOVER MORE ON ADDITIVE MANUFACTURING

Read the article '3D printing – A review of processes, materials and applications in industry 4.0' by Anketa Jandyal and colleages (2022) which explains the processes of 3D printing and the additives used.

6.5 ETHICAL DILEMMAS WITH EMERGING TECHNOLOGIES

Ethics is about doing the right thing, which provides us with moral codes to guide us, as well as legislation to ensure we follow the guidance. Emerging technologies that enable business practice raise many new ethical dilemmas, mainly around the use of data, personal privacy and systems design. There is an argument that if you have nothing to hide, it doesn't matter, but the data may be personal and it would be embarrassing if it were shared. You could be subject to blackmail if hackers discovered a deep secret that you'd rather your friends and employer didn't know about. Equally firms may have nothing to hide, but the information could be confidential and useful for competitors. As a result, there are many elements of ethics to consider with technology design and use, including:

- Roboethics and how we use robots for good, not harm
- Machine learning and algorithmic ethics which guide how coders build new systems without bias
- Information and communications technology (ICT) ethics which consider how we harvest and manage data

As there are many guidelines, as well as privacy and data-sharing legislation, it can be difficult to assess what is and isn't acceptable in different contexts. The United Nations has stepped into this conversation in different ways (see Digital Tool: **World Commission on the Ethics of Scientific Knowledge and Technology**).

DIGITAL TOOL   World Commission on the Ethics of Scientific Knowledge and Technology

As its website notes, 'The World Commission on the Ethics of Scientific Knowledge and Technology (COMEST) is an advisory body and forum of reflection that was set up by UNESCO in 1998'. It was established to develop ethical guidelines for the environment, nanotechnologies, information and science.

- You can explore it here: unesco.org/en/ethics-science-technology/comest

A different approach is to adopt corporate digital responsibility (CDR) which is defined as 'the set of values and specific norms that govern an organization's judgments and choices in matters that relate specifically to digital issues' (Lobschat et al., 2021: 876). This is a strategic way to ensure an organisation does the right thing, regardless of which new technologies may emerge. Researchers Lobschat et al. (2021) highlight 3 key factors to explain why this is needed. Firstly, technology keeps evolving; this could indicate that if new guidance appears, it would be out of date quickly. Secondly, the adaptability of technology means that it may not be used for the intended purpose, or its usage may change which was not foreseen. Thirdly, we use digital technologies daily in different ways without noticing. CDR moves the emphasis from organisations complying with specific laws to organisations adopting a holistic perspective that governs their use of all and any technology. This would require cultural changes to ensure employees at all levels, as well as their suppliers, understood CDR in the same way they follow corporate social responsibility policies, so they are not accused of **bluewashing** (see Key Term). Yet CDR may be a more ethical step forward.

KEY TERM   BLUEWASHING

According to Floridi (2019: 187), bluewashing is making 'misleading claims about, or implementing superficial measures in favour of, the ethical values and benefits of digital processes, products, services, or other solutions in order to appear more digitally ethical than one is'.

JOURNAL OF NOTE

The Journal of Information Technology is focused on new research addressing information, management, and communications technologies as applied to the digital worlds of business, government and non-governmental enterprises. The Journal is especially interested in studies that address emerging technologies and their convergence, including SMAC (social media, mobile, analytics, cloud) and BRAID (blockchain, robotics, automation of knowledge work, internet of things and digital fabrication).

CASE STUDY

PAYPAL'S FINTECH FUTURE

PayPal is a financial technology (fintech) platform that 'simplifies commerce experiences on behalf of merchants and consumers worldwide' (PayPal, 2021: 4). Fintech is described as 'breakthroughs in technology that potentially have the power to transform the provision of financial services, drive the creation of novel business models, applications, processes, and products, as well as lead to consumer gains' (Murinde

(Continued)

et al., 2022: 1). Fintech is a growing sector with many challenger banks and neobanks that offer lower costs with no physical presence and represent an issue for PayPal. Although it considers its financial competitors as:

- Intuit Inc which acquired MailChimp and QuickBooks
- JP Morgan Chase & Co., a traditional bank
- Mastercard, a credit payment system
- Meta Platforms, a social network platform
- Netflix, a movie-streaming platform
- Oracle Corporation, an enterprise management system which includes financial options
- Salesforce, a cloud-based customer relationship management system
- ServiceNow, a cloud-based workflow management system
- The Western Union Company, a traditional money transfer system

None of these competitors are challenger banks or neobanks, perhaps as they would be too small to offer the same range of services. Yet the longer-established banking firms have legacy systems; some may even rely on sending letters rather than emails! So it may take these firms longer to adopt new technology as their readiness levels are lower. The business faces ongoing challenges from competitors who offer a range of physical and electronic payments. To address this, PayPal notes that they employ directors with a background in 'developing technology businesses, anticipating technological trends and driving innovation and product development' (PayPal, 2022a: 14).

PayPal captures big data which is stored in cloud-based data centres as explained in its annual report (PayPal, 2022a: 8):

> The technology infrastructure supporting our payments platform simplifies the storage and processing of **large amounts of data** and facilitates the deployment and operation of large-scale global products and services in both our own **data centers** and when hosted by **third party cloud service** providers. Our technology infrastructure is designed around industry best practices intended to reduce downtime and help ensure the resiliency of our payments platform in the event of outages or catastrophic occurrences.

According to its Annual Report, the Blockchain, Crypto and Digital Currencies (BCDC) team is exploring blockchain and emerging technology. To support this, in 2021 the business spent over $3 billion on technology and development which was an increase of 15% from the previous year, partly as the cost of its cloud services increased.

Blockchain and cloud services require significant energy, and the business is aware of its energy use and its data centres run on 100% renewable energy. However, the greatest challenges the business encounters are cyberattacks and security vulnerabilities which could result in 'serious harm to our reputation, business, and financial condition' (PayPal, 2022a: 13). As a well-known brand name that collects and stores finances, the cyberattacks PayPal faces include 'cyberextortion, distributed denial-of-service attacks, ransomware, spear phishing and social engineering schemes, computer viruses or other malware' (PayPal, 2022a: 13). In January 2023 it was revealed that PayPal had suffered a major cyberattack in December 2022, which was not shared on its website, but in other news pages, such as CNET (Fowler, 2023: 1): 'Cybercriminals made off with the Social Security numbers and other personal information of about 35,000 PayPal customers after a December credential-stuffing attack.' According to a disclosure statement filed with the state of Maine, the attack occurred between December 6 and December 8 of 2022 and was discovered on December 20. In addition to social security numbers, usernames, addresses, dates of birth and individual tax identification numbers also may have been compromised.

There's no indication that any financial information was stolen, or that customer accounts were misused, PayPal said. The company's payment systems were also not affected.

In a statement released to CNET, PayPal said it has contacted affected customers and offered guidance on how to further protect their personal information. The company also reset the passwords of all of the affected accounts and is requiring their users to set new ones the next time they log in.

Managing cyberattacks is part of the day-to-day operations for fintech firms and this is likely to increase. It's likely that PayPal manages hundreds of attacks daily and only the larger ones breach their security systems. In the future a new technology may be able to identify attacks sooner and prevent further damage.

CASE QUESTIONS

PayPal must stay ahead with emerging technology and ensure it remains trusted and a secure environment to retain its customers.

- Why does PayPal consider Meta and Netflix as competitors?
- How can organisations like PayPal keep up to date with emerging technology?
- Why would PayPal exclude details of a security breach on its website?

FURTHER EXERCISES

1. Using Table 6.2 as a framework, assess a new technology. Create a survey and replace 'facial recognition systems' with terms relevant for your study. Use an online survey tool for the survey and discuss the results in a presentation.

2. The Internet of Everything (IoE) offers many opportunities. For an organisation of your choice, create a proposal identifying the benefits of relevant IoE to enhance processes within the organisation.

3. Consider the impact on society with 2 enabling or emerging technologies of your choice.

4. We are moving towards a fully connected world with the Internet of Everything and mobile broadband. Discuss.

(Continued)

SUMMARY

This chapter has explored:

- The hype cycle for emerging tech
- Technology, society and organisational readiness levels
- The extended technology acceptance model
- Technology enablers and ethical dilemmas

PART 3

DIGITAL BUSINESS INNOVATION, DISRUPTION AND TRANSFORMATION

CONTENTS

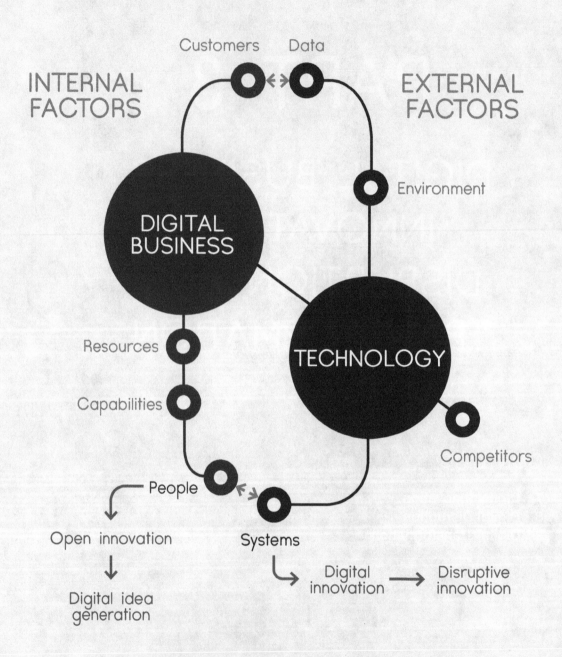

INTERNAL
FACTORS

EXTERNAL
FACTORS

Customers   Data

Environment

DIGITAL
BUSINESS

TECHNOLOGY

Resources

Competitors

Capabilities

People

Systems

Open innovation

Digital
innovation

Disruptive
innovation

Digital idea
generation

7
DIGITAL INNOVATION

LEARNING OUTCOMES

When you have read this chapter, you will be able to:

Understand the concept of digital innovation

Apply the Diffusion of Innovations framework

Analyse how disruptive innovation has impacted existing businesses

Evaluate options for crowd-based power

Create a plan for digital innovation using design thinking or crowdsourcing

PROFESSIONAL SKILLS

When you have worked through this chapter, you should be able to:

- Create a plan for digital innovation
- Select and apply the most appropriate innovation techniques

7.1 BACKGROUND TO INNOVATION

According to the *Merriam-Webster Dictionary* (2016: 1), innovation is either 'a new idea, method, or device' or 'the introduction of something new'. It can also involve invention which is 'usually something which has not previously been in existence'. The first mobile phone was an invention; the first smartphone was an innovation – a development of an existing device. When we think of innovation we may think of new products, yet it's not always new products that bring innovation. It can be:

- The place or access to the goods – introducing products from one country to another, for example taking TikTok (Douyin) from China to the USA and Europe
- The processes involved – using technology to improve customer journeys, for example booking hotel rooms via an app rather than via telephone or email
- The price which may be lower due to the business model – consumers selling to other consumers in a peer-to-peer (P2P) model, for example eBay, Vinted or SwapUp

Innovation is a driving goal within the United Nations. It is critical to society as it contributes to improving food supplies, healthcare and well-being, education, equality, water supplies, energy supplies, workplaces and infrastructures. It is also crucial for organisations to continue in business (Mariani et al., 2023). Yet many innovations fail. If you think of technology games companies, only around 20% of the games created succeed. The time taken to code and deliver the game can be wasted if gamers don't download it, or play once and delete – so 80% of games fail. Likewise less than 1% of apps uploaded to app stores are successful – so 99% of all apps are failures!

There are different ideas about what is the difference between success and failure for a new product. It is often related to research, but another key factor is sharing news about the innovation quickly, to gain attention and to grow many enthusiastic members quickly which is part of **network effects** (see Chapter 4). Looking at the different groups of people who decide when to adopt a new technology, whether that's a game, a piece of kit or something else, Professor Everett Rogers proposed the model 'Diffusion of Innovations' (Rogers, 1962), which explored the conditions that increased or decreased the likelihood of product adoption. This model is based on how a product gains momentum and spreads or diffuses through a group. Rogers proposed 5 adopter categories which considered when an individual adopted an innovation, as shown in Figure 7.1. Those adopting the product at the start are a small group and known as the innovators, actively seeking access to something new. They are keen to experiment and discover new concepts. At the other end of the scale, the laggards wait until they have no choice and need to acquire or use the new item, as they are more cautious. For example, the use of QR codes has become popular and early adopters may have been using these for 20 years, yet still some people prefer not to use them unless they have to – the laggards. The diffusion of innovation model has been adapted and changed over the years, yet it is still widely used. There have been discussions about the terms used as 'laggards' does not seem very complimentary. However, it provides a helpful framework to understand the different categories of adopters. It is important to understand the different adopters for marketing messages when launching innovations.

Figure 7.1 Diffusion of innovation

Source: Adapted from Rogers (1962: 247)

This chapter will explore different forms of innovation and consider the challenges for those managing innovation.

Activity 7.1 Apply the Diffusion of Innovations framework

Using the Diffusion of Innovations framework, consider a technology or social media platform which has been introduced in the last 5 years.

- Conduct research online to assess the number of adopters or users in the innovators, early adopters and early majority categories. Also consider whether some people are not yet using the technology or social media platform and why this may be.
- Discuss your findings in groups and compare your research.

DISCOVER MORE ON APP ADOPTION

Read 'Marketing research on mobile apps: Past, present and future' by Professor Lara Stocchi and colleagues (2022), published in *Journal of the Academy of Marketing Science*. This article explores research into mobile apps within the concept of the customer journey – from pre- to post-adoption – considering why consumers adopt and engage with apps.

7.2 DISRUPTIVE INNOVATION

Professor Clayton M. Christensen created the term 'disruptive innovation' in 1997. However, the original meaning was confused and the term is often used for *all innovation*, but not all innovation is disruptive. Disruptive innovation occurs when an existing market or product is challenged, rather than a completely new idea being introduced. According to later research by Christensen and colleagues (2018), there are 3 core elements of disruptive innovation:

- A gap at the *bottom of the market* for simpler offers
- *Inferior product attributes*, which represent what the customer wants
- Opportunities for new market entrants to invest in products that offer *lower margins, smaller markets*

Smartphone Sixty Seconds® – Seek disrupters

Using your mobile phones:

- Search for 'disruptive brands'.
- Pick one disruptive brand.
- In which sector are they based?
- Which companies will they most disrupt or damage in the next 12 months?
- Share findings with classmates.

7.2.1 CORE ELEMENTS OF DISRUPTIVE INNOVATION

A GAP AT THE BOTTOM OF THE MARKET FOR SIMPLER OFFERS

The gap at the bottom of the market makes businesses nervous. The top end of the market is considered more profitable and easier to serve. Many well-established businesses are less interested in smaller margins and smaller markets. Plus the idea of 'inferior products' may damage their brand. Can you imagine the French couture brand Chanel offering an everyday clothing line which was sold in supermarkets? Yet there are cases of addressing the gap at the bottom of the market with a simpler offer. For example, CDs (compact discs used for music and digital storage) were replaced with digital downloads, so the physical product is no longer required. This led to more innovation as instead of selling entire music albums, single tracks could be sold, a much simpler offer. The idea of selling individual music tracks at lower costs seemed like a bad idea to many firms. Why cannibalise an album into individual songs? This was the approach taken by firms like Spotify, and although its profits remain low it generates an annual revenue of over $10 billion compared to the longer-established Warner Music Group's revenue of $5 billion. The 2 businesses operate different business models. Spotify is a newer company and has a freemium business model. Warner Music Group uses a traditional model with revenue from licensing, publishing, streaming and its record labels.

INFERIOR PRODUCT ATTRIBUTES

Once again, the concept of inferior seems like a bad idea to many businesses. But sometimes a 'no frills' offer is exactly what the customer wants. Good examples of inferior product attributes can be found in:

- Airlines – budget airlines offering basic flights where passengers pay extra for food on board, luggage storage and seat selection, such as RyanAir and EasyJet
- Hotels – budget hotels offering low-cost room-only services, such as HotelF1 (previously Formula 1) in France

Once a market is established that demonstrates the opportunity to existing businesses, they may also change their behaviour. For example, British Airways offers a range of flight options which include 'lite', which is without luggage storage and seat selection.

LOWER MARGINS, SMALLER MARKETS

Opportunities for new market entrants to invest in products that offer lower margins and are in smaller markets include Spotify – much smaller margins and perhaps a smaller market, yet greater revenues than its rival Warner Music Group. Existing businesses often have a 'legacy system' in place which is a 'mission-critical system that supports the core business process of the organization with the restriction of outdated hardware, software, and resources to maintain' (Hasan et al., 2023: 1). These can slow down technology adoption and this is another reason why newer firms are more easily able to enter existing markets.

DISCOVER MORE ON LEGACY SYSTEMS

Read the article by Hasan et al. (2023) 'Legacy systems to cloud migration: A review from the architectural perspective', which explains more about legacy systems and discusses the challenges that they present for organisations.

7.2.2 MULTI-LEVEL INFLUENCE FACTORS

Expanding on earlier work (Christensen, 1997; Christensen et al., 2018), researchers Si and Chen (2020) suggest that there are multi-level influence factors that contribute to disruptive innovation. They state that there are 3 factors – internal, external and the wider network.

INTERNAL FACTORS

The internal factors include the individual approach and that of the firm. At an individual level it is about the manager leading the innovation which may be based on their own experience, their thought processes (mental model) and their ability to recognise threats or opportunities. There are well-known individual inventors, such as Steve Jobs of Apple who developed smartphones and Bill Gates who created computer code leading to Microsoft products. Yet there are other less well-known inventors such as:

- Frederick McKinley Jones, who invented a ticket machine that gave the correct change in 1939, an early form of a machine responding to different situations

- Karen Sparck-Jones, a self-taught programmer, who worked on natural language processing and in 1964 shared her research which underpins search engines such as Google
- Lonnie Johnson, who created a robot for a school project in 1968 and later worked for NASA

However, inventors are the exception and most disruptive innovation takes place at the firm level. Firms may change their strategy due to new resources, capabilities or processes. It can also be due to changes in customer demands. Firm-level innovation occurs when there are many competitors or issues inside the organisation and a change of strategy is needed. Firm-level innovation can happen when customers demand new products or change behaviour. For example, they may shop less frequently in store and spend more online. This level of innovation is also due to resources – the budget, people and technology available. For example, start-ups often have smaller budgets and need to adopt a more creative approach. For instance, Uber has low operational costs as it behaves like a start-up. When Uber moves into a new city, it does not rent smart offices in the centre, but often uses cheaper offices on industrial estates outside the city.

There are downsides too, as while the firm may foster innovation it can also block new ideas. The management team may be concerned about the risk of introducing new products or they might not have the infrastructure or technology to support the new product.

EXTERNAL FACTORS

The first external factor is the wider industry sector. The sector may have experienced change in market demand, for example during the pandemic when many art galleries had to close, but some adapted. Many galleries, including the National Gallery of Ireland and the Louvre in Paris, offered virtual tours when they were closed and have continued to provide this service. Technology has enabled this new innovation. Research demonstrates people like to plan before they visit, so this does not cannibalise the existing business, but expands the service to wider audiences who might never be able to visit.

At the nation and economy levels, policy makers may nurture innovation through new laws. For example, in 2022, President Biden in the USA signed the Inflation Reduction Act. This legislation provides many opportunities (and tax incentives) for firms to work on clean energy and climate change. It is likely to accelerate new products and services that reduce carbon emissions.

THE WIDER NETWORK

The last level in the multi-level influence factors of disruptive innovation model is the network/ecosystem. This considers the value of the wider network (see Chapter 4 'Network Effects') and how changes can bring innovation opportunities to entire communities, as demonstrated in Case Example 7.1: The Grameen Bank.

Figure 7.2 shows the different factors in the model of the multi-level influence factors of disruptive innovation.

Network:

- venture capitalists
- network of suppliers, customers and complementors
- formal strategic alliance
- cooperation (horizontally or vertically)
- disruptive susceptibility

EXTERNAL

Industry:

- market demand
- target market
- periodic variation of innovation in the industry economics of scale
- technological and customer capabilities of submarkets

Nation/ economy:

- emerging economies or mature economies
- government and policy makers (regulators)
- policies and instutions
- legistation
- tax preferences
- embeded social impacts

INTERNAL

Individual:

- manager's perception
- manager's inertia
- managers's experience
- manager's mental model
- manager's ability

Firm:

- strategy
- organization
- marketing
- resource

Figure 7.2   Multi-level influence factors of disruptive innovation

Source: Si & Chen (2020: 15). Printed with permission of Elsevier

CASE EXAMPLE 7.1   The Grameen Bank

In a Bangladeshi village in 1976 a pilot banking project was started by an economics lecturer, Professor Muhammad Yunus. Aiming to provide micro loans to people who are typically marginalised by mainstream banks, the Grameen Bank was launched. Eight years later the bank was formalised. It is described as a bank for the poor and focuses on helping those in most need. This is an example of *disruptive innovation* as an existing market was being challenged, rather than a completely new idea being introduced. Its mission is: 'Providing comprehensive financial services to empower the poor to realize their potential and to break out of the vicious cycle of poverty.'

Data from the International Monetary Fund shows that Bangladesh has a population of over 165 million. It is a fast-growing economy, moving away from agriculture and low-cost clothing manufacture. British American Tobacco is a major employer and 39% of the population (mainly male) smoke, by comparison to 8% in Sweden, 13% in Norway, 16% in Australia, 17% in Canada, 19% in the UK and 25% in the USA (see worldpopulationreview.com/country-rankings/smoking-rates-by-country).

One way to start and grow businesses is access to finance, but this can be challenging. As its website notes, 'the unique feature of Grameen Bank is that no collateral is required

(Continued)

to get the credit from the bank'. This means that people without a deposit or other income could gain financial support when needed. It offers different lending options, including:

- Microenterprise loans for people looking to start small businesses
- Crop loans for short-term investments for seasonal farming
- Livestock loans for purchasing and fattening cattle for special festivals and events
- Young Entrepreneur loans to the children of the members who are educated, enterprising, industrious, and willing to become entrepreneurs by creating self-employment
- Housing loans to build simple tin-roof houses
- Higher education loans for the children of members, so that they can pursue higher education at the highest level without facing any financial problems

This innovative bank has changed the entire community, by providing funding, education and support for all members of society. Grameen Bank has been able to further adopt digital innovation with its Village Pay Phone Programme, which World Habitat (2003: 1) explains:

> Bangladesh has one of the lowest phone penetration rates in the world. The Village Pay Phone Programme was developed by combining the Grameen Bank's expertise in micro-enterprise and micro-credit with the latest digital wireless technology.

A telephone in a village does not just ensure voice communication from village to village, but rather it can be treated as an important tool for development. The scheme to create a rural communications network by equipping one woman in each village with a cell phone is the most imaginative of several efforts to address one of the world's most basic technology gaps.

Grameen Bank's Annual Report confirms that, 'A borrower buys a mobile phone to become the "Telephone Lady of the village"'. She provides telecoms services to the village and makes a small profit. At the end of 2021 there were over 2 million 'village phone ladies'. This is an example of disruptive innovation where other banks were not interested in the bottom of the market. The products are simplified versions of complex loans although they are what the customer wants.

Access to funding changes lives and access to technology – something as simple as a telephone, which many of us take for granted, has the power to transform communities.

Case questions

- What do you think about how Grameen Bank operates? Why do other banks or organisations operate differently?
- What other examples of disruptive innovation can you think of, using mobile phones and why?
- What other disruptive innovations have transformed communities, like the example of Grameen Bank?

7.3 DIGITAL INNOVATION

Digital innovation is about using technology to deliver new ideas or processes. These innovations provide new opportunities for some organisations and challenges for others. Many new services are not new, but are novel approaches to well-established services and changes to one aspect of the marketing mix. For example, taxi services have been available for hundreds of years, yet Uber added technology to make the process of ordering a taxi easier. Friends have always swapped clothing, yet Vinted monetised the process, enabling people to re-sell older clothing and buy from others. Other examples of digital innovation that changed established services include those shown in Table 7.1.

Table 7.1 Types of digital innovation with examples

Type of digital innovation	Marketing mix element	Example
Developing new products	Product	Google and other search engines replaced traditional directories such as the Yellow Pages (also known as the Golden Pages)
Changing the product	Product	Deliveroo and Uber Eats collecting and delivering takeout food from several different restaurants at the same time for the consumer
Changing pricing	Price	The addition of buy now, pay later (BNPL) firms such as Klarna
Accessing new markets	Place	Canva, the Australian online image service, has expanded globally
Offering different forms of access	Place	Buying through the app rather than in store; for example, Mecca, the beauty brand store in Australia, allows customers to buy instore, online and via the app
Removing intermediaries	Place	Dell.com allows individuals to buy computers direct from their website
Adding intermediaries	Place	Airbnb acting as a broker between the accommodation provider and the visitors, as opposed to visitors choosing to book direct with a hotel chain
Varying methods of promotion	Promotion	Social media advertising or the use of influencers

According to Nambisan et al. (2017: 223), digital innovation is 'the use of digital technology during the process of innovating'. Varadarajan et al. (2022) suggest that digital innovations can impact the product, promotion and distribution – or a combination of these as **digital innovation for the greater good** (see Key Term).

KEY TERM DIGITAL INNOVATION FOR THE GREATER GOOD
(DIGITAL IGG)

Researchers Varadarajan et al. (2022: 487) took a different perspective on digital innovation and consider how it contributes to society. They propose that digital innovation for the greater good (digital IGG) is as 'a digital technology-based new product, process, or practice, or improvements in an existing product, process or practice, creating economic value for the innovating firm and environmental and social value for society'.

Varadarajan et al. (2022: 487) pointed out that innovations for the greater good are 'aligned with the United Nations (UN) Sustainable Development Goals (SDGs)'. They suggest there are 3 forms of digital innovation. The first form of digital innovation is through the product mix, for example, cloud computing (e.g. Dropbox, Apple iCloud or Google Drive), which means individuals do not require such high-powered or expensive computers and can share digital space online. This benefits individuals, firms and society who can access documents and other materials at any time from any place.

In addition to product innovation, we have seen changes to how goods are paid for, the pricing options. With financial credit widely available in Western countries, more organisations offer 'pay later' or instalment services.

The other form of digital innovation is through adding technology to distribution channels. Varadarajan et al. (2022) suggest this leads to **omnichannel marketing** (see Key Term), which provides better customer experiences, because it delivers what the customer needs, where and when it is needed – for example, customers buying through international sellers, or local businesses offering regional delivery or through live-streaming events, or via apps or social media platforms. A further aspect of changing place is the removal or addition of intermediaries. The concept of the **paradox of choice** (Sanders, 2022), where too much choice is overwhelming, has led to many intermediaries entering the market to simplify the decision-making process. For example, when searching for hotels it can be complicated, with so many brands to choose from, so booking sites such as Booking.com, GoSplitty, Kayak, MyHotelAfrica and Trivago provide filters to find accommodation based on location, price, ratings and more – reducing the choice but making the process easier.

KEY TERM   OMNICHANNEL

Omnichannel has been defined as 'the coordination and integration of a firm's marketing actions across multiple distribution channels, communication channels, and customer touchpoints to offer customers a seamless experience in their interactions with the firm, thereby enhancing firm performance' (Varadarajan et al., 2022: 495).

DISCOVER MORE ON THE PARADOX OF CHOICE

Read the article by Sanders (2022) 'Does the paradox of choice exist in theory? A behavioral search model and pareto-improving choice set reduction algorithm', which discusses the concept and the theories surrounding the paradox of choice.

Another form of digital innovation is through the promotion mix. For example, influencers communicate directly with the customers, rather than the traditional approach of delivering communications via the firm. Different influencers communicate with different audiences, which adds value as the different types of communication involve creative approaches that are more aligned with the customers.

Although not all innovation is disruptive, digital innovation aims to be disruptive by using technology. This changes the dynamics of how organisations provide goods and the value created – the benefits, for firms and customers.

CASE EXAMPLE 7.2 Easy Taxi

Brazilian entrepreneur Tallis Gomes was attending a start-up event in a district of Rio de Janeiro. He was attending Startup Rio 2011 and thinking about a bus app. But as he was standing in the rain and unable to get an Uber to his location, he thought of a different solution, using technology to work with local taxi firms, a form of digital innovation, which was named EasyTaxi.

Instead of waiting for a taxi to drive past, or calling one via Uber which may not have any drivers in the region, EasyTaxi works with local taxi firms who sign up to get notifications and pay a flat fee per trip. As a digital innovation, the EasyTaxi app finds drivers via local taxi firms, so instead of competing with existing businesses, EasyTaxi works with them. Users (riders) can download the app and use in any location. This means that when visitors are in an area they don't know, they can use the app to find a taxi cab which may be closer, have better local knowledge and be cheaper than a national company.

The business model is based on charging the driver and the rider. The fee paid by local firms was agreed at a fixed rate of BR$2 (less the 0.50 cents), which made it accessible. It was acquired by the Spanish company Cabify in 2019, which recognises that some ride-hailing apps are expensive and has stated that they don't need to be the most expensive cab company to make a profit. As an example, they suggested that in some cities taxis can use bus lanes and move around more swiftly, saving time and money.

When the acquisition took place, customers could use either app to find local taxi firms. This meant that the taxi firms and their customers were not disadvantaged with the changes.

It may seem that Cabify is competing with the largest firms in the taxi sector such as Uber, Didi, Grab, Lyft and Ola, but Madrid-based Cabify has a stronger vision and is working towards Mobility as a Service (MaaS). According to the MaaS Alliance, MaaS 'integrates various forms of transport and transport-related services into a single, comprehensive, and on-demand mobility service' (see maas-alliance.eu). For example, Mobility as a Service means people no longer need to own cars and can opt for ride-sharing or e-hailing or public transport as alternative means of transport. All platforms (and payments) would be contained on a single app.

Cabify is available in 7 countries – that's Spain and across Latin America. As a digital innovation, EasyTaxi/Cabify used technology to work with existing businesses and offer them access to customers they have previously missed.

Case questions

- EasyTaxi/Cabify applied innovation to the process of finding local taxi firms, but managed to keep the fees at an accessible level and worked with rather than against longer-established businesses. What were the benefits of this approach?
- It seems that Cabify isn't competing with Uber, but customers (riders) might not know this. How can small brands such as Cabify gain greater market share and move into more countries?
- What do you think about the concept of MaaS? What are the downsides?

7.4 OPEN INNOVATION

Innovation often took place behind closed doors within firms, as a closely guarded secret, with the end result being shared at a product launch. An alternative is the concept of 'open innovation' (OI), which was created by Henry Chesbrough as a 'new model for industrial innovation' (Chesbrough, 2012: 20). OI enables organisations to use their knowledge, exploit their technology or maximise their capabilities in new ways, increasing their usage and management of resources. For this reason OI was often a process adopted by larger firms, with greater access to a wider knowledge base, more technology or deeper capabilities. A criticism of OI is that smaller firms have been less involved due to the resources required (Carrasco-Carvajal et al., 2023).

> **KEY TERM**   OPEN INNOVATION
>
> 'Open innovation (OI) is a strategy that firms adopt to innovate by incorporating knowledge from both outside and inside their firms, exploiting their knowledge, and exploring the knowledge of their environment' (Carrasco-Carvajal et al., 2023: 397).

7.4.1 CLOSED INNOVATION

OI was intended as the opposite of closed innovation which takes place inside organisations where new activities are based on an internally focused perspective. Closed innovation starts with projects inside the organisation, based on research it has gathered. It takes a linear approach, step by step moving through different departments, such as research, prototype, testing, development and marketing, until there is a decision to abandon the idea or proceed to launch.

The challenge with closed innovation is that the organisation may feel it is a good idea, but customers cannot see the value. It could be described as innovation behind closed doors, but this may be to protect intellectual property or to gain a competitive advantage. In many ways, closed innovation is the traditional method for organisations to develop new product ideas, but it can fail. For example, we might consider Google Plus as an example of closed innovation. If you're not familiar with Google Plus (or Google +) it was designed as a business social network where you could join groups, post updates and share relevant information. It was Google's response to the growth of social media networks. But it never felt as if it was designed for users. One of the main questions about it was 'What's the point of Google+?' which eventually closed in 2019. On the other hand, Apple successfully works on its new product developments inside its organisation, not wishing to share its next big idea, but carefully monitors its online forums and engages developers at a major annual event.

7.4.2 OUTSIDE-IN, INSIDE-OUT AND COUPLED OPEN INNOVATION

Open innovation is more inclusive and actively seeks the external view. This means that OI is collaborative and engaged with the wider community and, at the same time, doesn't ignore ideas inside the organisation (Chesbrough, 2012). According to researchers, there are 3 types of open innovation: outside-in, inside-out and coupled (Carrasco-Carvajal et al., 2023; Chesbrough, 2012).

- **Outside-in or Inbound OI** – acquiring external knowledge and opening up a company's innovation processes to external inputs and contributions. Examples of inbound OI include start-up innovation awards or licensing the intellectual property. Lego holds competitions inviting users to do more with their products and Disney licenses their brand name and other intellectual property for a fee.
- **Inside-out or Outbound** – exploiting the organisation's resources where unused and underutilised ideas are shared outside the organisation for others to use in their businesses. Examples of outbound OI include joint-venture activities or spin-offs. For example the Google Play and Apple App store are based on outbound OI. They enable third-party firms to use their **software development kits** (see Key Term in Chapter 4) to create new product offers.
- **Coupled OI** – this blends inbound and outbound OI (Carrasco-Carvajal et al., 2023), working with partners to achieve common goals. This may take longer and involve more stakeholders. This is a form of co-creation where all parties share their knowledge and resources. For example, the development of COVID-19 vaccinations involved researchers, scientists, pharmaceutical manufacturers and health authorities working together to deliver a vaccination in record time.

Figure 7.3 illustrates the open innovation process.

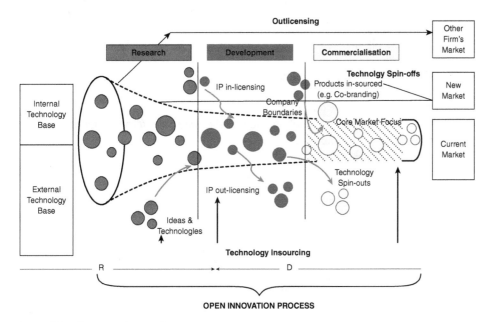

Figure 7.3 The open innovation process

Source: Adapted by Bujor & Avasilcai (2018: 3) from Chesbrough (2003) and Mortara & Minshall (2011)

The open innovation process requires research and development, but this varies depending on whether this is inbound or outbound. It can result in new products for the current market or technology spin-offs for new markets. Key factors in OI are external knowledge sources and collaboration, and technology exploitation and technology exploration.

One way to encourage OI is to hold hackathons, events where coders and companies meet to complete specific goals – known as 'hacks'. For example, EasyTaxi (bought by Cabify), founded in Brazil, is an app that, unlike Uber, connects users with local taxi firms and was created at a hackathon. Open innovation is more inclusive and actively seeks the external view. This means that OI is collaborative and engaged with the wider community and, at the same time, doesn't ignore ideas inside the organisation (Chesbrough, 2012).

DIGITAL TOOL   Open hackathons

The OpenACC Organization provides details of upcoming hackathons to help coders improve their skills, share and gain expertise by working on events together.

- You can explore it here: openhackathons.org/s/upcoming-events

Smartphone Sixty Seconds® – Discover the top hackathons

Using your mobile phones:

- Search for 'most famous hackathons'.
- Pick one and explore further.
- When and where does it take place?
- Who are the sponsors and what are the benefits they gain from this hackathon?
- Share findings with classmates.

DISCOVER MORE ON OPEN INNOVATION

Read the article by Carrasco-Carvajal et al. (2023) 'Measuring open innovation in SMEs: An overview of current research', which reviews the literature around OI and its application to smaller organisations.

7.5 DIGITAL IDEA GENERATION

Idea generation or ideation is the process of producing ideas. Ideas solve problems we know about (such as cures for major illnesses) and create opportunities that we hadn't recognised (such as developing new products, for example iPhones). Ideas can be generated by individuals and groups in different ways, such as inside or outside organisations. They can be based on customer feedback – where customers require new or adapted goods, or due to competitors entering a market. For example, following customer feedback, Uber and Airbnb have moved into the business market, providing dashboards and easier payment methods for customers using taxis or accommodation for work.

Activity 7.2 Generate ideas to reduce vaping by young people

An electronic cigarette (e-cigarette or vape pen) is a handheld device that works by heating a liquid that usually contains nicotine, flavourings and other industrial chemicals to create an aerosol that is inhaled. Using e-cigarettes is known as vaping and vapes were designed to help people quit smoking, but instead non-smokers have started to use them.

In some countries, vaping is becoming more popular than smoking, especially with younger people. Early research indicates it is addictive and could lead to diabetes with its high sugar content and other health issues.

In groups, generate novel and useful ideas to address the challenge of vaping.

Methods of idea generation include crowdsourcing and applying design thinking, which we will explore next.

7.5.1 CROWDSOURCING

Crowdsourcing has been described as 'a widely-used open innovation practice in which firms (called "seekers") publicly broadcast internal problems in the form of challenges to which individuals external to the firm (called "crowds" or "solvers") are invited to offer solutions' (Zaggl et al., 2023: 2). According to Steils and Hanine (2022: 296), although crowdsourcing is a form of co-creation, there are 3 main differences:

- the **electronic dimension**, as the internet and virtual communities provide fast access to the crowd
- the **strategic intention** behind the launch of the crowdsourcing operation
- the **open nature** of the call for contributions

Crowdsourcing can be used 'throughout the value chain of the product or service' (Steils & Hanine, 2022: 298), from idea generation and product design, to solving product challenges and resolving logistics issues, as well as customer communication. Crowdsourcing formats include creative and innovation contests (Steils & Hanine, 2022) which take place on crowdsourcing platforms, but only the preferred solution may result in payment for the solver. There are different types of crowdsourcing, with varying advantages and disadvantages as shown in Table 7.2.

Table 7.2 Advantages and disadvantages of different types of crowdsourcing with examples

Type of crowdsourcing	Advantages	Disadvantages	Examples
Fishing	• Useful for narrow problems • Open to a wide audience • Can be a lower cost for organisations as it may be payment upon selected solution	• Difficult to find solutions for broad problems • Individual solvers work alone so there is a lack of integration • Specialist knowledge may be required • Major time commitment for solvers • There can be too many solutions (paradox of choice) to choose from • Solvers who are not successful may share negative comments about the organisation	Elon Musk, X (formerly Twitter) owner has used fishing, asking users for solutions to problems
Collective production	• Useful for broad scope problems • Problems are shared among a crowd • Exchange of knowledge between the solvers • Less time commitment required from solvers who share the workload • Can result in higher quality results	• Solvers need to take on specific roles • Solvers may also work with competitors or share the knowledge gained • Solvers may gain access to valuable intellectual property • Moderators are required to answer questions and provide technical support	Working collectively, scientists solved the single problem of creating a COVID-19 vaccine, within an urgent context
Hunting	• Seekers identify the most relevant solvers who are often experts in the field • Can save significant time by seeking help from experts	• Pre-work is required to identify suitable criteria for solvers and to approach them • Solvers may not be interested in helping	In Ireland, the Best Doctors® programme is a worldwide network of over 50,000 medical experts who are approached for advice on specific medical cases

Source: Adapted from Gurca et al. (2023); Steils & Hanine (2022)

Organisations may use crowdsourcing for one element, such as fishing for new ideas. When the ideas have been shortlisted, they may move towards collective production to select the best ideas and refine the concept. Finally, hunting may be used to test the concept before launch.

Activity 7.3   Evaluate your options for crowd-based power

Find crowdsourcing websites and select one (you may need to sign up). Identify if there are any areas where you could contribute: perhaps designing a logo, conducting a digital marketing audit or building a website.

ETHICAL INSIGHTS   Payment fairness in crowdsourcing

Crowdsourcing is an effective way to generate new ideas and provides workers in any location the opportunity to earn money. Yet it has led to many debates about fairness of payments and exploitation of workers. Some platforms have even been called 'digital sweatshops' (Fowler et al., 2022).

There are different payment models (Salminen et al., 2022: 2) which all have challenges, including:

- Fixed flat rate – the main option as it is convenient
- Time-adjusted model – can be based on a specific hourly rate
- Quality-adjusted model – difficult to measure quality
- Cost of living adjusted model – difficult to know where workers are based and does not address quality of the work

The fixed flat rate for an activity or output is based on the volume of work done, with platforms such as Amazon's Mechanical Turk (MTurk). Time-adjusted payments take place where an estimate of the time required is offered as the fee. This works well if the worker is about to conduct the work in the given time, but it can take much longer. Payment based on quality is where a larger fee is offered and more work may be required; for example, for a new logo or idea for a business, where the winning person is paid a fixed amount when their idea or concept is accepted. The cost of living adjusted model is very challenging to operate as many platforms are international and, although someone in Australia may take the work, they may outsource to someone in a country where living costs are lower.

It may seem that output-based work, such as being paid a fixed flat rate per task (e.g. tagging photographs, answering questions, creating a new logo design), is reasonable as the worker agrees to take on the task. The reality is that this can result in payment that is less than any minimum wage, in some cases a few cents for many hours of work. Another aspect of fairness with contests, such as creating new logos or providing ideas for new concepts, is the lack of transparency as to which were selected and why (Abhari & McGuckin, 2023). Equally, submitting design ideas to an online platform in the hope that your proposal is accepted may mean delivering a lot of work free of charge and winning one project every few weeks. There can be a lot of competition on these websites; for example, 99 Designs claims to have '10,000 freelance designers across 144 countries'. The platforms also need to make money to provide the service and can charge an introduction fee and a commission on each project. According to Salminen et al. (2022), there is a challenge in agreeing what is the right amount to pay as there is no widespread agreement on 'fair compensation'. Buyers may be unaware of these issues and may follow the recommended guidelines from the platform.

- Have you ever participated (as a buyer or worker) in a crowdsourcing platform? What was your experience?
- What are your thoughts about payments in crowd-based platforms? How can payments be fair with workers from many countries with different living costs?
- Whose responsibility is it to ensure fairness in crowdsourcing platforms and why?

7.5.2 DESIGN THINKING

Design thinking is an approach to generating new ideas and finding solutions for challenges. It takes a customer-centric or people-first approach (Brown, 2008) as many new ideas start with the product, rather than the user. You could describe design thinking as adopting the customer experience perspective.

One of the early writers about design thinking, Brown (2008: 87) suggested the characteristics for design thinking involved:

- Empathy – seeing the issue from other people's point of view
- Integrative thinking – ensuring the issue is considered from a holistic viewpoint
- Optimism – a solution is better than the current situation
- Experimentalism – trying and refining the ideas
- Collaboration – working with others, similar to collective production

Brown (2008: 88–89) also suggested that there were 3 steps involved in design thinking. Crowdsourcing could be used for each stage to gain feedback from others (inspiration), testing ideas (ideation) and spreading the word (implementation).

- Inspiration – understanding the problem, getting others involved who have a range of skills and assessing how technology can help
- Ideation – brainstorm ideas and create scenarios to test the ideas, communicate with others and build prototypes to test the concern
- Implementation – should be planned in from the start, make the business case to spread the word

Although design thinking may seem like a logical idea, many organisations start with the product and consider the user or consumer later in the process.

7.5.3 MANAGING IDEA GENERATION

The process of generating ideas is complex and many ideas fail (Steils & Hanine, 2022). It can be expensive and ideas may not be implemented. To ensure a greater chance of success, idea generation requires a clear description of the problem and involvement by the users. According to Wrigley et al. (2020: 134), for design thinking to work successfully in organisations, these 4 elements must be connected:

- Strategic Vision—the organization's long-term strategic goals and intent.
- Facilities—the physical spaces and resources that are dedicated to design activities.
- Cultural Capital—the understanding, knowledge, and capability of the organization's workforce in relation to design.
- Directives—mandates that call for the use of design and hold the organization's staff accountable for using design.

Technology has provided different methods of digital innovation, yet they all require careful definition and management. AI may provide faster methods to assess ideas, but this would involve the organisations giving their ideas to AI platforms – which could be seen by competitors.

JOURNAL OF NOTE

The International Journal of Entrepreneurship and Innovation provides a worldwide forum for the exploration and dissemination of ideas and experience relating to the development and application of entrepreneurship.

CASE STUDY

PAYPAL DIGITAL INNOVATION

To stay relevant, PayPal must continue to innovate. Since launching in 1998 the company has had its ups and downs. The pandemic years were a challenge for everyone and, as many of PayPal's customers were unable to trade, this had a financial impact, but they recovered. As the 2022 Annual Report stated:

> In 2022, we delivered solid financial and operating results across our key performance metrics. This was accomplished during a challenging period of macroeconomic uncertainty, slowing e-commerce growth and geopolitical instability. (PayPal, 2023a: 3)

One of PayPal's leadership principles is innovation which aims to:

- Be a customer champion – focus on the customer not the products
- Never stand still – constantly seek ways to innovate
- Create simplicity and efficiency – ensure the user journey is frictionless

Of course technology and digital innovation is essential and so this is a skills requirement for directors joining the board: 'Because PayPal is a technology platform and digital payments company, we look for directors with a background in developing technology businesses, anticipating technological trends and driving innovation and product development' (PayPal, 2023a: 13). The board of directors includes the Former Chief Operating Officer of Airbnb, the President and CEO of HP, the President and Chief Executive Officer of Nike and the Former Board Chair and Chief Executive Officer of WarnerMedia Studios & Networks Group – all experienced people with knowledge and understanding of trading online and working on innovation.

PayPal is looking beyond digital innovation. It is looking to contribute to society and refers to its social innovation, to build a more inclusive digital economy and giving access to financial services to a wider group or people. Not everyone finds it easy to open a bank account, but PayPal does not require the same details, so can help those who need digital payments. The company has also provided consumers with pay later options which is a response to external factors, such as competitors already offering buy now, pay later.

The digital wallet is said to make PayPal easier to use and this is explained on their blog, to encourage more users to adopt this technology (PayPal Editorial Staff, 2023a: 1):

(Continued)

- A digital wallet is exactly what it sounds like: a digital app that makes it easy to store and use your various payment methods. Rather than holding physical cards like a physical wallet, a digital wallet stores information.

- A digital wallet can hold any type of account information: credit cards, debit cards, gift cards, loyalty cards, bank accounts, insurance information, concert tickets and more. In addition to storing this information, a digital wallet makes it easy to use those accounts to pay with just a tap of an app, perfect for small business transactions.

- To protect users, the app encrypts the account data to keep information secure during the transaction while using tokens to create a one-time number for each payment instead of using the account number.

- Digital wallets also make it easy to pay online by tapping the app at checkout instead of entering a credit card. Shoppers can also use their digital wallet to pay for products in store using tap-to-pay or QR code scans.

Offering new services may not be innovation, but with legacy systems that were established decades ago, it can involve digital innovation. Companies need to rethink how they use their systems and the changes required to provide greater efficiency for merchants and consumers alike.

Other digital innovations include: PayPal Rewards – a points system where consumers can earn, track and redeem points, and PayPal Honey – a browser extension which searches for voucher codes and applies at the checkout. These forms of digital innovation are about changing the processes rather than introducing new ideas.

As well as innovation through changing processes, PayPal has delivered innovation by changing the access (or place) to different services, such as 'access to $4.2 billion in capital for entrepreneurs and small businesses' (PayPal, 2023a: 11). This may seem very generous, although this expands PayPal's customer base and may have contributed to the organisation's post-pandemic recovery.

Innovation is so central to PayPal, to stay relevant in a fast-evolving sector, that the lack of being able to create new products and find solutions is recognised as a threat to the business: 'If we cannot keep pace with rapid technological developments to provide new and innovative products and services, the use of our products and services and, consequently, our revenues, could decline' (PayPal, 2023a: 15). However, most of the newness within PayPal seems to emerge from closed innovation, rather than actively seeking an external view.

CASE QUESTIONS

PayPal strives to be innovative and recognises the value of innovation, yet this brings online challenges.

- How does PayPal, as a large established business, stay relevant and continue to innovate?

- Why do companies like PayPal use closed rather than open innovation processes?

- What options are there for online payment systems to gain new ideas?

FURTHER EXERCISES

1. Analyse how disruptive innovation has impacted on existing businesses and the changes they have made to remain competitive.

2. Create a plan for digital innovation using design thinking or crowdsourcing.

3. Select a product or service of your choice. Assess whether this would gain most from Outside-In, Inside-Out, or Coupled Open Innovation.

4. Digital innovation leads to creative destruction. Discuss.

SUMMARY

This chapter has explored:

*   The concept of innovation
*   Core elements of disruptive innovation
*   How digital innovation uses technology to deliver new ideas or processes
*   Different forms of idea generation

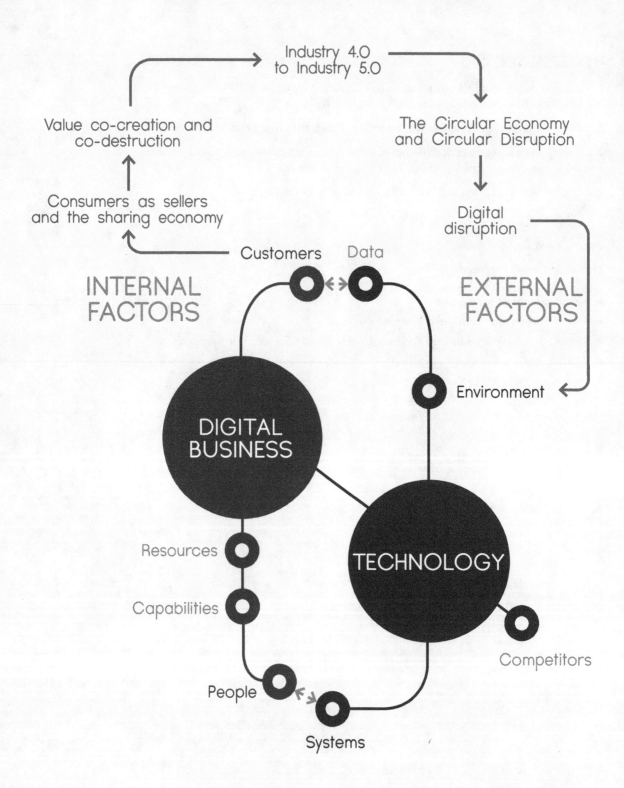

Industry 4.0
to Industry 5.0

The Circular Economy
and Circular Disruption

Value co-creation and
co-destruction

Consumers as sellers
and the sharing economy

Digital
disruption

Customers   Data

INTERNAL
FACTORS

EXTERNAL
FACTORS

Environment

DIGITAL
BUSINESS

Resources

Capabilities

TECHNOLOGY

Competitors

People

Systems

8

DIGITAL DISRUPTION

LEARNING OUTCOMES

When you have read this chapter, you will be able to:

- **Understand** the concept of digital disruption
- **Apply** disruptive technologies to your world
- **Analyse** the circular economy
- **Evaluate** value co-creation and co-destruction
- **Create** a plan to respond to digital disruption

PROFESSIONAL SKILLS

When you have worked through this chapter, you should be able to:

- Identify and discuss disruptive factors that may impact on future operations
- Manage, plan and report on digital projects concerning disruption

8.1 BACKGROUND TO DIGITAL DISRUPTION

As Zimand-Sheiner and Lahav (2022: 1) point out, 'in organizational management, disruption is defined as a radical change in industry, processes or business strategies that generates uncertainty'. Digital disruption can be described as a radical change introduced by the application of technology. It focuses on businesses, rather than individuals, and has been considered as 'originating in firm-level processes subsequently affecting industries' (Skog et al., 2018: 433).

Disruption is often perceived to be negative as it mainly impacts on older, existing firms, forcing them to change direction, adopt new processes or address. Yet digital disruption brings new innovations, improves services and enhances customer service. For example, Uber created digital disruption in the taxi business, to enable customers to find taxis, when and where they are needed. It created upset among existing taxi-cab organisations who took legal action to try and stop them. Yet when disruption occurs, a new market is created and other rivals can appear, such as Lyft and Ola in the taxi-cab sector. Overall, digital disruption provides customers with greater choice and existing businesses are improved as they adopt technology.

According to Skog et al. (2018), there are 3 key aspects of digital disruption which are shown in Table 8.1, with Uber applied as an example.

Table 8.1 Key aspects of digital disruption

Key aspects of digital disruption	What this means	Example
The processes originate from digital innovations and quickly erode competitive positions	A new product or service is introduced and reduces the power of existing firms	Uber displays the power over established taxi firms
They impact systems of value-creating actors by breaking and recombining linkages among resources, often facilitating more direct interactions and transactions	For a person needing a lift, the value is gaining a ride quickly. Knowing the type of car and driver provides direct interactions between the driver and rider	The Uber app enables driver and rider to learn more about each other such as the number of rides and feedback from others
The originating digital innovation processes are orchestrated by one or multiple firms, but effects on value creation and capture are systemic	Once the change is introduced, others jump into the sector with further innovations	Uber may have been the first e-hailing and ridesharing app, yet others such as EasyTaxi and Cabify have entered the market

Adapted from Skog et al. (2018)

The word innovation is a recurring theme in Table 8.1 and according to Thakur et al. (2023: 53), 'Digital disruption closely relates to, but differs from, the concept disruptive innovation'. Skog et al. (2018: 432) suggest that digital disruption is 'the rapidly unfolding processes through which digital innovation comes to fundamentally alter historically sustainable logics for value creation and capture by unbundling and recombining linkages among resources or generating new ones'. We can consider digital disruption as being a process that has negative and positive consequences for organisations and customers.

In this chapter we will explore the role of consumers as sellers in the sharing economy and how value is co-created and also destroyed. The circular economy and circular disruption are considered, as well as the concepts of Industry 4.0 and 5.0.

DIGITAL TOOL Table of disruptive technologies

Researchers at Imperial College in London created a table of disruptive technologies 'to make people think'. As their website notes, 'the table consists of 100 potentially disruptive technologies, which we have defined as those capable of significant social, economic or political upheaval'.

Registration may be required for the download.

- You can explore it here: imperialtechforesight.com/visions/table-of-disruptive-technologies-2

Activity 8.1 Apply disruptive technologies to your world

In groups, consider the different disruptive technologies that exist now and could exist in the future. Which of these do you believe will have most impact on your life – in a positive way? And which technologies might have a negative impact? Discuss why and use examples.

Also, explore how the negative impact could be positive in some situations. Prepare a short presentation to share in class which explains the choices you have made and why.

8.2 CONSUMERS AS SELLERS AND THE SHARING ECONOMY

The concept of more direct interactions and transactions was identified as a key aspect of digital disruption (Skog et al., 2018). An area where this takes place is where consumers become the sellers and share their possessions. This is known as the sharing economy (SE) and is also referred to as 'collaborative consumption, collaborative economy, peer-to-peer economy, platform economy and gig economy' (Rojanakit et al., 2022: 1317). The sharing economy is dependent on different elements shown in Figure 2.2 on p. 28. For example, easy-to-use technology is needed to facilitate the exchange process between providers and consumers. The exchange can be money, rewards or achieving social good – such as giving away items to someone who can use them, so that they are reused. For the sharing economy to succeed, enough people to buy and sell the goods or services are needed, which is why it is often **crowdsourced** (see Chapter 7). Another key factor is that the sharing economy experience can be *temporary*, as in many cases, the items are not sold or owned, but used on a short-term basis. For example, this could be a one-off ride with Lyft to get you to a job interview, a short stay at an Airbnb for a break with friends or a skill that's needed at that specific time, such as someone on 99 Designs creating a logo for your start-up business.

For the sharing economy to work, the interaction is often facilitated via technology, through a platform operator. For example, Uber is a platform operator: it connects buyers and sellers who need rides or food delivery. Uber charges buyers and sellers a platform fee in return for helping manage the processes for both parties. Many social media platforms are platform operators, such as Meta, which connects buyers and sellers at a local level with Facebook Marketplace.

8.2.1 SOCIETAL SUSTAINABILITY

The sharing economy is considered more sustainable and is the opposite of needing to own or consume goods which can occur with **overconsumption** (see ethical insights). It offers advantages such as **societal sustainability** (see Key Term) as goods are used and reused, so there is less environmental impact and this maximises the use of resources (Rojanakit et al., 2022).

ETHICAL INSIGHTS   Overconsumption

Owning the latest fashionable clothing is creating a sustainable nightmare. While many people are concerned about the planet and saving resources, there is a disconnect between the waste and energy reduction involved in clothing production. Clothing could last for years, but as Ting & Stagner (2021: 856) found, 'the life cycle of clothing has been constantly shortening; we are using and disposing of clothing faster and faster'.

There are bigger issues as over-consumption is a worldwide issue and our obsession for the latest fashion is damaging the planet for several reasons (Garcia-Ortega et al., 2023; Ting & Stagner, 2021):

- Clothing production often involves the use of polluting chemicals
- Clothing production generates more greenhouses gases than flying
- The clothing is so cheap that the factories may be making very little profit, so working conditions may be poor
- When donated to charities, most of the clothing is not good enough to sell, so it is destroyed
- Unsold goods are burned or added to landfill
- Returned or second-hand goods are sent to other countries and, as they may not be suitable or good enough to wear, they are added to landfill

To counter overconsumption, some companies are offering repair or refurbishment services. H&M is attempting to encourage customers to 'repair & remake' by providing instructions on how to 'cut jeans into shorts' or 'sew a button' (H&M, 2023). These initiatives only work if on a large scale, and these same companies' websites tag the latest fashion with 'new arrival', encouraging purchase of new goods.

Businesses such as Rent The Runway claim to support the planet by encouraging people to rent clothing instead of buying. Yet these firms often stock designer clothing so the rental costs are high. Plus the ongoing dry-cleaning processes also increase greenhouse gases.

There is a growing argument in favour of 'sufficient' consumption, where clothes are more durable and last longer, but in 2 years' time the trendy jacket you bought today may look very outdated. Some tech giants managed to avoid fashion statements by wearing the same clothing all the time (Bill Gates, Steve Jobs), but we don't know how many pairs of jeans, black polo neck tops or t-shirts they owned!

- What are your thoughts on overconsumption? Will clothing rental ever replace the need to buy?
- Is 'repair & remake' a genuine attempt to reduce consumption? How can this be encouraged?
- In a 24/7 Instagram world, how do we move towards 'sufficient' consumption and be seen wearing the same thing?

However, Rojanakit et al. (2022) identified that the benefits from the sharing economy are more often gained in developed economies (such as the United States and European countries) than in emerging economies (such as India and China in Asia). This was due to different perceptions in socio-cultural, legal, political, technological and economic factors in the different countries. For example, a major socio-cultural factor is trust, which is essential between the 2 parties and so this influences how a shared economy does or doesn't work. Trust can be built with knowledge and understanding and when this is lacking in emerging economies, the shared economy may not achieve the same success as in developed economies. However, elements of the sharing economy exist in less developed countries, such as **Dama** in Mali (see Case Example 8.1).

KEY TERM   SOCIETAL SUSTAINABILITY

Societal sustainability concerns the sustainability and survival 'of our institutions, political systems, and of civil society' (Arogyaswamy, 2020: 829).

DISCOVER MORE ON SOCIETAL SUSTAINABILITY

Read the article by Arogyaswamy (2020) 'Big tech and societal sustainability: An ethical framework', which evaluates the positive and negative outcomes we gain from technology, raising issues to consider as it changes our society.

CASE EXAMPLE 8.1   Dama: The gift economy in Mali

Mali is a landlocked West African country with a population of over 21 million. Primarily based on agriculture, for many years the country has had political and economic challenges, yet they have a cultural practice of gifting which is called Dama.

(Continued)

Dama is part of the sharing economy in Mali which has existed for many years. People provide a gift to others in the community. This can be an item that's no longer needed (such as furniture), a creation (such as a meal) or practical help (such as a bus fare). We consider this to be 'paying it forward' – doing something nice for someone, in the hope we might get something back later – but Dama is sharing with no expectation of a reward. Dama functions throughout a community and individuals pass on a gift when they can. So the consumer (recipient) might give a gift to another at a later time. In this example there is no technology, but an exchange of gratitude between the provider and the consumer. The processes are straightforward, such as hearing about a neighbour who needs help and providing the help.

The concept of Dama nurtures links between people and supports the local community. It celebrates the gift of giving. In a country with a challenging economy, little is wasted, so this is not about recycling, it is more about being part of a community.

Considering the gifting concept in a digital context, a similar example is the Freecycle Network. While this was started in the USA in 2003, its website notes that it 'covers 32 countries including Australia, New Zealand, Canada, the United States, and all European Union countries'. Like the notion of Dama, it is based around a local area and so Freecycle has '5,000+ groups with 7 million members across the globe'.

Freecycle's mission is 'to build a worldwide sharing movement that reduces waste, saves precious resources & eases the burden on our landfills while enabling our members to benefit from the strength of a larger community'. The executive director of the Freecycle Network claims, 'it is more than just a place to just go get free stuff for nothing. It is a place to give what you have and don't need, or receive what you need and don't have – a free cycle of giving which keeps good stuff out of landfills'.

Both Dama and Freecycle are community-focused, and operate on the principle of social good, yet Dama is about participating in the community and helping a person in need, whereas Freecycle is about reducing waste.

Case questions

- There are differences between the Dama concept and Freecycle – why is this?
- Have you participated in the gift economy and in what way? What recommendations would you give to someone who has not yet participated in the gift economy?
- Does technology help or hinder the gift economy?

8.3 VALUE CO-CREATION AND CO-DESTRUCTION

8.3.1 VALUE CO-CREATION

Another aspect of the sharing economy is value co-creation which was proposed by Vargo & Lusch (2004) at a time when marketing focused more on goods than services. This was based on the concept of **service dominant logic** (see Discover More). The idea was that customers were involved with the co-creation of the service. This is true in traditional businesses – you are advising your hairdresser or barber of your preferences when getting a haircut. But it is also applicable to digital business. For example, when ordering a pizza via an app, you select the size, the crust, the toppings – each order is unique as you create your perfect supper. Other examples of co-creation include customers receiving goods, filming the unboxing and sharing online with reviews – creating promotional videos for companies.

Value co-creation has been significantly researched in tourism. For example, co-creation in tourism includes holidaymakers recording and sharing their promotional videos of every step of their holiday, from boarding the plane and arriving at the hotel, to exploring many destinations. These holidaymakers are creating content and promoting destinations to wider audiences – sharing the benefits (or disappointment) of different locations, acting as mini tour guides, free of charge. The word guide is important here as Google recognises 'local guides' in its reviews. Consumers have become guides for other consumers.

DISCOVER MORE ON SERVICE DOMINANT LOGIC

The original article by Vargo & Lusch (2004), 'Evolving to a new dominant logic for marketing', published in the *Journal of Marketing*, explains the background to co-creation, where logic suggests that customers do not buy goods but offerings. The authors provided an update in 2017, 'Service-dominant logic 2025', published in the *International Journal of Research in Marketing*, where they reviewed the theory and considered the different aspects of marketing.

8.3.2 CO-DESTRUCTION

However, the sharing material might not always be positive! Value co-creation can take a different turn as business can be disrupted by co-destruction. Co-destruction occurs when customers share their displeasure with other customers or the organisation. Originally defined by Plé & Cáceres (2010: 431), co-destruction is 'an interactional process between service systems that results in a decline in at least one of the systems' well-being (which, given the nature of a service system, can be individual or organizational).'

While most services aim to co-create value, not destroy it, sometimes accidents happen and things go wrong (Plé & Cáceres, 2010). For example, this can take place when customers have been involved, as co-creators, but lack the capability or capacity to provide what is needed, leading to disappointment for all. For example, if you book a train to travel across Italy or France, you might not realise that there are different types of trains, with different tickets and very different prices. If you take the wrong train, you might blame the ticket company, because you were not aware of the differences – you lacked the capacity to make the decision with advice. This leads to many arguments for co-creation or co-design, especially in getting stakeholders involved, in the process. But there can be disadvantages such as the extra time needed to involve and organise the different groups. In some cases, to ensure that many diverse groups are represented, this can result in **tokenism** (see Key Term) where organisations wish to *appear* inclusive, rather than actually *being* inclusive which can 'result in interpersonal conflicts' (Kirk et al., 2021: 143). This can also backfire and lead to further co-destruction.

> **KEY TERM** TOKENISM
>
> According to the *Merriam-Webster Dictionary*, tokenism is 'the policy or practice of making only a symbolic effort (as to desegregate)'. Sometimes co-creation policies attempt to engage different members of the community, without fully engaging with that community, and this is where tokenism takes place.

Plé and Cáceres (2010: 433) suggest that another issue is 'the misuse of resources that can occur in the context of the role conflict felt by front-line service employees who have competing expectations from their employers and their customers'. That sounds complicated, but it is about juggling priorities. For example, if employees are allocated 5 minutes to find a customer's records via telephone and the customer keeps chatting, the customers are technically misusing the employees' time, even though they may be unaware of the policy. This means that part of the process has failed and there is a 'decrease in well-being', which is 'the result of a difference between the firm's value propositions and customer's perceived value during service process' (Hsu et al., 2021: 3). This can happen in different ways; for example:

- Poor interaction – slow responses to queries
- Negative service encounters – unwanted responses
- Due to the lack of collaboration between those involved – lack of clear information
- Unexpected situation – the goods or services are not as expected or as described

According to Ogunbodede et al. (2022), there are 2 dimensions to both co-creation and co-destruction. Co-creation involves participation and citizenship. Participation may involve trying to find information and then sharing this, for example in technology user groups (e.g. Apple, Samsung) where users share solutions to problems. It also involves supporting organisations (advocacy) and a desire to help others.

On the other hand, co-destruction is a form of non-cooperation or defiance and can involve acting irresponsibly. Defiance in co-destruction is where consumers purposefully do not follow the guidelines or fail to give the required information. For example, booking a delivery but not mentioning it is for an office on the 10th floor and the lift is not working is irresponsible. Consumers may also be rude to employees and not act in a responsible way, blaming the company for the situation, when they may be at fault.

Widely sharing negative information about the firm can be an act of subversion. This can damage the company and there is little action they can take. For example, an unhappy customer in Australia may leave negative feedback online and the organisation cannot delete the comments simply because they don't like them, as removal of negative reviews can be interpreted as misleading or deceptive conduct as outlined by the Australian Competition & Consumer Commission (2023). Table 8.2 notes the 2 dimensions for co-creation and co-destruction, as well as examples of consumer behaviour.

Table 8.2 Co-creation and co-destruction dimensions

Co-creation		Co-destruction	
Participation	Information seeking	**Defiance**	Ignoring information
	Information sharing		Withholding information
	Personal interaction		Impersonal interaction
			Irresponsible behaviour
	Responsible behaviour		
Citizenship	Feedback	**Subversion**	Negative feedback
	Advocacy		Opposition
	Helping		Neglecting Intolerance
	Tolerance		

Source: Ogunbodede et al. (2022: 1281)

Smartphone Sixty Seconds® – Search for negative reviews

Using your mobile phones:

- Search for reviews for a company or brand of your choice.
- What reviews did you find? Were these located on the brand website, or on third-party sites (e.g. TripAdvisor®, Yelp)?
- Look at the negative reviews – what do think about the content? Is it simply negative feedback or is it irresponsible behaviour? Did the brand or company respond?
- Share findings with classmates.

The legislation that exists in Australia is also present across the European Union to ensure that merchants do not simply delete negative reviews. However, a series of negative reviews for organisations can lead to co-destruction, which can result in companies losing listings in marketplaces such as Amazon, JD.com and Taobao. Because removing products from sale or delisting a company in the marketplace represents a major challenge, some organisations may engage in deceptive behaviour, such as **brushing** (see Chapter 3) to counter this.

Activity 8.2 Evaluate value co-creation and co-destruction

Value co-creation can help organisations, but sometimes consumers might get the facts wrong. In groups evaluate value co-creation. Consider a sports brand (e.g. sportswear or a sports club) that has successfully worked with consumers to co-create their brand. Reflect and explore why it was a success. Also assess other examples where this has not worked well.

Discuss why these situations occur and prepare recommendations for a sports brand to better manage co-creation.

8.4 THE CIRCULAR ECONOMY AND CIRCULAR DISRUPTION

8.4.1 THE CIRCULAR ECONOMY

Another concept that leads to digital disruption is the circular economy. This is defined as 'a model of production and consumption, which involves sharing, leasing, reusing, repairing, refurbishing and recycling existing materials and products as long as possible. In this way, the life cycle of products is extended' (European Parliament, 2023: 1). The aim is to reduce waste and when a product reaches the end of its life, such as a car, it is broken into pieces which can be recycled or better still, reused. Figure 8.1 shows the circular economy system at a top level where the energy and emissions involved in the production process are also considered.

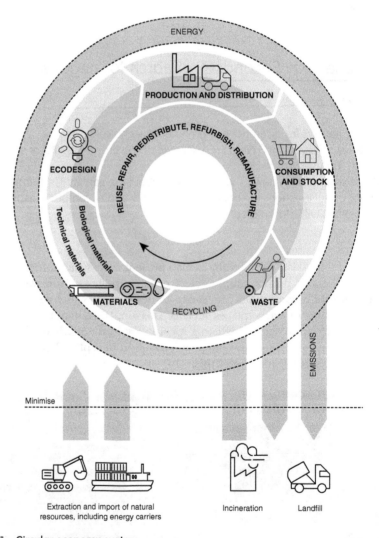

Figure 8.1   Circular economy system

Source: European Environment Agency (2020)

www.eea.europa.eu/soer/2020/soer-2020-visuals/circular-economy-system-diagram/view

The circular economy is largely credited to Ellen MacArthur, who was the fastest person to sail around the world solo. When at sea Ellen considered the vastness of the oceans and how precious the resources were. On returning home, Ellen established a foundation to encourage others to save resources. The website explains the difference between what we do (a linear economy) and what we should do (the circular economy):

> In our current economy, we take materials from the Earth, make products from them, and eventually throw them away as waste – the process is linear. In a circular economy, by contrast, we stop waste being produced in the first place. (Ellen MacArthur Foundation, 2023: 1)

This is disruptive as instead of companies making more items and selling them, they need to consider how they can be reused or recycled. Technology creates challenges for the circular economy as it generates more waste than many other items. Mobile phones use rare earth minerals such as lanthanum for colours on screen, plus neodymium and dysprosium for haptic vibrations (Dayaram, 2023), which need to be extracted from specific locations and processed for use. For example, in their latest report, The Global E-waste Monitor notes that 'in 2019, the world generated 53.6 million metric tons (Mt), and only 17.4% of this was officially documented as properly collected and recycled' (Forti et al., 2020: 9). To put this into context, the average adult elephant weights about 1 metric ton, so the non-recycled e-waste is about 44 million elephants! This is why the circular economy is being considered as circular disruption.

Activity 8.3   Analyse e-waste

Think about your old laptops, computers or other devices. When you no longer need or use them, they can become 'e-waste'. Sadly in many cases, they are disposed, without being recycled, repaired, refurbished or reused.

In groups, discuss when you last upgraded to a new device. What happened to the older model? Did you manage to sell or trade it (reused)? Or could it be repaired or refurbished? Would you consider buying repaired or refurbished goods? In your groups consider the amount of waste created and how this could be avoided in the future.

DIGITAL TOOL   Global E-waste Monitor

According to their website, the 'Global E-waste Monitor 2020 (www.globalewaste.org) is a collaborative product of the Global E-waste Statistics Partnership (GESP), formed by UN University (UNU), the International Telecommunication Union (ITU), and the International Solid Waste Association (ISWA), in close collaboration with the UN Environment Programme (UNEP). The World Health Organization (WHO) and the German Ministry of Economic Cooperation and Development (BMZ) also substantially contributed to this year's Global E-waste Monitor 2020'. (Unitar – United Nations Institute for Training and Research, 2023: 1)

Explore their latest datasheets for different parts of the world.

- You can explore it here: ewastemonitor.info

8.4.2 CIRCULAR DISRUPTION

The circular economy is naturally disruptive as it seeks ways to move from a throwaway economy towards sustainable production, where goods can be reduced, reused and recycled, with waste management built in from the start. However, **circular disruption** (see Key Term) has greater urgency attached and Blomsma et al. (2023) suggest there are 3 phases, as shown in Table 8.3, with examples from the automotive sector.

Table 8.3   Phases of disruption

Disruption phase	What this means	Example
Pre-disruption	Where 'doing more of the same' no longer works	Diesel cars are being phased out as they are considered to be harmful to the planet and are more expensive to maintain
Disruption	When there is a crisis or a need to change	Climate change has highlighted the need to review modes of transport and move away from fossil fuels
Post-disruption	There is an uptake of new innovations and policies	Electric cars are slowly becoming more affordable

> **KEY TERM**   CIRCULAR DISRUPTION
>
> According to Blomsma et al. (2023: 1011) circular disruption is, 'A transformation in a socio-technical system which causes the systemic, widespread, and fast change from the harmful "take-make-use-dispose" model to a socially and environmentally desirable and sustainable model that reduces resource consumption and addresses structural waste through the deployment of circular strategies'.

In a digital setting, we have seen better recycling of older technology, due to European legislation such as the Waste Electrical and Electronic Equipment (WEEE) recycling. But old technology is not just about computers and can include microwaves, washing machines, televisions and money dispensers!

Smartphone Sixty Seconds® – Explore International E-Waste Day

Using your mobile phones:

- Search for 'International E-Waste Day'.
- When and where does it take place?
- What activities are taking place near you and were you aware of these?
- Share findings with classmates.

> ## DISCOVER MORE ON CIRCULAR DISRUPTION
>
> The article by Blomsma et al. (2023), 'The 'need for speed': Towards circular disruption—What it is, how to make it happen and how to know it's happening', published in *Business Strategy and the Environment*, explains the background to co-creation, where logic suggests that customers do not buy goods but offerings.

8.4.3 ANTI-CONSUMPTION

While circular disruption seeks to move faster to reduce waste, a form of consumer disruptive behaviour is anti-consumption. This can be a refusal to buy specific goods or aiming to repair and reuse (Armstrong Soule & Sekhon, 2022). This is an intentional behaviour and considered as subversive co-destruction. At a low level this may be avoiding website tracking and using incognito browsing, to a high level where consumers organise high-profile campaigns to boycott companies. In some cases consumers are proactive and intentionally seek co-destruction, but sometimes it may be reactive, when something goes wrong. The role of the firm also varies from being the main focus of attention or simply an incidental element. For example, sharing passwords to save subscription fees can be incidental, unless the focus is on a specific firm. Wilson et al. (2022) created a typology of these different subversive behaviours which is shown in Figure 8.2. These all contribute to co-destruction and may seem negative, although the *activists* are often seeking circular disruption and ensuring businesses change unacceptable behaviours.

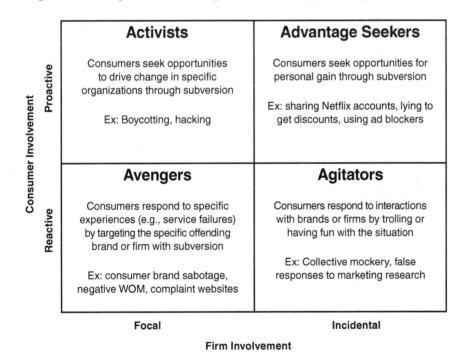

Figure 8.2 Typology of consumer subversion

Source: Wilson et al. (2022: 605). Printed with permission of John Wiley

8.5 THE FUTURE OF DISRUPTION, INDUSTRY 4.0 TO INDUSTRY 5.0

Looking at disruption across a country, **Industry 4.0** or Industrie 4.0 (see Key Term) was proposed by the German government as the fourth industrial revolution. To put this into context, Figure 8.3 shows the various stages of the industrial revolution and while the 4th industrial revolution is in place now, the 5th is imminent.

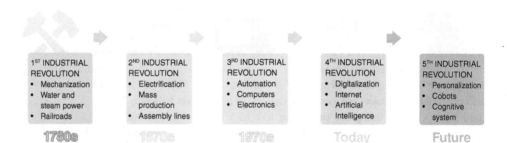

Figure 8.3 The various stages of the industrial revolution

Source: Raja Santhi & Muthuswamy (2023: 948). Printed with permission of Springer Nature

Industry 4.0 has such importance that it is a central part of the Federal Government's Digital Agenda. It involves making factories smarter, with greater automation, bringing more efficiency and improving processes.

KEY TERM INDUSTRY 4.0

According to the Federal Ministry for Economic Affairs and Climate Action in Germany (2023: 1), Industrie 4.0 means that 'factories' smart machines control production processes by themselves. Service robots help people do physically demanding work in the assembly shop. Driverless transport vehicles manage the logistics processes and the flow of materials without any human intervention. But it is not only "smart factories" that are becoming increasingly connected. Across company and industry borders, a wide range of economic stakeholders are also becoming part of this trend: from medium-sized logistics companies to specialised technical service providers and creative start-ups'.

DISCOVER MORE ON INDUSTRY 4.0 AND INDUSTRY 5.0

Read 'Industry 4.0 and Industry 5.0—Inception, conception and perception' by Xu et al. (2021), published in the *Journal of Manufacturing Systems*. This article explains the concepts and provides the background to Industry 4.0 and 5.0.

However, like the example of anti-consumerism where individuals believe that companies are failing to take action regarding climate change, there is concern that digital disruption through technologies such as artificial intelligence (see Chapter 5) may take away work and create unemployment. This may occur in routine-based, repetitive tasks, but non-routine work requiring specialist skills needs human intervention or guidance. Industry 5.0 is an extension of Industry 4.0, but instead of focusing on the factory, Industry 5.0 takes a humanitarian view with a human-centred approach, moving away from just economic and technological factors. Industry 5.0 considers the workers and their well-being within the workplace (Xu et al., 2021).

Xu et al. (2021) suggest that Industry 5.0 comprises 3 connected core values: human-centricity, sustainability and resilience. Perhaps we need Disruptive Consumerism 5.0 which fosters change to balance the needs of consumers with the resources available?

Disruption in the competitive landscape will continue. Högberg & Willermark (2022: 1) refer to this as 'disruptive digital innovations (DDI)' which impact on the business and how we do business. For example, in the hospitality sector, there have been a series of DDIs:

- Digital disruption of guest behaviour – when booking a hotel, guests have become travel agents, checking online reviews, looking at photos of the hotel location and assessing whether or not to book
- Digital disruption of the relationship between hotels and guests – as many use 'online travel agents' such as Trivago or Booking.com, so the hotel does not capture the guest data – who they are, where they are travelling from, how many trips this year – as the data stays with the online travel agents
- Digital disruption of competition – as guests have become hosts and can rent out their homes through platforms such as Airbnb

As a result, the entire hospitality industry is experiencing disruptive digital innovations and seeking other ways to create value for guests. Hospitality is a visible industry, but many more sectors are experiencing disruptive digital innovations, for example:

- Advertising placements – these are mainly programmatic, the guidelines are set and the process is automated
- Financial services – neobanks are taking market share from banks that have been established for hundreds of years
- Manufacturing – the use of robots on the factory floor is commonplace

Recognising that digital disruption will accelerate, the concept of Industry 5.0 will become more important, ensuring we consider the workforce, adopt flexible approaches and address sustainability.

CASE EXAMPLE 8.2   The Digital Stage: DigitalScenen

During the COVID-19 pandemic, many organisations had to adapt to being closed and looking for ways to communicate with their audiences, using technology. In many countries,

(Continued)

the culture and arts sector had challenges with many actors, performers, musicians and others finding themselves out of work. At the same time, many consumers were looking for activities to cope with being at home all day. In Norway a response to this was the Digital Stage, known as DigitalScenen. It enabled productions to be made and to be viewed in consumers' homes. As a radical change introduced by the application of technology, this was a form of digital disruption. Although this digital disruption took place in many countries, Norway is considered to be one of the world's most digitally advanced countries (European Commission, 2022b) and they took a humanistic viewpoint, looking at how the performers could be supported and the adaptations that were needed.

The discussion on the potentially dire consequences for the cultural sector started immediately. One of the first suggestions on how to do something about the situation came through a campaign on social media, called #ingenrefusjon ('no refunds'). The idea was that no organiser of performances should demand a refund from the artists who had to cancel their shows because of the lockdown. So, technology was applied very quickly – within w48 hours in Norway. According to Hylland (2022: 4), the first step was to adopt Facebook (now Meta) with its live-streaming potential and 'after two days, DigitalScenen had 50,000 members/subscribers, with this number later increasing to over 150,000 members'. This may not seem such a large number, but with a total of 5.4 million people living in Norway in 2022, this represents 3% of the population. If you compared this to India, the equivalent number would be over 42 million people. Within a few weeks, there were 400 digital concerts per month.

The technology had been available for years, but was not used as people enjoy attending performances and being present with others. The pandemic changed this and suddenly introduced audiences to performers' homes, who gained close-up views of their favourite artistes' living rooms! There were challenges, as attending events involves participation and publicly expressing emotions – clapping, cheering and feeding back to the performers. Yet with audiences sitting in their own homes, this aspect was missing, making it difficult for performers to gauge audience reactions.

Post-pandemic, some aspects of The Digital Stage – DigitalScenen still exist but at a reduced scale. The question is whether The Digital Stage will continue at a much smaller scale for specialised events and specific audiences.

Case questions

- How do you feel about participating in digital festivals? What are the benefits of attending digital events?
- Which audiences gain most from the digital stage? Why is this?
- What types of online events do you believe would be useful or entertaining?

JOURNAL OF NOTE

Organization Studies is published in collaboration with the European Group for Organization Studies (EGOS). It 'promotes the understanding of organizations, organizing and the organized, and the societal relevance of that understanding. OS prompts engagement with organizations and organizing as psychological, social, economic, cultural, political, historical and philosophical phenomena', which includes digital disruption.

CASE STUDY

PAYPAL DIGITAL DISRUPTERS THREATEN THE COMPETITIVE POSITION

The financial technology or fintech sector has seen significant digital disruption. Fintech is described as 'financial service delivery by leveraging technology to execute many traditional banking functions in a superior manner' (Almansour, 2023: 1) and adopted Industry 4.0 to make financial transactions smarter, with greater automation, bringing more efficiency and improving processes. One area of growth in fintech has been the emergence of neobanks, disrupting the traditional banking system. Neobanks are different from traditional banks because they:

Don't have branches, as they operate online or via apps

Are open to wider groups of people, as the restrictions for opening an account are better assessed by AI

Don't have complex legacy software systems, so they can start from the perspective of the customer, not the processes, using design thinking (see Chapter 7)

This has resulted in neobanks appearing in many countries, such as Revolut, Bunq, Lunar and Wise.

These digital disrupters have eroded PayPal's initially strong competitive position. Plus new fintech services are built around an app, enabling consumers to directly interact with helpdesks (or well-trained bots) and simplify transactions. These characteristics represent the key aspects of digital disruption, as once change is introduced in the fintech sector others jump in with further innovations. There are different approaches to addressing disrupters and in East Africa M-PESA held a dominant position in mobile banking, but instead of reacting against neobanks, it is supporting them; for example, Fingo, promoted as 'Youth Focused Banking', with its infrastructure. PayPal has responded to these disruptions by creating a mega-app which functions like a credit card and much more. For example, PayPal has joined the sharing economy as consumers can send and lend money to each other, request money and split bills using the app.

PayPal is also investing in disruptive fintech. For example, the digital wallet and identity service Magic (see magic.link) has gained significant funding from PayPal. So has the German fintech Finanzguru, an app that offers money management and advice. By investing in these other companies, PayPal continues to learn how consumers are using different apps, as well as what works well.

When PayPal was launched in 1998 it demonstrated digital disruption, changing the traditional banking sector. One of the key questions about new banking systems is whether they are safe. PayPal promoted an extra layer of trust, which still exists today: 'We differentiate ourselves to consumers through the ability to use our products and services across multiple commerce channels, including e-commerce, mobile, and payments at the point of sale, and without sharing their financial information with the merchant or any other party they are paying' (PayPal, 2023a: 7).

Thinking about disruptions connected to the circular economy, it may seem that PayPal does not need to address these issues as it is not manufacturing goods and

(Continued)

so recycling may seem less obvious. After all, it is providing financial services. However, its Financial Stability Board has established the Task Force on Climate-related Financial Disclosures (TCFD) to develop recommendations for more effective climate-related disclosures. As a digital payments company, PayPal's greenhouse gas (GHG) emissions footprint is relatively small (PayPal, 2023b: 3). Yet it recognises that it has 'a public goal to achieve 100% renewable energy for our data centers by 2023 and our long term goal to reach net-zero emissions across our value chain by 2040' (PayPal, 2023b: 3).

Payment processing involves significant energy consumption. And PayPal is currently disrupting one of its core business processes, data centres. These are used to store customer data and require energy for processing as well as teams to manage the systems. The company has a 'mission to move to zero data center ownership' (Google, 2023: 1). This means that instead of buying more computers to store data and manage payments at certain times of the year only, the company works with Google's Cloud space which can be increased and reduced when needed. For example, peak processing times include holidays, as well as Black Friday and Cyber Monday where 'PayPal processed 1,000 payments per second' (Google, 2023: 1).

PayPal started as a digital disrupter and continues to radically change its processes and business strategies, to stay ahead.

CASE QUESTIONS

PayPal started as a digital disrupter and continues to bring digital disruption into the financial sector.

- What would be PayPal's next big disruption and why?
- How can PayPal adopt Industry 5.0? What actions would be needed and how can these actions be managed?
- How else can PayPal address the circular economy and reduce, reuse or recycle?

FURTHER EXERCISES

1. Analyse how an organisation of your choice addresses the circular economy.

2. Using Table 8.1 evaluate the key aspects of digital disruption in the entertainment or restaurant sectors.

3. For an organisation of your choice, create a plan to respond to digital disruption.

4. Businesses need to disrupt or they will disappear. Discuss.

SUMMARY

This chapter has explored:

- How consumers have become sellers and are disrupting industries
- Value co-creation and value co-destruction
- Circular economy and circular disruption
- Industry 4.0 and Industry 5.0

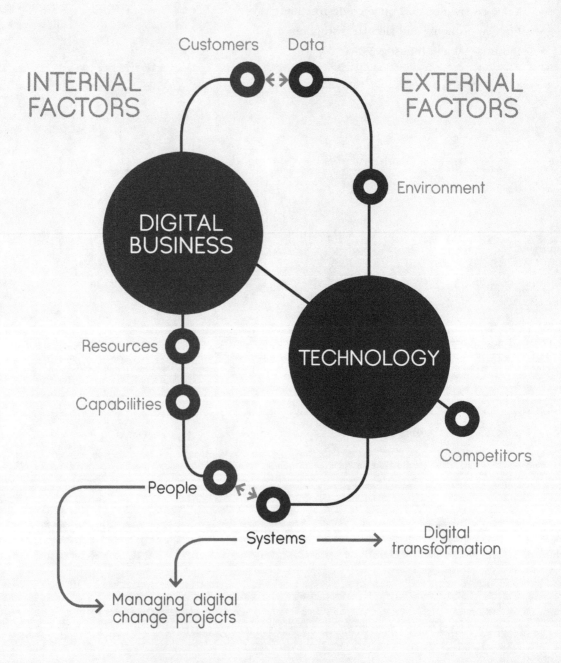

Customers   Data

INTERNAL
FACTORS

EXTERNAL
FACTORS

Environment

DIGITAL
BUSINESS

TECHNOLOGY

Resources

Capabilities

Competitors

People

Systems

Digital
transformation

Managing digital
change projects

9

DIGITAL TRANSFORMATION

LEARNING OUTCOMES

When you have read this chapter, you will be able to:

Understand digital transformation

Apply advantages of introducing technology

Analyse opportunities for a digital super-wallet

Evaluate the main issues in addressing digital transformation

Create an enterprise architecture plan

PROFESSIONAL SKILLS

When you have worked through this chapter, you should be able to:

- Identify opportunities for digital transformation
- Apply the principles of business transformation in the context of technological change

9.1 BACKGROUND TO DIGITAL TRANSFORMATION

Digital transformation has been described as 'a process that aims to improve an entity by triggering significant changes to its properties through combinations of information, computing, communication, and connectivity technologies' (Vial, 2019: 188). The essential factors are change and technology, across an entire organisation. It is often an iterative process, taking place step by step, over some time.

It's important to note that digital transformation is connected to digital innovation and digital disruption. Sometimes a digital disruption occurs which causes businesses to transform their processes. Or an innovation can be developed which transforms a business. The connections between digital transformation, digital innovation and digital disruption are shown in Table 9.1. The primary connection is technology, but the difference with digital transformation is that it is not a single activity that transforms the business, it is a series of activities over a longer period of time.

Table 9.1 The connections between digital transformation, digital innovation and digital disruption

Digital element	Overview	Timescale	Example
Digital innovation	Using technology to deliver new ideas or processes	Varies, once available different businesses take different amounts of time to adopt the innovation	Cloud computing – storing data online rather than on individual computers – was available for decades, yet it became widely adopted during the pandemic as organisations realised that they needed to access their files from any location at any time
Digital disruption	A radical change introduced by the application of technology	Can appear sudden, but may have been building over time	For example, generative AI has the potential to disrupt many businesses, such as the automation of routine processes: creating agendas for meetings, building a slide deck and gathering background information
Digital transformation	Applying technological change across an organisation	Longer period of time	Using additive manufacturing (3D printing) to manufacture prosthetics instead of traditional manufacturing processes which are slower and more expensive

In this chapter we will explore the digital transformation process that's involved in the preparation and planning. We will then explore the key issues in managing digital transformation projects and the challenges that can occur.

9.2 THE DIGITAL TRANSFORMATION PROCESS

Digital transformation is a process and rarely takes place overnight! It starts with changing traditional analogue processes to digital systems (digitisation). From here technology is introduced into specific parts of an organisation (digitalisation), until technology is applied across the organisation (digital transformation) as outlined in Figure 9.1.

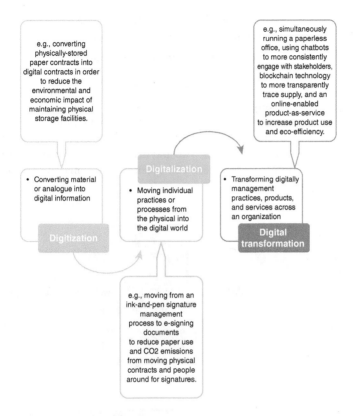

Figure 9.1 The process of digital transformation

Source: Hanlon & Laasch (2024)

9.2.1 DIGITISATION

Digitisation involves converting analogue processes to digital systems. For example:

- A paper form becomes an electronic form
- A physical loyalty card becomes an e-card that can be added to your digital wallet
- An emailed survey to complete in a document becomes a Google form where the data is analysed automatically
- A catalogue becomes an app
- Cash becomes digital payments

Although these digitising examples seem simple, there are processes in the background which need to be resolved. For example, if you think of a market trader selling vegetables, typically they take cash as payment. To move from cash to digital payments, they need to:

- Set up a merchant account, the contract between the acquiring merchant (e.g. VISA, Mastercard) and the business bank
- Confirm finance approval limits (e.g. maximum €100, £100, $100 per transaction)

- Select and pay for payment hardware – a register, terminal or card reader
- Connect to the payment hardware to the business bank account
- Connect the merchant account to the accounting system

In the medium term there are more benefits to taking payments digitally; for example, taking payments at any time, sending digital receipts, building customer profiles, enabling customers to pre-order at busy times and perhaps increasing the amount spent. In the short term there is a learning curve in understanding how the systems work. There are also increased costs with paying for the payment hardware rental and paying a transaction fee – for every €25 spent, the fees may be €0.25. Plus some customers might prefer using cash.

DIGITAL TOOL   How much to make an app?

Apps can seem to be a good solution, but they require investment. The online calculator 'How much to make an app' provides an indication of the budget involved.

- You can explore it here: howmuchtomakeanapp.com

Activity 9.1   Evaluate digitisation challenges

Imagine you have a stand at a farmer's market, selling fruit and vegetables. Your regular customers always pay with cash. You have had a few requests to take card payment and have been thinking about this.

In groups, discuss how you will communicate this to your regular customers. What objections might they have? Will particular groups be affected in any way? How will you address these issues?

It's not only businesses that are digitising. Chemify, a project started at Glasgow University, has gained significant funding from external investors to digitise chemistry (Cookson, 2023). They have added technology to chemical design which allows the team to design and discover new molecules. This means they can help speed up the process of developing new pharmaceuticals for illnesses and diseases.

9.2.2 DIGITALISATION

Once a business has started the process of digitising, it may move to digitalising and making greater changes with technology. Table 9.2 shows the digitalisation opportunities for different types of businesses.

Table 9.2 Digitalisation opportunities

Type of business	Types of customers	Examples of digitalisation opportunities
Small retailer	Local customers	As well as taking card payments, retailers can communicate with customers about new products through e-newsletters and social media
Regional healthcare provider	Regional patients	As well as storing patient data online, establishing an automated appointment reminder system will save time and reduce no-shows
Restaurant chain	Customers across a region	As well as accepting online bookings, customers are sent booking reminders which saves time and reduces no-shows
Medium-sized IT company	Customers across a region	As well as recording clients' details, all support requests from specific individuals are stored on a central system which can assess who makes the most calls and see if more support is needed

Digitisation seems to be the solution for all businesses, but it is not without risk and may not be accessible to all. Some businesses may not have the finances, internal capability or capacity to introduce and manage new systems. Some customers may be excluded as a result of digitisation.

ETHICAL INSIGHTS   Digital exclusion

We often take access to digital devices and connectivity for granted. We nearly consider this as a human right. Yet as we move towards digital transformation in many sectors, not everyone can be included. According to the United Nations (2020a: 1): 'Half of the world's population currently does not have access to the Internet. By 2030, every person should have safe and affordable access to the Internet, including meaningful use of digitally enabled services in line with the Sustainable Development Goals.'

The United Nations has outlined different factors that create the digital divide which centres around governments and citizens:

- Government: access to finance is less available to install broadband in countries where there are other priorities
- Government: High charges from telecoms companies providing access to broadband connectivity in smaller countries with less purchasing power
- Government: Lack of incentive to use Wi-Fi as an alternative due to the costs of establishing the network
- Citizens: Lack of finance to acquire digital devices
- Citizens: Lack of finance to pay for software
- Citizens: Lack of skills to use digital devices

(Continued)

Yet there are other issues as the United Nations has stated that 'Digital technology does not exist in a vacuum – it has enormous potential for positive change, but can also reinforce and magnify existing fault lines and worsen economic and other inequalities' (2020a: 3).

- Can you imagine a region where there is little – or no – Wi-Fi? What changes would you need to make to adapt to living without Wi-Fi?
- What actions can wealthier countries take to support those without access to connectivity?
- What are the downsides of being digitally included with 24/7 access to devices and software?

Smartphone Sixty Seconds® – Identify digital exclusion

Using your mobile phones:

- Search for 'digital exclusion'.
- What types of documents did you find?
- Were any from official sources (government bodies, international organisations) and were you aware of these?
- Share findings with classmates.

DISCOVER MORE ON DIGITISATION RISKS

Read 'A general framework of digitization risks in international business' by Luo (2022) published in the *Journal of International Business Studies*. This article examines the types of risks associated with digitisation and how these may be managed in an international setting.

9.2.3 DIGITAL TRANSFORMATION

Taking the digitalisation process further towards digital transformation takes longer. Some transformation projects take place in 24 months – but this is unusual. It can take many years to fully implement all the different elements, as well as the staff training and recruitment which may be needed. Table 9.3 shows examples of the key changes and opportunities with digital transformation for the same business types shown in Table 9.2.

Table 9.3 Digital transformation key changes and opportunities

Type of business	Types of customers	Key change towards transformation	Examples of digital transformation opportunities
Small retailer	Local customers	A website with greater functionality becomes the central hub for all transactions	• Changing the website to an online store, to expand the customer base • Providing online gift cards to be spent in store or online • Accepting orders online, via phone or in store • Organising pickup and delivery, which is tracked and communicated to customers • Customer reviews are automated
Regional healthcare provider	Regional patients	A patient management system is established	• Patient history is available across the region, to the healthcare providers and the patient, with a record of any required medication • Patients are sent automated reminders before appointments • Regular check-up appointments are automated and added to the healthcare provider's calendar system
Restaurant chain	Customers across a region	An integrated restaurant management system is established	• Customers' details are captured in the system • Deposit payments are taken for large bookings • Bookings are automated • Booking reminders are automated • Employee management of shifts and staff needed is based on the bookings • Customer feedback is gathered and published • Tips are pooled and shared each month • Newsletters about new menus are automated based on customer preferences • Management reports showing best-selling dishes, locations and average spend per table are created
Medium-sized IT company	Customers across a region	An integrated client service and support management system is established	• Clients' details include the number of pieces of hardware and types of software used • Regular requests for support are analysed to assess if training is needed • Service requests are attached to specific pieces of hardware to diagnose problem machinery early • Sales teams are sent reports of older hardware to organise meetings with clients to discuss upgrading

Digital transformation can be considered as a journey. One of the ways to start the journey is to understand the advantages of technology in the business. This helps to prepare the business case to convince stakeholders such as employees, managers, the directors and investors.

9.3 PREPARING AND PLANNING FOR DIGITAL TRANSFORMATION

9.3.1 THE ADVANTAGES OF TECHNOLOGY IN BUSINESS

In preparing for digital transformation it is essential to understand the benefits of employing technology (Kraus et al., 2021). Kraus et al. (2021) also found that adopting digital technologies provided wider benefits than the technology alone as the process can change existing business models.

If you think about logistics firms, such as DHL, DPD or Fedex, as examples, in the past these businesses communicated to their stakeholders through 'official channels' such as newspapers or TV advertisements, whereas using social media changed the relationship and the interactions between these businesses and their stakeholders. With a TV ad, you can watch it, but it's a monologue, a one-way conversation. An advertisement on YouTube, TikTok or Instagram enables a dialogue and more feedback for the business in real time.

Technology also offers **network effects** (see Chapter 4) and mobile phones are an example of a technology that is widespread. This means that the large numbers of mobile-phone users worldwide make it worthwhile for businesses to create apps, such as Airbnb or Uber, which have benefited from network effects. Logistics firms usage of smartphones has changed their business models. They are used for real-time tracking (of delivery staff and parcel), order management (scanning and consigning parcels), analytics and reporting (showing optimal delivery routes), as well as communication. This encourages businesses to be more agile, being able to respond faster and automatically. Kraus and colleagues also discuss cloud-based computing as a mechanism which adds value to a business by providing 'location-independent

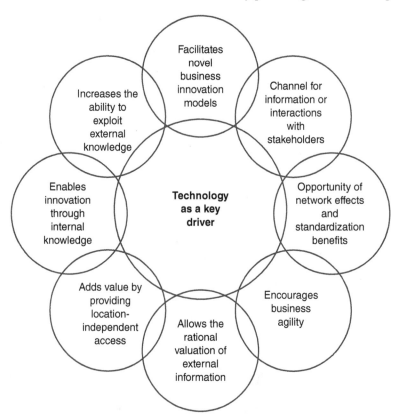

Figure 9.2 Advantages of introducing technology into business

Source: Kraus et al. (2021: 11)

access', so employees no longer need to travel to the office to view or edit key documents; they can do this from wherever they are located. This means that employees in logistics companies can access all the data needed from their smartphones.

Another advantage was innovation through internal knowledge which may include the employees available for work, number of vehicles available and parcels to be delivered. Having this information can lead to innovative solutions, such as grouping consignments or planning staff needs. External knowledge is available through many sources – GPS tracking of drivers' vehicles, real-time traffic data providing more accurate estimates of arrival times. When these different elements are combined, they have the power to transform business. Figure 9.2 shows the advantages of introducing technology into business.

Activity 9.2   Apply advantages of introducing technology

Using Figure 9.2, consider which of these would apply to a food service provider or restaurant near your university.

In groups, discuss the advantages firstly from the point of view of a customer, and secondly from the point of view of the restaurant.

9.3.2 ENTERPRISE ARCHITECTURE

A method of combining these advantages is reviewing the **enterprise architecture** (see Key Term) within a business. This ensures all the key elements are planned out and integrated from the beginning.

> **KEY TERM   ENTERPRISE ARCHITECTURE**
>
> Enterprise architecture uses the concept of architecture – creating plans and blueprints and applying this to an organisation. According to Bokolo Jnr & Petersen (2023), enterprise architecture (EA) is the overview of an organisation's IT systems and business processes and how these are shared by different teams within the organisation.

The Open Group Architecture Forum established the TOGAF® Standard for enterprise architecture which is shown in Figure 9.3. The TOGAF® Standard forces the business to consider what they are trying to achieve (A architect vision) and from here map out the business, information systems and technology plans (B, C, D). The opportunities for the transformation, along with solutions for any issues, need to be identified, as does the move, or migration to the new systems (F). Once this is in place, the implementation starts which should be carefully managed (G). Along the journey changes may occur which should be noted in the architecture change management step (H). The TOGAF® standard should be considered as a toolkit rather than a step-by-step method as this might not occur in a straightforward circular process. However, it is a useful framework for considering enterprise architecture projects.

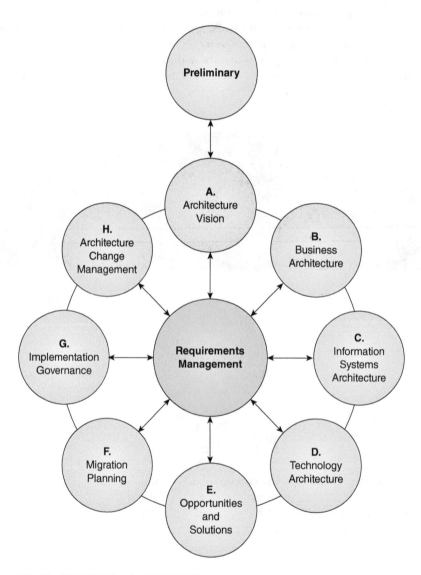

Figure 9.3   The TOGAF® Standard, 10th Edition

Source: The Open Group (2023)

One example of digital transformation, where an organisation worked on its enterprise architecture and adopted an integrated process, is **Entur**, which changed travel planning across Norway (see Case Example 9.1).

DISCOVER MORE ON ENTERPRISE ARCHITECTURE

Enterprise architecture was proposed by Zachman in 1996. Since then there has been further development of the subject. This more recent article 'Exploring the future of enterprise architecture: A Zachman perspective' (Lapalme et al., 2016) includes the original author and explains more about the concept.

CASE EXAMPLE 9.1 Entur

There are many travel planning apps for navigating around cities such as CityMapper, which covers several cities around the world, but has gained mixed reviews due to charging a subscription, and Moovit, which is free but has confusing adverts that look like instruction buttons. Overall, there are fewer apps which cover transport for the whole country, although one example is Incredible India, launched by the Ministry of Tourism, mainly for tourists. Yet in Norway they have launched a national travel planner app, Entur, which connects all Norway's public transport systems. Its website (Entur, 2023b: 1) notes:

> The travel planner suggests itineraries based on all modes of transport in Norway. The service finds the best options for you, based on your criteria.

> Travel by bus, train, ferry, metro, plane, or you can even hop on an e-scooter or city bike. Entur finds journeys across all transport options in all cities. Our goal is to make it easier to choose public transport in all of Norway.

> The Entur website has all the features you need to plan and book travel in Norway. By using our iOS or Android app, you get access to more features, options and tickets.

This is a form of mobility-as-a-service (MaaS) that 'enables citizens to buy public transport as part of a broader bundle of transport options' (Rudmark et al., 2023: 62). The state-sponsored company gathers data from all transport companies and provides travellers with optimal routes. Their goal is 'to make it easier to choose public transport in all of Norway'. The slogan on their website notes: 'En reise, en billet, en app' (one journey, one ticket, one app). The app is free and does not contain adverts. It allows users to indicate their preferred lines (e.g. bus), which types of travel they prefer (e.g. cycles) and to buy tickets for yourself or for others. The app is available in Norwegian languages and English.

The app is very useful for travellers, whether a tourist or local, but the main reason for the app is to support Norway's climate change goals. The website states:

> Entur contributes to achieving important transport policy goals such as simpler everyday travel, increased value, efficient use of new technology, Norway's climate and environmental goals and a zero-vision for those killed and seriously injured in traffic. Entur connects public transport in Norway, and collaborates with the actors in the public transport sector to achieve simple, sustainable travels. (Entur, 2023a: 1)

(Continued)

Norway is recognised worldwide for its efficient public transport network. Public transport saves energy with many people sharing the same transport which is more efficient than private cars, but for the system to work, the processes need to be easy. The Entur app is an example of how governments transform public transport using technology. Entur also notes that the app 'is intended to offer basic public transport services within travel planning and ticketing on competition-neutral terms'.

This lack of competition makes it seamless for the traveller and without the irritating adverts that appear on other apps. Many other locations have multiple apps that often separate the travel based on mode of transport (e.g. several bus apps, multiple train apps, separate apps for specific cities). Entur is transforming country-wide travel planning.

Case questions

- How can governments be encouraged to adopt a single country-wide travel app such as Entur?
- What processes do you think were involved in the creation of an app like Entur? What may be involved in gaining agreement from all train and bus companies in an area?
- Would Entur work in your country? If not, why not and if you are in Norway, what are the downsides of Entur?

9.4 MANAGING DIGITAL CHANGE PROJECTS

According to Nadkarni & Prügl (2021), the 2 recurring themes in the research on digital transformation are technology and actors (people). These researchers explored scientific articles about digital transformation and the main themes identified are shown in Figure 9.4.

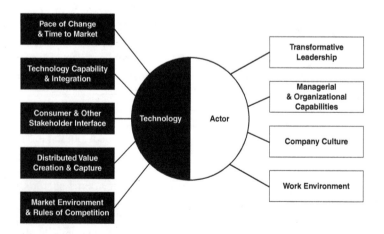

Figure 9.4 Digital transformation high-level thematic map emerging from the analysis of the literature

Source: Nadkarni & Prügl (2021: 240). Printed with permission of Springer Nature

9.4.1 THE ROLE OF TECHNOLOGY IN MANAGING DIGITAL TRANSFORMATION

Technology is less easy to manage and control. External suppliers may provide the systems needed and the pace of change has increased, so in some cases there is little time to respond. New technology is often launched quickly, before being tested. For example, Google's AI GPS tool, Bard, was not ready when it went to launch, but Google recognised the urgency in getting to market as ChatGPT was gaining worldwide headlines, so launched as an 'experimental tool'. Microsoft did the same and launched its GPS product in the same week (Mondal et al., 2023).

Technology capability and integration have moved from joining up internal processes to working on all processes together. We can call this an omni-process approach. For example, **Entur** (see Case Example 9.1) worked with others and made faster progress. Plus, by using Open-Source software, Entur did not need to code from scratch, which enabled the organisation to leverage its digital transformation (Rudmark et al., 2023).

Consumer and other stakeholder interface concerns the changes in consumer behaviour. As Nadkarni & Prügl (2021) found, consumers no longer rely on business websites, they rely on other consumers as guides (see Chapter 8 'Consumers as Sellers'). These guides are co-creating and sharing what are considered to be more authentic stories about organisations.

Value creation and value capture are recurring themes in this textbook as they sit at the core of digital business. Digital transformation must provide some value to justify the investment. Digital transformation may be distributed, providing value for the business, its stakeholders and customers. For example, the Apple app store provides value for Apple, but also for its developers. Customers provide value in sharing feedback via reviews, which in turn improves the apps available. We could call this circular value.

According to Nadkarni & Prügl (2021), the last theme linked to technology is the market environment and rules of competition. They comment that 'digital transformation redefines, blurs and even dissolves existing industry boundaries' (Nadkarni & Prügl, 2021: 250). Thinking about Airbnb, as a disrupter in the hospitality sector, this blurs all boundaries. Hosts can register their room with Airbnb, but hosts can also be guests and small hotels can also list their rooms with the platform. There is no longer a clear separation between who is the host and who is the guest.

9.4.2 THE ROLE OF PEOPLE IN MANAGING DIGITAL TRANSFORMATION

The actors involved in digital transformation include many stakeholders (see Chapters 1 and 2). If they are not involved in the process, they may not adopt or accept the technology (see 'technology acceptance model' in Chapter 6). So the first theme in actors identified by Nadkarni & Prügl (2021) is transformative leadership. Today's leaders need a **digital mindset** in their organisations (see Key Term) which may be supported by chief digital officers 'to help navigate a more complex and technical environment' (Fernandez-Vidal et al., 2022: 10).

KEY TERM   DIGITAL MINDSET

According to Solberg et al. (2020: 107) a digital mindset is 'having an organizational climate or culture that emphasizes the importance of, and supports, digital transformation'. It is less about the individual and more about the organisation.

DISCOVER MORE ON DIGITAL MINDSETS

Read 'Digital mindsets: Recognizing and leveraging individual beliefs for digital transformation' by Solberg et al. (2020) published in the *California Management Review*. This article explains digital mindsets, how these relate to employees and how they react to digital transformation.

Managerial and organisational capabilities involve enhanced abilities. This means that with technology at the core of the business, new skills may be required. For example, managers may be managing staff who are working remotely and having to find new ways to plan team meetings and monitor progress. This can lead to more changes within the organisation. For example:

- A small retailer working with local customers may need to learn how to write successful newsletters and process online orders
- A reception team working in a restaurant chain may need to do more than meet and greet customers, but also reply online, manage the online booking system and add new content to the website
- Regional healthcare providers may need greater IT management skills, for accurately recording every episode between patients and healthcare providers

These new capabilities may require upskilling or retraining which is recognised as a key goal within the United Nations (2021). This also leads to changes in the company culture where not only the managers, but the employees need to adopt the digital mindset (Nadkarni & Prügl, 2021; Solberg et al., 2020). Finally, the work environment is ever-changing (see Chapter 2) and, due to remote working, some valuable skills may be missed or accidently not be shared (Nadkarni & Prügl, 2021).

Managing digital change projects needs a leader that supports a digital mindset, or with the ability to engage such support. Read Case Example 9.2 'DigiLocker' to see how a government took this approach.

CASE EXAMPLE 9.2   DigiLocker

DigiLocker is an app launched in India to safely store all the documents a citizen may possess. It is an example of digital transformation within government, changing the traditional processes of providing pieces of paper, which would need to be witnessed in a lawyer's office as being authentic.

Like a digital wallet, but containing all your key papers in one secure digital document wallet, this is a government concept co-created with a high-tech entrepreneur, Amit Ranjan, who co-founded SlideShare which was acquired by LinkedIn in 2012. With a great understanding of building a tech business, Ranjan joined the Government of India's Digital India programme within the Ministry of Electronics & IT (MeitY). MeitY's aim is to support 'digital empowerment' for citizens. This was a courageous approach by the government, recognising they needed external help. Ranjan's approach was to ensure the system was open and accessible to all and so DigiLocker was created using **Open API** (see Key Term) which supports co-creation.

This means that a wide range of organisations could partner with the service, making it more valuable to citizens and organisations. For example, if you're a university, you can create a plugin to enable students to upload their grades and certificates to their DigiLocker. Or if you're a recruiter you can allow candidates to upload their CV and evidence of their employment history, such as references. This means individuals only need to upload once, rather than constantly emailing different documents to different organisations. The Open API has succeeded as DigiLocker is used not only by government agencies and educational institutions, but also by private organisations such as financial institutions, recruitment services and employers.

Leading the project, Ranjan ensured that value co-creation was embedded within the DigiLocker business model. The DigiLocker team promoted the value for organisations as:

- Reduced Administrative Overhead: Aimed at the concept of paperless governance. It reduces the administrative overhead by minimizing the use of paper and curtailing the verification process.
- Digital Transformation: Provides trusted issued documents. Issued documents available via DigiLocker are fetched in real time directly from the issuing agency.
- Secure Document Gateway: Acts as a secure document exchange platform like payment gateway between trusted issuer and trusted requester/verifier with the consent of the citizen.
- Real Time Verification: Provides a verification module enabling government agencies to verify data directly from issuers after obtaining user consent.

Another factor and a key challenge in gaining technology adoption (see technology adoption in Chapter 6) is providing a solution that is useful and easy to use. In terms of its usefulness, DigiLocker can store documents, including education records (exam certificates), identity documents (passport), health records, travel documents (driving licence, rail and air tickets), local government papers, work records. When trying to encourage adoption by citizens, the benefits were noted as:

- Important Documents Anytime, Anywhere!
- Authentic Documents, Legally at Par with Originals.
- Digital Document Exchange with the consent of the citizen.
- Faster Service Delivery – Government Benefits, Employment, Financial Inclusion, Education, Health.

(continued)

As its website notes, 'DigiLocker aims at "Digital Empowerment" of citizen by providing access to authentic digital documents to citizen's digital document wallet'. DigiLocker is part of the Digital India programme (see digilocker.gov.in) which is disrupting how governments and citizens co-exist. This is a major undertaking, as legislation was changed so that DigiLocker is considered the same as providing the original documents.

Case questions

- DigiLocker seems to be the perfect digital super-wallet. What may be the downsides of systems like this and how could they be addressed?
- What documents would you find it useful to store in a DigiLocker so they could be accessed anytime, anywhere?
- Many governments are looking to use technology and transform how they function and provide services to citizens, as it saves money and provides greater efficiency. What are the key considerations for governments when exploring digital transformation?

KEY TERM   OPEN API

An API is an application programming interface, which is a piece of software that allows 2 applications to talk to each other. Having an open API means that the developer shares some code which the user organisation can access, to link the software to their website. Open APIs facilitate co-creation as the developer and recipient organisation can work together. For example, Apple and Google share their APIs so developers can create apps that may be added to the app stores.

Activity 9.3   Analyse opportunities for a digital super-wallet

With the DigiLocker case as an inspiration, analyse opportunities for a digital super-wallet that works for you and your classmates.

If you already access the DigiLocker, how can this be enhanced and who would need to be involved to make this happen?

9.5 CHALLENGES WITH DIGITAL TRANSFORMATION

Digital transformation may seem to be a straightforward process, but it is complex, so can go wrong and often does (Alnuaimi et al., 2022; Kraus et al., 2021). Challenges identified by various researchers (Brunetti et al., 2020; Saarikko et al., 2020) centre around:

- Culture and skills
- Ecosystems
- Infrastructure and technologies

9.5.1 CULTURE AND SKILLS

The culture within an organisation starts with the CEO leading the team, which is responsible for its success. If the CEO does not understand the challenges and opportunities of digital transformation, or lacks transformational leadership abilities, or fails to create a digital mindset, this has an impact on the likelihood of success (Alnuaimi et al., 2022; Fernandez-Vidal et al., 2022).

Other senior team members may feel threatened as they see their roles changing or being replaced, which causes personnel difficulties (Kraus et al., 2021). Employees may also resist change, which can lead 'to difficulties in implementing DT in the organization' (Kraus et al., 2021: 10). Unless the cultural issues are addressed from the start, digital transformation is unlikely to succeed. This may also involve reviewing skills within the business. Digital skills are a priority worldwide, as part of the United Nations Sustainable Development Goals, 1 of the 5 foundational pillars of the Digital Economy for Africa (DE4A) initiative, launched by the World Bank and a key initiative across Europe.

9.5.2 ECOSYSTEMS

Ecosystems consider the wider environment, beyond the individual company. For digital transformation this includes both public and private organisations. Public institutions such as government administration supporting innovation, as well as universities where research can take place, are considered critical in a digital ecosystem. Private companies may seem like competitors, yet other companies may share resources so the entire sector improves. Researcher Karina Von Dem Berge investigated business-to-business (B2B) resource sharing in Switzerland and concluded that creating a sharing inventory (what's available) and matching partners saves resources as well as building skills in the community.

9.5.3 INFRASTRUCTURE AND TECHNOLOGIES

For technology to work efficiently, access to high-speed broadband is needed. This means if the infrastructure is not in place, the transformation project will fail before it starts. Researchers also identified 'data security and reliability of the connection infrastructure' as essential (Brunetti et al., 2020: 711) to protect data and knowhow.

Long-established businesses may struggle to work in ecosystems and be less used to sharing knowledge and resources (Saarikko et al., 2020). This is similar to the concepts of closed and open innovation (see Chapter 7), where open innovation shares the difficulties faced and seeks help from the crowd. Traditional businesses are less keen on this approach, perhaps because it seems to be a sign of weakness. Sharing issues and working within an ecosystem requires organisations to adopt a digital mindset.

Smartphone Sixty Seconds® – Find digital transformation failures

Using your mobile phones:

- Search for 'digital transformation projects that failed'.
- What did you discover, what were the main reasons for failure?
- What were the costs involved?
- Share findings with classmates.

Digital transformation is a long and complex process that requires businesses to adopt a more open approach and to carefully blueprint their future. This is a path many organisations will need to face if they wish to survive.

JOURNAL OF NOTE

SAGE Open aims to be 'the world's most important social science journal'. Its focus is broad and its editorial board represents researchers from across the world. Several of the articles in this chapter were sourced from *SAGE Open*.

CASE STUDY

PAYPAL MANAGING DIGITAL TRANSFORMATION

Operating in 165 countries with offices in the Americas, Asia Pacific, Australasia, Europe and the Gulf region, with around 30,000 employees, undertaking a digital transformation journey is challenging. The business already manages many different cultures and within this has its own 'PayPal culture'. The PayPal culture is 'welcoming and fun' and there is support for employees 'by valuing inclusion, innovation, collaboration, and wellness' (PayPal, 2023b: 1) where individuals are rewarded for their contribution. This sounds like a great place to work, which has been recognised with many awards. There may be changes ahead as President and CEO Dan Schulman has retired. Schulman is recognised as a transformative leader and appointed most of the current board of directors. The new CEO Alex Chriss may make changes or take a different approach that could be better – or worse.

As a technology company, PayPal has been constantly involved with digital transformation processes. Adopting new technologies, 'while driving cultural change' (PayPal, 2023a: 28), seems to be an everyday occurrence. Part of driving change is listening to employees and feedback is gathered on a regular basis. Recent feedback stats are impressive: 'in our 2022 employee engagement survey, we heard from 83% of PayPal's employees globally' (PayPal, 2023a: 42). With engaged employees, changing processes can be much easier, but it's not clear whether the 83% are all positive, or negative or mixed.

Although PayPal was formed over 25 years ago, it works within an open ecosystem for card processing payments. This is because they offer their merchants and consumers flexibility to pay when and where they need to. However, PayPal still has many legacy systems and is working towards a full digital transformation. To do this the CEO notes that the business has had to 'streamline our operating model and sharpen our focus' (PayPal, 2023a: 3).

The business also promotes the opportunity of digital transformation to smaller merchants – 'Accelerate your digital transformation with PayPal' (PayPal Editorial Staff, 2023: 1) – which demonstrates a lack of understanding about digital transformation. It is not just about the technology and it is rarely fast. Yet adopting PayPal can help businesses win more customers. To support this with external evidence, the business invests in research from well-known consultancy firms. This is available in the website section 'Reports and Insights' (see www.paypal.com/us/brc/resources/reports-insights).

Within a transformation process there are risks with new technology. PayPal recognises these issues as 'Cyberattacks and security vulnerabilities could result in serious harm to our reputation, business, and financial condition' (PayPal, 2023a: 14). PayPal states that this could include: 'cybersecurity threats, including advanced and persisting cyberattacks, cyberextortion, distributed denial-of-service attacks, ransomware, spear phishing and social engineering schemes, the introduction of computer viruses or other malware, and the physical destruction of all or portions of our information technology and infrastructure' (PayPal, 2023a: 14). While it seems like digital innovation as PayPal has taken a lead in consumer data protection through education and tools, this is part of a wider strategy reducing opportunities for cybercrime.

The real question is whether PayPal is in a state of constant digital transformation where it recruits people who fit the positive and agile culture, works – or perhaps leads the ecosystem and identifies the latest technology to enhance business performance. Feedback on Glassdoor mentions the great culture, but also the need to be agile and the constant change, which doesn't suit everyone.

CASE QUESTIONS

PayPal's digital transformation will never end as it is an ongoing process.

- Although digital transformation is a journey, PayPal seems to be on a constant journey. What do you think are the main challenges and benefits working in this type of environment?
- How can PayPal support digital inclusion? What practical actions could the business take?
- How can large organisations sustain digital transformation?

(Continued)

FURTHER EXERCISES

1. Digital transformation is easier for larger established businesses with the investment required. This means some smaller businesses may be excluded and unable to compete. For a traditional organisation of your choice, evaluate the main issues in addressing digital transformation.

2. Using Figure 9.3, The TOGAF® Standard, 10th Edition as a framework, create an enterprise architecture plan to map out digital transformation for an organisation of your choice.

3. Prepare a newsletter for a community group or charity explaining why a digital transformation project is needed.

4. Digital transformation is no longer a choice for business, it's essential for survival. Discuss.

SUMMARY

This chapter has explored:

*   The stages in the digital transformation process
*   Preparing and planning for digital transformation
*   The concept of the digital mindset
*   Challenges with digital transformation projects

PART 4

DIGITAL BUSINESS STRATEGY AND MANAGEMENT

CONTENTS

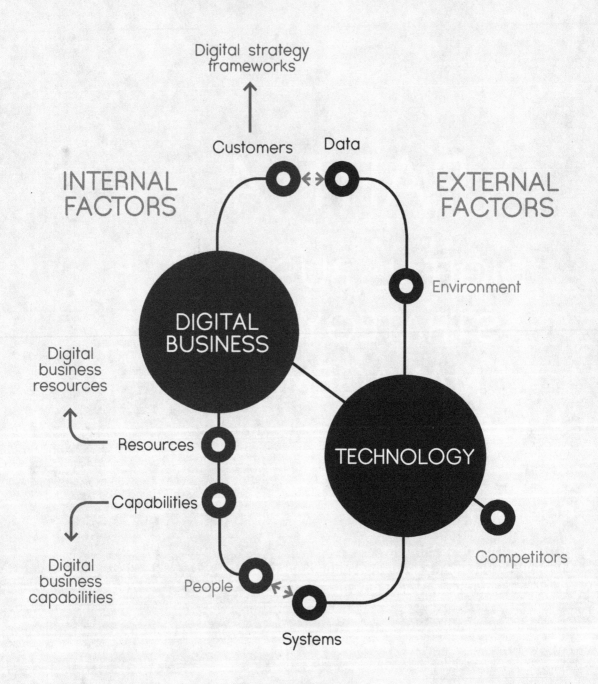

Digital strategy
frameworks

Customers   Data

INTERNAL
FACTORS

EXTERNAL
FACTORS

Environment

DIGITAL
BUSINESS

Digital
business
resources

TECHNOLOGY

Resources

Capabilities

Digital
business
capabilities

People

Systems

Competitors

10

DIGITAL BUSINESS STRATEGY

LEARNING OUTCOMES

When you have read this chapter, you will be able to:

Understand digital business capabilities and resources

Apply the VRIN framework

Analyse digital business strategy

Evaluate your digital skills

Create a digital business strategy

PROFESSIONAL SKILLS

When you have worked through this chapter, you should be able to:

- Interpret, communicate and brief internal or external stakeholders on digital business requirements
- Critically evaluate arguments about digital capabilities to enable a business solution to be achieved

10.1 INTRODUCTION TO DIGITAL BUSINESS STRATEGY

Digital business strategy is more than a business strategy or a digital strategy.

- A strategy is a plan or programme, to achieve your aim or vision
- A *business* strategy is a plan for the business

Digital strategies are often confused with an IT or technology strategy which is the business programme to improve IT in an organisation. According to Bharadwaj et al. (2013: 472), digital business strategy is an 'organizational strategy formulated and executed by leveraging digital resources to create differential value'. The difference is that digital business strategy harnesses digital assets, whether that's cloud computing, artificial intelligence or data management to create value for stakeholders.

Bharadwaj et al. (2013: 473) expand on this theme and explain:

> Digital business strategy is different from traditional IT strategy in the sense that it is much more than a cross-functional strategy, and it transcends traditional functional areas (such as marketing, procurement, logistics, operations, or others) and various IT-enabled business processes (such as order management, customer service, and others). Therefore, digital business strategy can be viewed as being inherently transfunctional.

A digital business strategy is usually shared in a document that explains the overarching aim or plan that the company has and how the different elements fit together to achieve the plan. A strategy is essential for businesses as it provides direction and common goals. Without a strategy there are risks of: duplication, which increases costs and wastes time; failing to understand customers' needs, so they stop buying from the business; employees lacking guidance, so they leave the company; and increased costs as different departments work in an unconnected way.

In Chapter 1 we looked at the digital business framework. The key internal factors were customers, resources, capabilities and people. The external factors centred around technology and included data, environment, competitors and systems. Creating a digital business strategy requires all of these elements to be integrated. We considered data, environment and competitors in Chapter 1, systems in Chapter 4 (platform ecosystems) and digital technologies in Chapter 6. In Chapter 11 we will examine *customers* in more depth and in Chapter 12 we will address the *people* element. In this chapter we will explore resources and capabilities in more detail.

10.2 DIGITAL BUSINESS CAPABILITIES

According to Ritter & Pedersen (2020: 182), 'a capability is a qualification or skill necessary to perform a certain activity'. While it seems that all businesses would possess the capabilities needed to deliver their customer offer, when the environment changes, the skills needed may change too. This is a major challenge for long-established businesses that have worked the same way for many years, as not all workers may possess the new capabilities.

Activity 10.1   Evaluate your digital skills

As many jobs require digital skills, the European Union has created a test to evaluate your skills. This test is 'based on the European Digital Competences Framework for Citizens, developed by the Joint Research Centre and the European Commission'. The assessment is available online in 29 languages.

Go to the website europa.eu/europass/digitalskills and take the test to assess your digital skills. Compare your results with classmates and discuss the differences. Consider sharing the digital skills test with other members of your family to evaluate their digital skills.

Capabilities are about the skills of the individual worker, which contributes to the entire business. If some workers have the skills, but other workers don't, this reduces the capabilities of the business. Capabilities are also about the skills of the business – the workers and its resources. But there are challenges because there is no common understanding of digital business capability (Wielgos et al., 2021). In assessing the components of digital business capability, Wielgos et al. (2021) suggested that there were 3 main elements: digital strategy (focusing on what the business needed to do), digital integration (focusing on how the business joins up all the elements) and digital control (ongoing monitoring and measurement). In each of these 3 areas, there were separate capabilities needed. These are shown in Figure 10.1.

Digital strategy
- Create new value for customers through digital technologies
- Create new value for the firm and its partners through digital technologies
- Deliver digital product and service innovations
- Make digital business transformation a strategic priority

Digital integration
- Interconnect business processes along value chain
- Interconnect all areas of the firm (e.g., marketing, sales, IT)
- Interconnect with customers, suppliers, and partners
- Interconnect with actors on digital platforms
- Redesign business processes

Digital control
- Establish specifications to implement digital business transformation
- Monitor digital business transformation
- Analyze performance metrics

Figure 10.1   Digital business capabilities

Source: Adapted from Wielgos et al. (2021)

Let's explore each of these elements in the next sections.

10.2.1 DIGITAL STRATEGY

Digital strategy is often more visible, which makes it easier to assess. For example, you may be a customer of a local food business, and if they offer an app for online ordering, you can see that they have created new value for customers by using digital technology. You might not be able to judge whether a business has created new value for the firm and its partners through digital technologies, unless they share stories about how they have both benefited. Sometimes this happens in business-to-business (B2B) where firms publish good news about how their systems have helped other organisations in case studies. This is because delivering digital product and service innovations is often announced to show the skills of a company. For example, when Tesla adds new features to its cars, it launches major promotional campaigns to make customers aware of the innovation.

Making digital business transformation a strategic priority is information that can only be gathered from larger businesses with shareholders, who produce annual reports. The annual reports often explain the actions they are taking or planning. For example, PayPal informs its investors about their activities: 'This was a year of transformation for PayPal, as we increased our operating discipline while continuing to invest in innovation at scale' (PayPal, 2023a: v).

Smartphone Sixty Seconds® – Search for case studies

- Oracle is a global B2B provider of enterprise information technology (IT) systems. Take out your mobile phone and search for 'case study Oracle'.
- Select one case study that looks interesting.
- Who did they help and what was the main benefit?
- How did this create new value for the firm? Which digital technologies were used?
- How did this create new value for its partners?

10.2.2 DIGITAL INTEGRATION

The second theme, digital integration (Wielgos et al., 2021), involves integrating different parts of the business. This ensures that silos, or parts of the business that are disconnected, are joined up. But an understanding of whether business processes, departments, partners or suppliers are linked up is difficult to assess unless you're inside the business.

10.2.3 DIGITAL CONTROL

In the same way, unless you are working within a business, it can be difficult to assess its digital control capabilities. As we noted in Chapter 9, digital transformation is a process that can take many years and may not always be obvious until much later. Plus access to a business's metrics is difficult, even when you are working there!

Activity 10.2 Analyse digital business strategy

Consider a sports or food brand that you believe you know well. Analyse their digital business strategy and identify areas where they are performing well – or less well.

Compare your findings with classmates. Who has selected the business with the strongest digital strategy? Why is this? Are there any businesses where the digital strategy seems weak? What makes it difficult to analyse the digital strategy?

Sometimes a change of strategy is needed when an organisation does not possess the marketing capabilities. There may be gaps in their capabilities to address a market and they may need to make major changes, as Case Example 10.1 National Australia Bank demonstrates.

CASE EXAMPLE 10.1 National Australia Bank

National Australia Bank (NAB) was a traditional bank with customers comfortable with visiting the branch to conduct their financial business. However, NAB had a challenge. Younger, more digital-savvy customers were not using NAB. They didn't want to visit a branch and wanted an app to manage their money. Plus they never received or issued old-fashioned paper cheques and they had no need for cash as they carried a digital wallet. As a result, they were applying for accounts with other organisations as NAB was unable to deliver these services. This showed a weakness within NAB's capabilities. They simply continued doing what they had done for many years, without identifying the need to deliver digital product and service innovation to its customers. It seems as if its digital strategy capabilities were not in place and, without these, the bank lacked digital integration or control.

However, it is not surprising as NAB was established in 1981, a pre-digital age. This is before digital capabilities were considered as a requirement. When they started over 40 years' ago NAB had all the capabilities that it needed – and more, as the bank gained many awards for its traditional banking services. When NAB assessed the capabilities that were required to launch digital bank services, they realised there were major gaps.

This was then a difficult decision. Should NAB participate in digital banking or not? NAB realised that they needed to create value for customers through digital technologies. But how could they achieve this? They had 2 main options. Firstly, they could have started a major re-training and recruitment campaign, but this would disrupt their everyday activities and could result in a reduction in the NAB service. Or secondly, they could have created a separate department to focus on digital capabilities. However, to address this issue, NAB took a different option and created a new bank; not just a separate department, but a totally new business with its own identity – Ubank.

As Ubank was born in a digital age, the bank recruited the capabilities needed, such as product analysts, IT support specialists and cyber security engineers. Plus, as a digital-first

(Continued)

bank which offers online and telephone banking, it has no physical branches, so there was no need to invest in property and spend months fitting out buildings. As an online bank with no branches, staff could work remotely or in a hybrid pattern, so Ubank could recruit from a wider pool of people.

Since launching, the Ubank app has attracted many new customers. As its website states: 'Think of us as your daily money companion. One that gives you the ability to see your money in one place, with smart features and real-time insights designed to help you get ahead' (Ubank, 2023: 1). Without the legacy of a traditional bank with restrictive procedures Ubank took a creative approach to managing customer services and created a YouTube channel called Ubank Moneybox. Ubank Moneybox answers many frequently asked questions about savings, investment, loans and other aspects of finance. The easy-to-use app has won many awards with its innovative approach to banking.

Case questions

- One solution for National Australia Bank was to open a separate division, not start a separate company. What are the advantages and disadvantages of starting a separate division?
- What do you believe is the long-term future for banks like NAB? Will they still exist in 30 years' time? Why is this?
- Are there organisations that you are familiar with, which have had challenges when they started new divisions, or upskilled existing staff? Why was this?

10.3 DIGITAL BUSINESS RESOURCES

10.3.1 ORGANISATIONAL RESOURCES

As well as capabilities, according to Barney (1995) an organisation has many resources, including:

- Financial resources – money in the bank, the ability to borrow
- Physical resources – offices, retail stores
- Machines and manufacturing facilities – specialist equipment
- Human resources – expertise in recruitment and retention
- Know-how – the experience, knowledge and wisdom of workers
- Organisational culture – its history and relationships

These are traditional resources which organisations such as NAB (see Case Example 10.1 National Australia Bank) possessed and managed well. But to survive in a digital environment, businesses need digital resources too. Digital resources include expertise and know-how, intellectual property, technology, data and analytics.

10.3.2 EXPERTISE AND KNOW-HOW

The capabilities of teams in a business can offer great advantage over competitors. This is because skilled teams can deliver results faster and provide better customer service. For example, Amazon has know-how in cataloguing huge volumes of products and managing the associated data (product descriptions, pricing, sellers, images, reviews) which require online storage, so the business created an internal system which is now known as Amazon Web Services (AWS), a cloud-based storage system. AWS has expanded into a range of web services which are sold to other businesses. Effectively AWS sell the know-how developed for their own business to other businesses.

Expertise and know-how can expand businesses, as Uber has demonstrated. It has created a technology platform which matches one group with another. This has allowed the business to move into different markets. For example, Uber matches drivers and passengers, Uber Eats matches restaurants with hungry people, and Uber Freight matches carriers with shippers. This means that Uber is not a taxi business, but a technology platform business.

10.3.3 INTELLECTUAL PROPERTY

When the know-how has distinctive benefits, it can be legally recognised through registration of trademarks or patents which can be managed through licenses. Intellectual property gives the owner legal protection and they can monetise their goods through licensing. For example, Friedchillies Media from Malaysia licenses its food-related content, such as recipes and hacks, to appear on other food websites that need ongoing content. Another example is where Google and Universal Music are exploring licensing artists' voices to create AI-generated music. Intellectual property has a value when managed well and can be a digital resource.

DIGITAL TOOL Online trademark checker

The European Union intellectual property office (euipo.europa.eu) has created an online trademark checker.

- You can explore it here: tmdn.org/tmview

10.3.4 TECHNOLOGY

Technology as a digital resource includes all forms of automated systems, such as AI, customer relationship management and commercial systems. For example, DigiLocker in India is the ultimate digital super-wallet which holds all personal ID and other data in one place, or DataRobot, an AI Platform which integrates with business apps and other data platforms.

When a business creates a technology platform, it can allow others to use the platform, which adds value to customers and partners. For example, Bol.com, a **B Corporation** (see Key Term) based in the Netherlands, created an online shopping platform and sells goods from over 50,000 sales partners. This enables businesses to sell via a ready-made platform and provides a wide range of goods to its 13 million customers.

KEY TERM   B CORPORATION

A business that benefits a wider group of stakeholders is known as a B Corporation. In 2006, 'B Lab became known for certifying B Corporations, which are companies that meet high standards of social and environmental performance, accountability, and transparency' (B Labs, 2023: 1). There are B Corporations in nearly 100 countries and over 160 industries.

DIGITAL TOOL   B Corporations directory

B-Lab has an online directory of B Corporations around the world.

- You can explore it here: bcorporation.net/en-us/find-a-b-corp

10.3.5 DATA

Data includes personal details (name, age), work records (employer, wages) and state records (where you live, household details). Data may seem to be a strange digital resource, but **rich data** (see Key Term) 'signals our waking hours (behaviours), recognizes our online likes and dislikes (psychographics), shares our browsing and shopping habits (webographics) and monitors our family and friendship bonds (demographics)' and can be used by advertisers (Hanlon et al., 2023: 1).

KEY TERM   RICH DATA

Rich data is the blend of different pieces of data. This leads to greater depth and detail than a single piece of data. Rich data enables businesses to make informed decisions, such as who will respond to which offers and when. Described by Schultze & Avital (2011: 3), 'rich data, like rich soil, is also fertile and generative, capable of producing a diversity of new ideas and insights'.

There are also special categories of data that are recognised within legislation in many countries; for example, race, ethnic origin, political opinions, religious or philosophical beliefs, trade union membership, genetic data, biometric data (where used for identification purposes), health data, sex life or sexual orientation. Therefore, protecting personal data is a major responsibility. But, as the United Nations Conference on Trade and Development (2021) has noted, some countries have no data protection in place. This means they can use the data in any way they choose.

Within businesses, the main data collected is about customers, who they are, where they are based, when and what they buy. Data has a value as it can be traded, as long as it follows the legislation. For example, the Irish airline Ryanair has a massive database of travellers and can recognise frequent flyers or party people. This allows Ryanair to offer car hire to some travellers and last-minute getaway breaks for others.

DISCOVER MORE ON PRIVACY AND DATA

Read 'Ethical concerns about social media privacy policies: Do users have the ability to comprehend their consent actions?' by Annmarie Hanlon & Karen Jones (2023), published in the *Journal of Strategic Marketing*. This article explores the complexity of social media privacy policies and raises ethical concerns about users' understanding of how their data.

ETHICAL INSIGHTS Data breaches

You may be aware of the Cambridge Analytica scandal where Facebook sold user data about millions of people, which may have influenced election results (Hanlon et al., 2023). Although the firm was fined and this was a public event, there have been many data breaches where businesses have accidentally disclosed personal data, which is an ongoing problem and may be less public. The top 4 business sectors where breaches occur most frequently are healthcare, financial services, pharmaceutical and energy.

A data breach typically occurs due to weaknesses in technology or user behaviour. As the European Commission (2023) website notes:

A data breach occurs when the data for which your company/organisation is responsible suffers a security incident resulting in a breach of confidentiality, availability or integrity. If that occurs, and it is likely that the breach poses a risk to an individual's rights and freedoms, your company/organisation has to notify the supervisory authority without undue delay, and at the latest within 72 hours after having become aware of the breach. If your company/organisation is a data processor it must notify every data breach to the data controller.

(Continued)

If the data breach poses a high risk to those individuals affected then they should all also be informed, unless there are effective technical and organisational protection measures that have been put in place, or other measures that ensure that the risk is no longer likely to materialise.

As an organisation it is vital to implement appropriate technical and organisational measures to avoid possible data breaches.

However, they still occur. In their *Cost of a Data Breach Report* (2023), IBM states that the cost of a data breach to a business in the USA can be $4.45 million. This is because some breaches can take over 200 days to resolve, finding out what happened and why, then restoring the systems and paying compensation to those involved.

The costs in a data breach include:

- Downtime – systems may be closed until repaired; for factories this is an expensive process
- The cost of the response – placing advertisements online and offline to advise customers
- Reputational damage – some customers may cancel contracts as customers lose trust in the business
- Fines from government – these are fixed depending on the geographical location and size of the breach
- Users taking action – in the US users may decide to take legal action against the business

Plus after a data breach the operating costs inside the business often increase as their insurance premiums escalate and they may need better ongoing IT support. Yet the customers suffer as a result because the business may need to pass costs to the customers. The data stolen may include personal identifiable information (name, age, workplace, government records), which increases the fines but also makes the customer vulnerable to their details being hacked.

Ways the data are stolen include:

- Phishing – an employee receives an email that looks realistic, asking them to send money or share some details
- Accidental loss of a device – such as a laptop left on a train
- Screen not locked in a public building – someone may gain access and use the device

It can take months to identify that an attack has occurred as the attacker may be inside the system and gathering data before they are discovered. You may think over 200 days is a long time not to discover the data breach, but Toyota Japan revealed that the vehicle data of 2.15 million users had mistakenly been made publicly available for 10 years due to poor training! The company says this data was mistakenly set to public view, and included 'registered email addresses; vehicle-unique chassis and navigation terminal numbers; the location of vehicles and what time they were there; and videos from the vehicle's "drive recorder" which records footage from the car' (Whittaker, 2023: 1). Toyota was lucky as the data was not used maliciously, but that's not always the case.

- Were you aware of the cost of data breaches?
- What do you do to protect your data? Have you ever had training about this?
- With advances in computer technology, has it become impossible to protect data?

Smartphone Sixty Seconds® – Find types of phishing

- Phishing or fishing for information takes place in many different ways. Take out your mobile phone and search for 'Types of phishing attack'.
- What types of phishing attack did you discover?
- Have you or anyone you know fallen into a phishing trap?
- What were the consequences?
- What advice would you give others to ensure they ignore phishing scams?

DIGITAL TOOL   Have my details been hacked?

Troy Hunt, a Microsoft Regional Director and Developer Security professional, created this tool 'as a free resource for anyone to quickly assess if they may have been put at risk due to an online account of theirs having been compromised or "pwned" in a data breach'. It lists all the recent attacks and will let you know if your data has been compromised through a third party.

- You can explore it here: haveibeenpwned.com

10.3.6 ANALYTICS

Analytics has become a digital resource and this is about making sense of the data. Analytics is about the ability to analyse data and gain insights from which specific valuable actions can be taken. There are 4 main types of data:

- Descriptive – what happened? For example, how many customers visited the bol.com website on Sunday evening? What was the average amount spent per customer? How many were new customers?

- Diagnostic – why did it happen? For example, did any of the sales relate to a newsletter or social media post? If yes, which were most successful?

- Predictive – what may happen in the future? For example, if another newsletter is issued, how many more sales might this create?

- Prescriptive – what is the best response? For example, would a newsletter or social media post be better?

For instance, recognising that specific travellers book on Sunday evenings could allow businesses like Ryanair to offer car hire and other packages, creating value for the firm and its partners through analysing customer behaviour across its digital technology platforms (website and app).

According to Ritter (2020), businesses need to consider how they manage data, the process of gathering the permissions required to process the data and how the analytics will be managed. Table 10.1 shows the areas to be explored. These issues highlight the importance of treating data with care.

Table 10.1 Conceptualisation of a firm's digitisation capability

Dimension components	Data	Permission	Analytics
Individuals	What kinds of employees are working with data generation, transmission, storage, and access for the firm, and how many? Which new roles will be needed?	What kinds of employees are working with permissions for the firm, and how many? Which new roles will be needed?	What kinds of employees are working with analytics for the firm, and how many? Which new roles will be needed?
Processes	What kinds of processes related to data generation, transmission, storage, and access are established in the firm?	What kinds of processes related to permissions are established in the firm?	What kinds of processes related to analytics are established in the firm?
Structure	What kind of structure governs data generation, transmission, storage, and access in the firm?	What kind of structure related to permissions exists in the firm?	What kind of structure governs analytics in the firm?

Source: Ritter & Pedersen (2020: 183). Printed with permission of Elsevier

Activity 10.3   Apply digital business resources

Use the information from the digital business resources (expertise and know-how, intellectual property, technology, data and analytics) and apply it to a sports, food, music or other business of your choice. Demonstrate how the business uses their resources with examples. Consider where they have strengths and weaknesses, and which resources provide the greatest value.

10.3.7 RESOURCE-BASED VIEW

It's not enough to simply have the resources; they need to be distinctive. If all competitors possess the same resources, they don't deliver real value as there is no difference. According to Barney (1991), resources should be valuable, rare, inimitable and non-substitutable – VRIN, as shown in Table 10.2.

Table 10.2   The VRIN resources

VRIN resource	What this means	Example	Alternative approaches
Valuable resources	These are resources that have value for the organisation, although they may be common to other organisations.	Disney possesses trademarks which allow the business to gain ongoing income from third parties for using film footage in their apps. Other businesses may also have trademarks, but Disney has a strong brand name which has a track record of appealing to many generations of children.	An organisation could decide not to use Disney, but select an alternative children's favourite instead.
Rare resources	These are resources that are rare, or unique to the organisation, otherwise competitors could offer the same advantages.	A patented technology indicates rarity. Apple is expanding its Siri software to explore how it can respond to lip reading.	Patents are published documents which competitors can review and assess. They may not be able to be replicated, but may be able to be adapted, yet this could take significant time and investment.
Inimitable resources	These are resources that are difficult to be copied or obtained by others. So while copying or imitating may be possible in some cases, the original item cannot be replicated.	ChatGPT has a unique historical condition of being the first generative artificial intelligence system. While others followed, it has become a brand name overnight which is difficult to copy.	One solution may be to buy the organisation which has the inimitable resources – this is a practice that Google adopted for many years. For example, Google bought an analytics firm, Urchin, which later became Google Analytics, as it was a superior way of analysing web data.
Non-substitutable	The resource cannot be replaced with another.	Many mobile phones are non-substitutable for their owners. If you have a Samsung mobile phone, when you upgrade, it may be to another Samsung device as your data is already stored and the switching process is easy.	Over time some resources could be substituted. For example, the challenge for ChatGPT is that substitutes have started to emerge, so while it seems valuable today, it will need to evolve to find resources that are more difficult to substitute.

When capabilities and VRIN resources are combined, this leads to superior performance (Barney, 1991). This is known as the resource-based theory (RBT) or the resourced-based view (RBV) and leads to sustained competitive advantage. This is a planned and strategic process, and is why some businesses are more successful than others.

DISCOVER MORE ON RESOURCE-BASED THEORY

Read 'Firm Resources and Sustained Competitive Advantage' by Jay Barney (1991) published in the *Journal of Management*. This was the article that introduced the concept of resource-based theory.

10.4 DIGITAL STRATEGY FRAMEWORKS

When considering digital business models, Ritter & Pedersen (2020) noted that it was based on what was offered to customers (the digital value proposition) and how customers could perceive this (digital value demonstration), an understanding of who the customer is (data) and which capabilities were needed to deliver this (digital organisation and digitisation). This is shown in Figure 10.2.

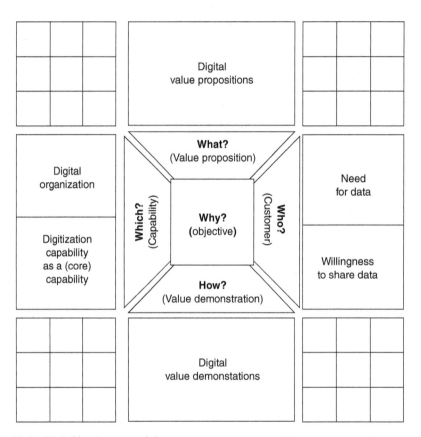

Figure 10.2   Digital business models

Source: Ritter & Pedersen (2020: 184). Printed with permission of Elsevier

Let's apply this model to Amazon Web Services (AWS) who provide cloud and IT services to businesses in many locations:

- Why does the business exist (what is the business objective)? To provide premium cloud services for B2B customers in Norway, Finland, Denmark and Sweden
- What is offered to customers? Cloud services
- How do customers perceive this? Case studies shared online from well-known companies
- Who is the customer? AWS holds significant customer data and can target those most likely to use its services

- Which capabilities are needed to deliver this? Expertise and skills in managing cloud services for many organisations at the same time

This may seem to be a simple structure, but it includes the key elements of a digital strategy.

DISCOVER MORE ON CAPABILITY AND BUSINESS MODELS

Read 'Digitization capability and the digitalization of business models in business-to-business firms: Past, present, and future' by Thomas Ritter & Carsten Lund Pedersen (2020), published in *Industrial Marketing Management*. This article provides an overview of research on digitisation and digitalisation in business-to-business markets with a proposed business model.

CASE EXAMPLE 10.2   X-Road®

Estonia is a small country with a population of 1.3 million. On gaining independence they made some big decisions, including adoption of digital technologies. The support for digitalisation of the country was strong and Estonia is recognised as the most digitally advanced country in the world. Most state services are online and 99% of residents have a digital ID card.

To become digital Estonia needed a shared system that worked across the entire country. Rather than work alone, they formed a partnership with Finland, another digitally focused country. With a population of 5.5 million the Finnish government established the Finnish Digital Agency, which 'promotes the digitalisation of society, secures the availability of data, and provides services for the life events of its customers'.

The partnership formed a joint association, the Nordic Institute for Interoperability Solutions (NIIS). The purpose of NIIS was to create a secure software system that would enable data sharing and data transfer. This became X-Road®, a digital ecosystem that enables citizens to share specific data with government and allows government to communicate with its citizens. The aim was to build an ecosystem which 'includes a full range of services for the general public' (E-Estonia, 2021: 1).

The system is described as 'an open-source software and ecosystem solution that provides unified and secure data exchange between private and public sector organisations'. It is not a blockchain, but a sharing data and communication ecosystem which 'allows the nation's various public and private sector e-service information systems to link up and function in harmony'. The X-Road® links all the services you might need and has saved thousands of administration hours within government. A graphic illustration of the X-Road® demonstrating the links between the different organisations is shown in Figure 10.3.

(Continued)

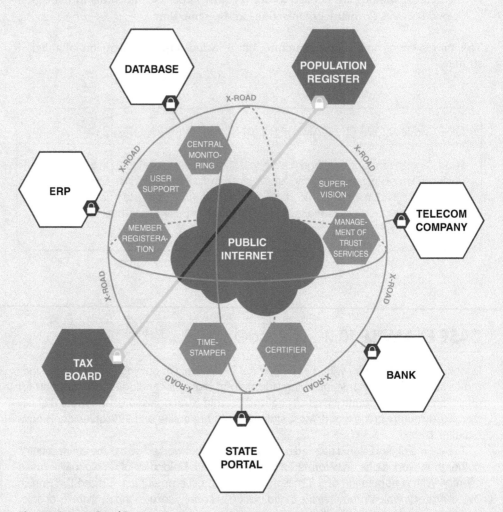

Figure 10.3   X-Road® system

Source: https://e-estonia.com/wp-content/uploads/e-estonia-050623_eng.pdf. Printed with permission of e-Estonia

The governments also needed citizens to feel confident that their data was secure. This required several security protocols to protect the data: 'to ensure secure transfers, all outgoing data is digitally signed and encrypted, and all incoming data is authenticated and logged'. The data is always exchanged between the service provider (such as the tax board) and the service user (i.e. a citizen). Third parties are not able to access the system.

The benefits of the ecosystem have encouraged other services to participate, such as banking or enterprise resource planning (ERP). This allows businesses to connect their systems into the X-Road® and provide a smoother customer experience. Because the system has successfully and securely connected different data sets, it has been adopted by other governments including Iceland, Mexico, Japan and India. This was a form of digital strategy, with a plan to make citizens digital and worked well due to the capabilities and application of technology.

Case questions

- X-Road® sounds like the perfect system for citizens to access, more efficient than having to access one platform to pay local taxes, another to register for healthcare and another for ID services such as passports. Why do you think the citizens of Estonia and Finland supported X-Road®?
- Estonia and Finland are smaller countries – what barriers would larger countries need to address to ensure its citizens would use this type of system?
- How many government or state departments have you encountered and what was your experience?

A digital business strategy should address the key internal and external factors. We've discovered that the strategy is the overall aim, plan or vision. To deliver the strategy, this is supported by the objectives and from this the actions (tactics) are created, which relate to the internal and external factors. Figure 10.4 shows an alternative framework for a digital business strategy.

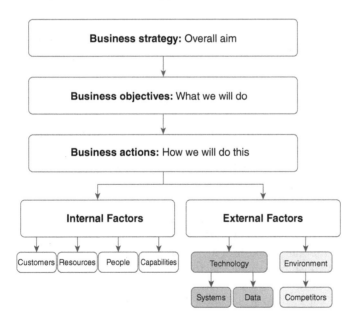

Figure 10.4   Digital business strategy

It is not uncommon for organisations to confuse strategy, objectives and actions. Objectives should be SMART (specific, measurable, achievable, realistic and timed) and state the specific action to be taken. For example, 'to offer value for customers' is vague and difficult to assess, but 'to offer the citizens of Iceland an integrated system for all state departments, by July' is specific and can be assessed and measured. This would be classed as a strong objective. The actions to achieve the objectives are often a long list of tasks. When this is completed it may require an assessment of internal and external factors, as not all the capabilities or resources may be available.

10.5 THE FUTURE OF STRATEGY

Technology is changing how we live at a record pace. When ChatGPT was launched, many students tried using it for assignments and universities struggled to catch up and find a solution that would identify work not created by the students. Governments reacted in different ways, with some, like the Italian government, initially banning ChatGPT and then changing its mind. Companies also issued policies to ensure their most valuable content wasn't added to ChatGPT to be recycled by their competitors. This is not the first new technology that has changed our lives and will not be the last.

At the same time consumer behaviour is changing. High streets are struggling to encourage people to visit stores as online shopping is so easy. We are witnessing new phenomena such as **deshopping** (see Chapter 3) as consumers buy, wear and return goods. Many face-to-face meetings in a B2B environment have been replaced by faster Zoom or Teams calls – they're efficient but may not nurture strong relationships.

10.5.1 DYNAMIC CAPABILITIES

So how do businesses adapt? A traditional strategy was often shared in a document which was intended to last for 5, 7 or even 10 years. But changes are happening fast and strategies may soon be out of date. One argument to manage this change is that dynamic capabilities (Eisenhardt & Martin, 2000) are needed. According to Eisenhardt & Martin (2000: 1106) 'dynamic capabilities consist of specific strategic and organisational processes like product development, alliancing, and strategic decision making'. Eisenhardt & Martin (2000: 1107) suggest that dynamic capabilities should be 'the organizational and strategic routines by which firms achieve new resource configurations as markets emerge, collide, split, evolve, and die'. Dynamic capabilities then become a way of life for business.

Looking at business such as Apple and Tesla, they have demonstrated dynamic capabilities. They are 'research-first' businesses and produced new products that consumers had not realised they needed. The first iPhone changed how we communicate and transformed a mobile phone into a mobile personal computer. When there was a reluctance from consumers to buy electric vehicles due to the lack of charging stations, Tesla created a network of electric vehicle (EV) charging points. These businesses adopt dynamic capabilities which have 3 parts (Teece, 2007):

- Sensing
- Seizing
- Reconfiguring capabilities

Sensing involves conducting research to understand what is happening in the market and scanning for new opportunities. It is not enough to understand what is happening in the market and so seizing is required. Seizing concerns taking advantage of the opportunity to be addressed. At this stage the business may need to reconfigure its capabilities to address the opportunity. To do this a digital mindset may be required, as well as workers with the right capabilities to be able to adapt quickly.

JOURNAL OF NOTE

The *Journal of Business Strategy* is dedicated to business strategy. It 'defines strategy in the broadest sense and thus covers topics as diverse as marketing strategy, innovation, developments in the global economy, mergers & acquisition integration and human resources'.

CASE STUDY
PAYPAL DIGITAL CAPABILITIES AND RESOURCES

PayPal has adopted a growth strategy to 'grow its business, expand its value proposition' (PayPal, 2023a: 13). To do this, the firm recognises the importance of capabilities and is actively buildings its skills. Its annual report comments that they need to 'Enhance our Commerce Enablement Capabilities' (PayPal, 2022a: iv). The business notes key areas where more capabilities are needed:

> We are focused on investing in our foundational capabilities, such as identity, data insights and our shared tools and platforms to create better and more meaningful experiences for our customers as we work to bring new capabilities to the market. These investments will bolster our reliability and availability, helping to ensure that we are best in class at the basics. (PayPal, 2022a: iv)

Recognising the need for the whole team to stay ahead, PayPal focuses on 'Developing talent to ensure they have the critical skills and capabilities to excel in current and future roles' (PayPal, 2022a: 42). To help employees develop these skills further, they are encouraged to support local communities and volunteer their skills to help small businesses or underrepresented groups. It's not only the employees who need the right level of capabilities as the business ensures its senior leadership team has the skills needed: 'The Board reviews and discusses the capabilities of our executive management' (PayPal, 2022a: 32). If further training is needed, this is arranged.

According to its latest annual report, 'The Board is responsible for providing advice and oversight of PayPal's strategic and operational direction and overseeing its executive management to support the long-term interests of the Company and its

(Continued)

stockholders' (PayPal, 2023: 26). In addition to the employees and senior managers, the capabilities of the board of directors are assessed. This is carried out using the PayPal board skills matrix which reviews the experience, expertise and attributes of those serving on, or nominated to, the board of directors. The capabilities at this level include:

- Payments, financial services and fintech
- Technology and innovation
- Global business
- Senior leadership
- Business development and strategy
- Legal/regulatory/governmental
- Cybersecurity/information security
- Finance/accounting
- Consumer/sales/marketing/brand management
- Environmental, social and/or governance (ESG)
- Talent management

Not all directors have all skills on the list. To ensure the business can easily see whether they may need further support, all skills are plotted onto a graphic, as shown in Figure 10.5. This means that when a director leaves, they can easily see which capabilities need to be replaced.

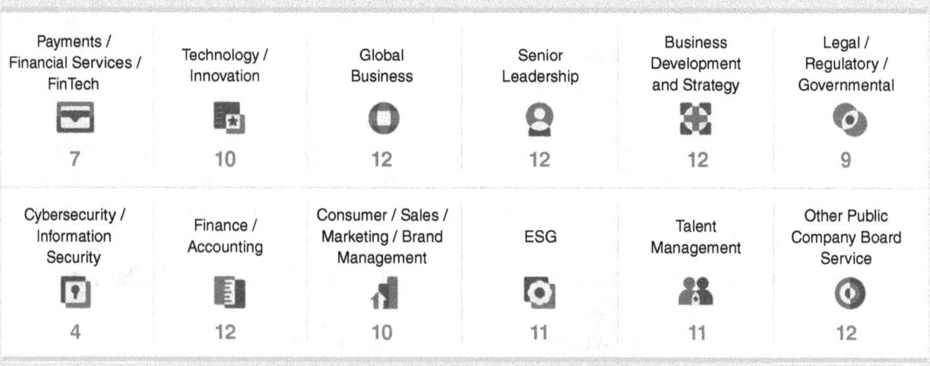

Payments / Financial Services / FinTech	Technology / Innovation	Global Business	Senior Leadership	Business Development and Strategy	Legal / Regulatory / Governmental
7	10	12	12	12	9
Cybersecurity / Information Security	Finance / Accounting	Consumer / Sales / Marketing / Brand Management	ESG	Talent Management	Other Public Company Board Service
4	12	10	11	11	12

Figure 10.5   Directors' skills and experience

Source: PayPal (2023a: 8). Printed with permission of PayPal

Key aspects of digital strategy are capabilities and also resources: 'We invest resources towards improving our products and services, offering choice in payment options, providing excellent customer service, and building brands that merchants and consumers trust' (PayPal, 2023a: 7). PayPal's digital resources include expertise and know-how, intellectual property, technology, data and analytics. The expertise and know-how come from the employees as well as the staff. Plus the business acquires other companies to bring in new skills,

Its intellectual property includes a range of brands: PayPal, Braintree, Venmo, Xoom, Hyperwallet, PayPal Zettle, PayPal Honey and Paidy. As a technology business, its data is well managed and the 'technology infrastructure supporting our payments platform is designed to simplify the storage and processing of large amounts of data … in both our own data centers and when hosted by third-party cloud service providers' (PayPal, 2023a: 8). The business understands analytics to such an extent that it helps its customers better understand their customers through their analytics dashboards. This helps the merchants to convert and retain its customers.

CASE QUESTIONS

- PayPal is aiming to grow its business. How much can the business grow and what are the risks?
- The requirement to meet its capabilities means that many of the directors on the board are older. Does this matter? Or how could younger directors be recruited and to which of PayPal's capabilities would they contribute?
- PayPal is a global business – how can smaller companies ensure they have the right capabilities to meet their business needs?

FURTHER EXERCISES

1. Evaluate the digital business capabilities for a business of your choice. Try and find its careers page to identify which skills are valued and where there are gaps.

2. Apply the VRIN framework to a product of your choice. Consider how they can retain their valuable, rare, inimitable or non-substitutable resources.

3. For an organisation of your choice create a digital business strategy.

4. Digital strategy is a waste of time as the environment changes too quickly. Discuss and justify your response.

SUMMARY

This chapter has explored:

- The components in a digital business strategy
- Different aspects of digital business capabilities
- The resource-based view and the VRIN framework
- Digital strategy frameworks

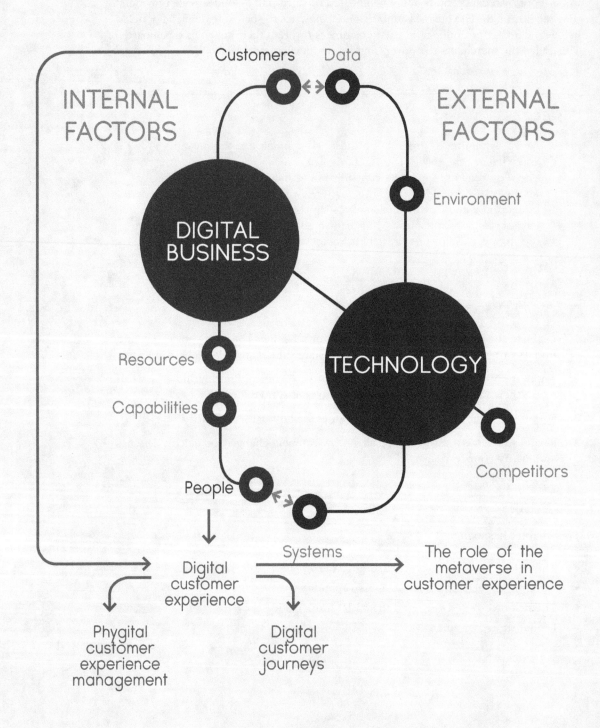

INTERNAL FACTORS

EXTERNAL FACTORS

Customers

Data

Environment

DIGITAL BUSINESS

TECHNOLOGY

Resources

Capabilities

Competitors

People

Systems

Digital customer experience

The role of the metaverse in customer experience

Phygital customer experience management

Digital customer journeys

11

DIGITAL CUSTOMER EXPERIENCE MANAGEMENT

Annmarie Hanlon and Graham Bell

LEARNING OUTCOMES

When you have read this chapter, you will be able to:

Understand the role of the metaverse in customer experience

Apply the phygital customer experience (PH-CX) framework

Analyse the role of social media in the digital customer experience

Evaluate the potential for chatbots

Create a customer journey map

PROFESSIONAL SKILLS

When you have worked through this chapter, you should be able to:

- Set the strategic direction for customer experience
- Provide direction and technical guidance in using AI and the metaverse

11.1 BACKGROUND TO DIGITAL CUSTOMER EXPERIENCE

Customer experience (CX) is considered a critical element in marketing management (Lemon & Verhoef, 2016). It involves different aspects of marketing, including levels of engagement, loyalty (Waqas et al., 2021) and satisfaction (Roy et al., 2022; Waqas et al., 2021). It's also about whether the consumption is **utilitarian or hedonic** (see Key Term). This means that it impacts on the competitiveness of a business (Becker & Jaakkola, 2020) and whether a customer intends to re-buy.

There are challenges with the concept of customer experience as it involves many elements. This is recognised in one definition: 'Customer Experience is comprised of the cognitive, emotional, physical, sensorial, and social elements that mark the customer's direct or indirect interaction with a (set of) market actor(s)' (De Keyser et al., 2015: 14). These elements contribute to different stages of the customer experience. For example, the customer experience may be more important at the start when a consumer is thinking about making a purchase (the consideration stage), especially where they are unaware of the brand. If they are aware of the brand, it may be after they've bought it (post-purchase) that the experience is more critical. Table 11.1 provides examples of the consideration and post-purchase stages in buying a laptop.

Table 11.1   Different elements in customer experience

Elements	What this means	Consideration stage	Post-purchase stage
Cognitive	A rational or **utilitarian** (see Key Term) approach	I need a new laptop because this one is broken and I have an assignment to submit next week	My new laptop is easy to use
Emotional	An emotional or **hedonistic** (see Key Term) response	I want a purple laptop as it makes me feel happy	I love my new purple laptop, I am so pleased I bought it
Physical	Physical enablers or limitations	The laptop I want is available for next day delivery	My laptop arrived the next day and I was using it within a couple of hours
Sensorial	The senses (see hear, smell, taste, touch)	The laptop I want is lightweight and the keyboard feels good to use	My laptop is easy to add to my bag and the keyboard feels great
Social	Responding to social or environmental contexts	All my friends have purple laptops	My friends love my new purple laptop, I will take a photo and share online

KEY TERMS   UTILITARIAN AND HEDONIC CONSUMPTION

Utilitarian consumption is buying something that is needed, such as water, a snack or a travel ticket. It has been described as the functional, instrumental and practical attributes of the item (Chitturi et al., 2008). Hedonic consumption is more about pleasure than need – something you want, rather than an essential item. Hirschman & Holbrook (1982: 92) described it as 'consumer behavior that relates to the multi-sensory, fantasy, and emotive aspects of one's experience with products'.

Activity 11.1   Apply customer experience elements

Using Table 11.1 as a framework, in groups, think about a recent purchase that went wrong. Discuss the situation and assess the consideration and the post-purchase stages. Explore whether this could have been improved and at which stage.

According to Becker & Jaakkola (2020), there are 2 main viewpoints around the consideration and post-purchase stages:

- CX is the response to *managerial stimuli* – that means customers reacting to brand names, packaging, advertising, pricing, which are all controlled by the business
- CX is the customer reaction to *consumption* – that means when the customer decides to use the item, which is controlled by the customer.

Digital CX situates the customer experience in a digital setting where responses to the managerial stimuli can be tested in real time and where the customer reaction to consumption is transparent and visible. One mistake and it's across social media.

This chapter will explore phygital customer experience management, then we will explore the elements in the digital customer experience and the role of the metaverse. Finally we shall examine digital customer journeys.

Smartphone Sixty Seconds® – Find managerial stimuli

- Take out your mobile phone and select your preferred social media platform.
- Scroll down until you find managerial stimuli such as an advert or brand message.
- What is the message and would the message encourage you to explore further? If yes why and if no why not?
- Compare your examples with classmates.

11.2 PHYGITAL CUSTOMER EXPERIENCE MANAGEMENT

The blurred boundaries where physical and digital meet are referred to as the *phygital*. Phygital is more than a range of channels for customers to discover goods, which we call omnichannel; instead it is an ecosystem that 'uses a combination of both physical elements and digital devices, platforms, technologies, extended realities, online platforms, and so forth to offer unique and immersive experiences' (Batat, 2022: 2). Phygital moves seamlessly between the physical and digital elements of all aspects of the customer experience, so there is no difference whether you buy online or in store.

Although phygital CX combines the physical and digital, these were separated when customers believed the 2 were not the same and offered different benefits. This was found in **webrooming and showrooming** (see Key Terms) where customers would take out their mobile phones in store to search online for better prices or faster delivery for the same products. In a phygital world, this would be encouraged and stores would provide the devices!

KEY TERMS   WEBROOMING AND SHOWROOMING

Webrooming is looking online to gather all the details and then purchasing offline at the store offering the best options. Showrooming involves visiting stores and checking out the products and returning home to buy online (Wolny & Charoensuksai, 2014).

Digital devices and technologies involved with the phygital customer experience include:

- Tablets and mobile apps – to facilitate 'smart shopping' and often found in retail stores, enabling customers to check whether a product is in stock or online
- Augmented reality – used in virtual fitting rooms where customers use their smartphones to see how a pair of shoes would look, or how clothing would fit, without trying on the items
- QR codes – to discover more about a single item which may be a product in store (e.g. pair of shoes) or a location (e.g. museum, outdoor event)
- Automatic checkouts – popular in supermarkets, with the aim of speeding up the process

Having understood more about the phygital customer experience, let's explore a framework to put this into context.

11.2.1 THE PHYGITAL CUSTOMER EXPERIENCE (PH-CX) FRAMEWORK

It can be difficult to know how the physical and digital connect and Professor Batat created a phygital customer experience framework to explain further. This framework provides an overview of the 3 main aspects: driving forces, connectors and pillars.

DRIVING FORCES

Driving forces is about the consumer and what they perceive they will gain from the purchase. This may bring extrinsic (external) or intrinsic (internal) values. Batat suggests that the extrinsic consumer value is where consumers evaluate economic and social factors or the **utilitarian** (see Key Term) aspects of the purchase, such as what does it cost, how well will it work for me and what will my friends think? The intrinsic consumer value is about the feelings from the consumption process, which Becker & Jaakkola (2020) also identified, and involves **hedonism** (see Key Term earlier) as consumers are seeking pleasure from the purchase (Batat, 2022). Or it may be for altruistic or ethical reasons, such as buying vintage clothing or recycled computer equipment to reduce waste.

CONNECTORS

In customer experience we often refer to a customer journey (see Section 11.5) and the different touchpoints that a consumer experiences during the purchase process. For example, this could be an email or social media post which prompts a visit to a website or a visit to a store. The in-store experience is another touchpoint and, depending on the instore experience, the purchase may go ahead – or not. Batat explains that connectors in the phygital customer experience framework are much more than touchpoints; they are about the *impact* of the interactions. The connectors are in 4 groups:

- Media – promotional messages or other managerial stimuli
- Digital – devices and technologies
- Physical – merchandising techniques, such as in-store personalisation
- Human – staff and employees who have contact with the customers

The connectors can provide a positive or negative CX, but they are all involved in the phygital CX. For this to be successful, the business needs to adopt new technology to integrate its systems and provide high levels of staff training.

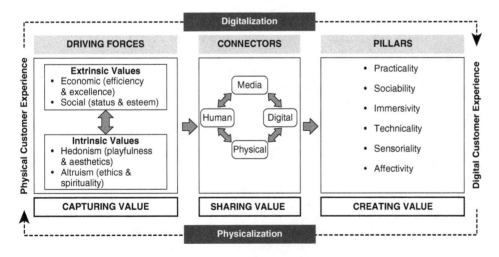

Figure 11.1   The phygital customer experience (PH-CX) framework

Source: Batat (2022: 12). Printed with permission of Taylor & Francis

PILLARS

The phygital CX is a holistic experience that includes 6 pillars which create the value. These pillars provide the customer with their utilitarian needs (practicality), which are easy to use (technicality), social interaction (sociability) and fun from the experience (immersivity) that impacts the senses (sensoriality) and the emotions (affectivity). Figure 11.1 shows the phygital customer experience (PH-CX) framework.

The phygital customer experience (PH-CX) framework demonstrates how the digital and physical elements are joined, to provide customers with the value they are seeking. This may seem like a long list of factors to achieve, but read Case Example 11.1 Lacoste Arena to see how this has been achieved.

CASE EXAMPLE 11.1   Lacoste Arena

Lacoste is an iconic French brand, founded by the tennis legend René Lacoste, an international champion 4 times and recognised as the world's best player in 1926–1927. The brand has a long heritage and a distinctive crocodile logo, representing the tennis star's nickname, with his tenacious approach to not giving up.

Nearly 100 years later, Lacoste has over 1,000 stores in nearly 100 countries and is the official sponsor of the Roland Garros tennis stadium in Paris. It employs 8,500 people worldwide and runs manufacturing facilities in France, Japan and Puerto Rico. Its polo shirts are known for their durability – you could say their tenacity! Lacoste's clothing ranges are subject to rigorous material testing, to ensure the colours won't fade after the first wash. This demonstrates that the functional aspect of the product is important to the company. As well as the practical side, the polo shirts are recognised which provides social interaction. The brand is working hard to improve its offer to customers and their website shows their focus on CX which they see are part of their brand consistency – delivering the same service across the world. To do this they have a dedicated training academy:

> The Group's Customer Experience Academy (CXA) promotes the "Lacoste attitude" across the globe, showcasing values, key products from seasonal collections, brand history and the latest news. The Crocodile has a reputation to live up to!

While many shops are closing down, Lacoste opened a megastore on the Champs-Élysées in the centre of Paris. At 17,200 square feet or nearly 1,600 square metres, that's equivalent to 80 student studio bedrooms! The megastore combines many digital elements to build on the experience. This includes:

- An in-store photo booth for customers to take photos and share on giant digital screens
- An app to find sports shoes to try on, so there is no need to wait for an assistant!
- Customisation kiosks which allow customers to select their preferred shirt, bag or shoes and personalise with their initials or other details
- The latest items of clothing which are displayed on a rotating carousel

By blending digital devices and technologies Lacoste has created much more than a retail environment; this is an experience, a fun day out to share with friends and family. This hedonic experience encourages customers to spend more time browsing, promote the store via social media posts and buy goods.

Case questions

- Many traditional shopping malls are closing or have empty stores. Are megastores like the Lacoste Arena a solution to encourage customers to shop in real life?
- The Lacoste Arena has carefully blended technology into the store. How can its phygital experience be developed further?
- What other stores are you aware of that offer a phygital customer experience?

11.3 DIGITAL CUSTOMER EXPERIENCE

Digital CX is no longer simply about visiting a website and buying online. As technology evolves, artificial intelligence (AI) is becoming the central hub within digital customer experience. With big data in **customer relationship management** systems (see Key Term in Chapter 1) AI can identify relevant social media posts and automate advertising responses, support the customer journey with augmented reality and embed brand messages in the right places within the metaverse. This means that the digital CX encompasses a wider set of digital tools and spaces, including:

- The role of social media
- Chatbots
- Voice technology
- Augmented reality
- The metaverse

The rest of this section will explore social media, chatbots, voice technology and augmented reality. Section 11.4 will examine the metaverse.

11.3.1 THE ROLE OF SOCIAL MEDIA

Social media is the facilitation of interactive, connected platforms at organisational, peer-to-peer and personal levels. While the social media platforms may change their names or launch new brands, the purpose is the same – connecting people and things to perform actions. These actions may be to send messages, ask questions, like brand posts, provide feedback or click to shop. Social media has a role in the digital customer experience as consumers may be involved in a conversation with friends, or looking through short videos and responding to managerial stimuli such as an advert or brand message (Becker & Jaakkola, 2020). Or consumers may be watching their favourite influencer showcasing a range of branded products, via a social media platform.

AI has been part of the digital customer experience in social media for many years. For example, businesses have been able to test which posts are most and least successful through basic AI. This includes identifying posts that gain more likes, shares or comments, or which posts lead to decisions such as making a purchase, downloading content or sharing data. This allows businesses to optimise posts in their marketing campaigns and use this knowledge when planning future campaigns.

Combining AI and CRM systems enables businesses to personalise marketing messages further (Libai et al., 2020). For example, customers who shop on Thursday lunchtimes may be sent an offer code or early access to new clothing. This rewards loyal customers and enables firms to measure the exact results from marketing campaigns. But it can work the other way too. Weak customers who frequently participate in **deshopping** (see Key Term in Chapter 3) could be excluded from targeted social media posts.

As the use of cookies to track customers declines (see Chapter 4), businesses need to encourage customers to provide a unique identifiable piece of data, such as their most-used email address or their mobile phone number. If the email or mobile phone number is contained in social media data, and also within the business CRM, it is easier to identify and target specific groups of customers with more relevant messages. This is where AI saves businesses time and money, removing the guesswork from marketing activities.

11.3.2 CHATBOTS

Chatbots were originally described as 'computer software employed a text-based dialogue process to imitate natural conversation' (Shaalan et al., 2022: 369). The first chatbot was called Eliza and aimed to respond like a psychotherapist, as the individual was encouraged to 'talk to it'. Chatbots have evolved and are better described as intelligent virtual assistants (IVAs). According to Shaalan et al. (2022), chatbots were originally intended as tools to carry out operational rather than customer-facing tasks, but their role has evolved as they have become part of the digital customer experience. They provide customer service by helping provide order updates, booking tickets and providing advice on purchases. Table 11.2 shows the different formats of chatbots based on the services provided.

Table 11.2   Chatbot formats

Type	What this means	Example
Template-based chatbots	They select responses from predefined templates but there is limited data based on keyword identification to provide simple responses	Often used for travel timetables, buses, trains and planes, where the responses are predictable
Corpus-based chatbots	Select responses from large databases and construct the results	Customer services chatbots: 'it looks like you need help with …'
Intent-based chatbots	They identify the action verbs (I want to **book, make** …') and provide responses and are linked to other systems	Widely used for task-oriented systems such as booking tickets, making reservations
Neural-based chatbots (RNN chatbots)	Recurrent Neural Network chatbots use a deep learning model dedicated to the handling of sequences	Apple's Siri and Google's voice searches use RNN as you might ask one question and then a supplementary question (what time does the movie start, can I book tickets)

Adapted from: Luo et al. (2022)

One of the best-known chatbots is ChatGPT, which has mastered responses that seem to be part of a real conversation (Taecharungroj, 2023). It claims it can 'admit its mistakes, challenge incorrect premises, and reject inappropriate requests' (OpenAI, 2022: 1). ChatGPT is trained to challenge mistaken beliefs (incorrect premises) so should reject hate speech or offensive text. Admitting errors is more straightforward; for example, when advised that some of the references provided were wrong, ChatGPT responds: 'I apologize if there were inaccuracies in the references I provided. My knowledge is based on information available up until September 2021, and I strive to provide accurate and reliable information. However, errors can occur, and information can change over time.'

An inappropriate request may be to ask 'Can you write my essay for me?, and the response from ChatGPT is: 'I can certainly help you with your essay by providing information, suggestions, and guidance on how to structure and write it, but I cannot write it for you. Writing an essay is a valuable skill, and it's important to learn and practice it yourself.'

The advantages of chatbots (Shaalan et al., 2022) include being cost effective as they are cheaper to manage than humans and provide effective communication as they can link one query to an earlier query, or find customers' details more quickly. However, the disadvantages (Shaalan et al., 2022) include user acceptance, which is a common theme in technology. Plus there are concerns about data and privacy. They are not yet an answer to all customer service issues as 'there is still a notable gap between customer expectation and chatbot performance' (Luo et al., 2022: 13).

Chatbots are generally considered to provide text rather than voice responses; however, as technology has evolved, chatbots as intelligent or digital virtual assistants now include natural spoken language. This is explored in the next section.

DIGITAL TOOL   Build a chatbot

Building a chatbot is complex. Intelliticks provides a simple way to start a chatbot. Registration is required and you'll need to verify your email address. It is not a complete chatbot, but shows the initial elements to consider.

- You can explore it here: intelliticks.com/registration

11.3.3 VOICE TECHNOLOGY

Voice technology has been part of the customer experience process for years. For example, its use with telephones and 'Interactive Voice Response (IVR) systems can respond to consumers' requests anytime and anywhere with synthetic or recorded voices. This type of interaction is, however, limited to specific options selected via the phone keypad ("to reach … press 1") or orally ("to reach … say …")' (Zoghaib, 2022: 394). As a customer service tool, voice technology has had received mixed responses (Zoghaib, 2022). In some cases voice customer services 'have positive effects on firm's competitiveness as well as on consumers' responses' (Zoghaib, 2022: 398). But in other situations, customers are unhappy with the lack of human contact.

Consumers are adopting voice technology (Aw et al., 2022). But there are barriers to adoption by businesses, including poor results, poor comprehension of responses and the costs involved (Statista, 2023a). However, artificial intelligence has enhanced voice technology as shown in Table 11.3.

Table 11.3   Definitions of key terminology

Term	Definition
Digital voice assistants (DVA)	"software applications based on Artificial Intelligence (AI), which communicate with people through natural, spoken language" (Ewers et al., 2020: 55)
Conversational agents	"physical or virtual autonomous technological entities that recognize and understand voice-based user requests in real time and communicate using natural language to accomplish a wide variety of tasks" (Fernandes & Oliveira, 2021: 181)
Smart voice interaction technologies	"internet-connected devices that, depending on their technical functionalities, incorporate some degree of autonomy, authority, and agency and allow for voice-based conversational interaction between consumers and technology, for instance, within the fixed contextual boundaries and domestic routines of consumer homes" (Foehr & Germelmann, 2020: 182)
Smart speaker	"a wireless device with artificial intelligence that can be activated through voice command" (Smith, 2020: 150)

Source: Tuzovic (2022: 530)

Although the market for digital voice assistants is growing, according to Tuzovic (2022: 531) it is 'dominated by four main players: Apple *Siri*, Amazon *Alexa/Echo*, Google *Assistant*, and Microsoft *Cortana*'. Voice assistants include more than smartphones and include smart speakers (your TV, Echo), smart mirrors and vehicles (Aw et al., 2022). Digital voice assistants are changing consumer consumption, in how they conduct research, purchase goods and connect with businesses (Aw et al., 2022).

DISCOVER MORE ON VOICE ASSISTANTS

Read 'Alexa, what's on my shopping list? Transforming customer experience with digital voice assistants' by Aw et al. (2022), published in *Technological Forecasting and Social Change*. This article explores the characteristics of voice assistants and adoption by consumers.

Activity 11.2   Assess digital technology or customer experience

Assess the potential for social media, chatbots and voice technology to provide customer services for a sports or fashion organisation. Consider how these technologies could enhance the digital customer experience and how they would be integrated within the organisation.

11.3.4 AUGMENTED REALITY

Augmented reality (AR) 'supplements reality, rather than completely replacing it' (Azuma, 1997: 356). Whether as an overlay or filter, AR provides rich and new ways to engage with customers (Devagiri et al., 2022) and can enhance the customer experience.

According to Rauschnabe et al. (2022: 1140) there are 4 main reasons why businesses use AR, which they describe as the 'BICK four framework'. This is shown in Table 11.4.

Table 11.4 The BICK four framework

BICK framework elements	What this means	Example
Branding (the business)	<ul><li>Build brand awareness</li><li>Strengthen brand image</li><li>Increase employer attractiveness</li><li>Reach new target groups with our brand</li><li>Present our offerings</li></ul>	Businesses such as AMD computer chips and Beats earbuds promote their brand in AR games
Inspiring (customers)	<ul><li>Inspire customers</li><li>Generate customer needs</li></ul>	Cosmetics brands such as Sephora and Esteé Lauder allow customers to try out make up in AR before deciding to buy
Convincing (customers)	<ul><li>Generate buying interest</li><li>Enforce willingness to pay</li><li>Generate sales</li><li>Promote cross-selling/upselling</li></ul>	Nike has stores within games where customers can buy goods Ariane Grande sold virtual goods in an online concert with Fortnite
Keeping (customers)	<ul><li>Increase customer loyalty.</li><li>Improve customer service (after service)</li><li>Offer additional services to products</li><li>Offer customers added value through AR content</li><li>Keep customers in the loop (top of mind)</li></ul>	The LEGO® App allows customers to enhance their use of LEGO

Adapted from: Rauschnabe et al. (2022)

AR is involved with many aspects of the customer experience, from making customers aware of the brand, to inspiring and suggesting ideas, to convincing or persuading customers to make a decision and finally keeping customers so they recommend. This is a growing area and the global augmented reality market size was 'estimated at US$40.12 billion in 2022 and is predicted to hit around US$1,188.98 billion by 2032' (Precedence Research, 2023: 1).

> ### DISCOVER MORE ON AUGMENTED REALITY IN MARKETING
>
> Read 'What is augmented reality marketing? Its definition, complexity, and future' by Rauschnabe and colleagues (2022) published in the *Journal of Business Research*. This article explains more about the BICK framework and provides examples of how AR is used in marketing.

11.4 THE ROLE OF THE METAVERSE IN CUSTOMER EXPERIENCE

The metaverse was once considered to be exclusive for gamers, with big headsets and big screens. As headsets have become cheaper and more widely used, the metaverse has become part of the digital customer experience. For example, many people have participated in concerts in the Metaverse, where from their own homes they have been part of a worldwide event. Other organisations use the metaverse for advertising and brand promotion. For example, Sephora (cosmetics) has used adverts in the Second Life game and Gucci (luxury goods) has held virtual fashion shows in the game Roblox. More traditional businesses such as banks are exploring providing alternative customer service channels through the metaverse. For example the Union Bank of India has created its Uni-Verse, a customer experience lounge in this virtual world.

As well as a B2C service, many manufacturing companies are creating their own metaverse. They are building **digital twins** (see Key Term). These digital twins allow engineers and product developers to walk around the factory or to get inside a machine and understand why an issue may have arisen, such as a fault or problem in the system, and then test effective solutions. This takes managing the customer experience to a new level. Digital twins are also used by government to replicate buildings and cities such as Helsinki and Singapore.

KEY TERM   DIGITAL TWIN

A digital twin is a copy or model which represents the object in accurate detail. This can be a replica of a physical object such as a machine in a factory, a building or an entire factory. Having a digital twin means that when there are challenges, they can be tested on the digital twin first, to see if it works. For example, Microsoft has made digital twins of its cloud storage facilities. So if there is a problem on one server, they can check on the twin.

ETHICAL INSIGHTS   Evil twins

Digital twins are useful replicas that enable users to practise and make assessments virtually before taking action in real life. However, time has demonstrated that where new technology provides an upside, there can be a downside too.

An evil twin is a malicious virtual software model of a digital twin (Kasten, 2023). Evil twins could be used to harm people or infrastructure and are a growing concern. For example, a digital twin of a city includes data about all the essential services in the city such as water supply, energy hubs and communication networks. It shows how different buildings connect to each other, the traffic routes through the city, as well as the health and education services. Hackers could create evil twins which could access and change the data. This could result in chaos for a city, with water, power supplies or communications being disrupted. For hackers to gain access, they may impersonate a well-known individual in a city. To counter this in the USA, the Department of Defense (2022) has adopted a Zero Trust policy. This means that employees should 'never trust, always verify' (Department of Defense, 2022: ii). To support the zero-trust approach, they have shared their strategy document which explains that they adopt 'multi-factor authentication, micro-segmentation, advanced encryption, endpoint security, analytics, and robust auditing' (Department of Defense, 2022: iv). They encourage organisations to adopt the same levels of security and a zero-trust mindset, questioning and verifying all requests for access to data.

- In addition to zero trust policies, what steps can be taken to guard against evil twins gaining access to digital twins?
- How did we reach Zero Trust and what does this mean to you?
- 'Evil twins' sounds like science fiction – what other aspects of science fiction have become real and how has this changed how you live or work?

As a virtual world accessed via headsets, the metaverse was initially perceived as a tool for getting things done in a way that 'complement(ed) the real world' (Dwivedi et al., 2022: 5). One use of the metaverse is in healthcare where surgeons can practise specific operations which could be fatal if they went wrong. A virtual patient in the metaverse makes it easier for surgeons to see where there could be mistakes and how these could be avoided. We might not consider patients to be customers, but this healthcare metaverse is a training space that results in a more positive experience for everyone involved.

DISCOVER MORE ON THE METAVERSE

Read 'Metaverse beyond the hype: Multidisciplinary perspectives on emerging challenges, opportunities, and agenda for research, practice and policy' by Dwivedi et al. (2022), published in the *International Journal of Information Management*. This is an extended article by many academics which examines many different aspects of the metaverse.

CASE EXAMPLE 11.2   Accenture's Nth Floor

When the global pandemic struck, Accenture, a global professional services and consulting company, had to find new ways to help its staff and clients communicate and collaborate. With over 500,000 employees globally and 9,000 clients (representing some of the largest companies worldwide), Accenture was under pressure to find ways to enable its teams to function in what had become a totally digital environment almost overnight.

Due to a strong future vision and collaboration between Accenture and Microsoft, a metaverse environment called the 'Nth Floor' had been developed. Jason Warnke, Senior

(Continued)

Managing Director at Accenture, recognised the opportunity and commented, 'physical and virtual experiences will co-exist in future ways of working, Accenture is moving boldly into the metaverse, to create workplace experiences, where our people can participate, contribute and feel like they belong, regardless of where they work' (Warnke, 2022: 1). This move towards phygital provides a better digital staff and client experience. The Nth Floor is a digital twin that looks and feels like Accenture offices. It was possible due to advancements in virtual reality software, combined with greater affordability and better hardware availability.

Before bringing customers into the Nth Floor, Accenture used its metaverse for new employees. By creating digital twins of key offices around the world, Accenture can introduce new team members to each other in familiar surroundings.

To complement the digital twins an exclusive metaverse location 'One Accenture Park' was created. This digital space was designed for new employees to begin their professional careers with the organisation. One Accenture Park provides opportunities for developing relationships and collaborating with colleagues. Allowing staff members to attend training sessions and collaborate on company projects are some examples of how the Nth Floor metaverse has modified interactions.

Another benefit of the Nth Floor is that it provides a platform to create immersive and engaging virtual events. This is an upgrade from standard style videoconference calls, as the metaverse makes attending events such as virtual presentations more engaging for clients. By creating a unique metaverse-based experience Accenture has provided its globally based workforce and customers with innovative and immersive opportunities to connect and collaborate.

Case questions

- Accenture is addressing the phygital setting of work, yet other firms want employees to return to their offices. How will Accenture maintain the engagement and benefits from the Nth Floor in the longer term?
- New employees are taken through an induction programme using the Nth Floor. Do you feel this virtual onboarding process helps or hinders new staff?
- What other benefits can a digital twin of key offices provide?

11.5 DIGITAL CUSTOMER JOURNEYS

Digital CX is part of a wider customer journey. A customer journey is the process or steps that a customer takes from considering to buying a product or service. Each step in the journey is recognised as a touchpoint. For example, in downloading an app, the first touchpoint may be visiting the app store to find the app. The second touchpoint may be reading reviews and the next is making the download. In the next touchpoint the app is opened and the customer decides whether to delete or keep the app. In another example, you might book a hotel room online – that's the first touchpoint. At each touchpoint the customer makes a cognitive, affective and sensory evaluation (Kranzbühler et al., 2018) and continues or abandons the journey.

Smartphone Sixty Seconds® – Search for customer journey maps

- Take out your mobile phone and search for 'customer journey maps' in images.
- Look at several customer journey maps and assess the differences.
- What are the key steps or stages in the journey?
- What information is needed to create a customer journey map?

Customer journeys are also known as shopper and buyer journeys. Originally considered as a linear process, research has shown that it can move forwards and backwards several times. The journey may take seconds, minutes, hours or more – depending on the cost of the item and the context. For example, a customer journey to buy a mobile phone may take a few weeks. You may check online review sites, speak to friends and then decide when and where to make the purchase.

11.5.1 BUSINESS-TO-BUSINESS CUSTOMER JOURNEYS

Business-to-business (B2B) journeys can take months – or years. For example, consider the process involved in a business deciding to invest in a new IT system.

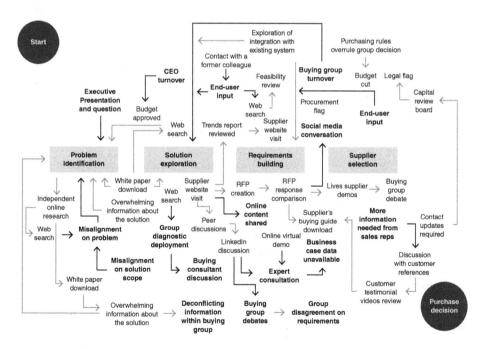

Figure 11.2 The business-to-business buying journey

Source: Adamson (2019). Printed with permission of Gartner

They need to understand what functions are required from the system, the numbers of users and where they are based (all in the office, all working from home or hybrid). This is not a quick decision. Plus, the business may have an arrangement in place with an existing firm, so is unable to switch suppliers until the contract is ended. IT contracts are often in place for 2 or 3 years, so this adds to the time involved.

As buying goods in a business context involves more investment, the process involves more information and research. Gartner, the consulting firm, has conducted research to explore a business-to-business buying journey. This involves multiple steps from online searching, reading material and conversations with colleagues. As the buying group becomes more informed, a request for proposal (RFP) can be created which is shared with suppliers, in order to provide a quote. Figure 11.2 shows an example of a business-to-business buying journey.

11.5.2 SOCIAL CUSTOMER JOURNEYS

B2C customer journeys were considered to be a solitary experience where the customer travelled alone. Yet the introduction of social media has opened the journey to a wider group. This means that customers seek recommendations through:

- Social media – guidance from those well known to the individual, for example friends and family
- Blogging sites – guidance from those not known to the individual such as those in similar situations
- Expert sites – guidance from those known to the individual, for example expert bloggers
- Professional social media – guidance from those partly known to the individual, for example colleagues in another departments

According to Hamilton et al. (2021: 69), customer journeys are no longer isolated experiences: individuals take the journeys with their friends or 'traveling companions' as we seek opinions and guidance before making the purchase.

The steps seem linear, but loop around with other people – travelling companions, at different stages. These travelling companies provide recommendations or guidance. At the start, the customer was motivated to buy something and searched for information, evaluated the options, made a decision, and decided they were satisfied and shared the results. The social customer journey is shown in Figure 11.3.

Customer journeys are dynamic and include many different environments (Hoyer et al., 2020), from traditional to phygital, operating across social media and within the metaverse.

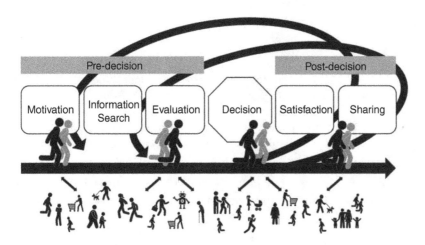

Figure 11.3 The social customer journey

Source: Hamilton et al. (2021)

DIGITAL TOOL   Figma

Customer journey mapping usually takes place with teams of people adding their thoughts and evidence. Figma is an online design tool and enables collaborators to work together. It includes a range of templates, including customer journey mapping. Registration may be required.

- You can explore it here: figma.com/templates/customer-journey-mapping

Activity 11.3   Create a customer journey map

Thinking of yourself as a customer, create a customer journey map for a recent purchase. Identify which 'companions' were involved on the journey and the time it took from start to finish. You could create the map using online software or pieces of paper.

JOURNAL OF NOTE

The *Journal of Strategic Marketing* is the 'interface between marketing and strategic management'. It explores marketing philosophy and marketing-led strategic change with many articles on the customer experience.

CASE STUDY

PAYPAL – THE OMNICHANNEL CHECKOUT EXPERIENCE

PayPal's goal is to 'deliver seamless and trusted payment experiences for our customers' (PayPal, 2023a: 101). This is not without challenges as PayPal has over 425 million customers. As an online payment system, its customers are 2-sided. On one side are the merchants providing the goods and on the other are the consumers making the purchases. To ensure that both sides work effectively the process must be seamless; there should be no gaps in service on either side.

Customer experience is important to PayPal and customer satisfaction metrics are part of the performance-based reward system. As a result, PayPal listens to what customers value and noted that (PayPal Editorial Staff, 2022: 1):

> 47% of PayPal customers ranked experiences as one of their top 10 values. Over one-third of respondents had considered 'breaking up' with a brand, not because of their products or services, but because of what they perceived to be a poor customer experience. 58% of surveyed consumers said customer experience is one of the most important factors when making a purchase decision.

This is enhanced by a long-standing leadership principle which includes 'be a customer champion', which means 'giving consumers choice … to pay how and where they want, in new ways' (Shulman, 2016: 1). To strengthen the Customer Champion strategy PayPal launched a 'Customer Immersion Experience (Immerse), designed to reinforce our Customer Champion strategy among Director + employees through live side-by-side experiences with our customer service operations team' (PayPal, 2021: 12).

One way to ensure there are no gaps in service is through 'better checkout experiences' (PayPal, 2023a: 3). This has been achieved by improving the digital wallet, as consumers want to access a payment system regardless of where they are. This needs to be simple and work at any time on any device and with any payment form. Sometimes consumers might want to take credit options (buy now, pay later) or send money to friends or family.

Digital wallets have become critical as a payment method. According to PayPal (PayPal Editorial Staff, 2023: 1), these include:

- Apple Pay is built into Apple Wallet and is available on eligible Apple devices, including Mac computers, iPhones, iPads and the Apple Watches
- Google Pay is the in-built digital wallet for Android OS devices, which is the dominant OS for Google devices
- Samsung Pay is the in-built digital wallet for Samsung devices, which is one of the most popular manufacturers of smartphones and wearables

PayPal has observed 'nearly a third of global point-of-scale (POS) transactions took place through a digital wallet in 2021, accounting for nearly half of global e-commerce transaction value' (PayPal Editorial Staff, 2023: 1). But sometimes there are challenges for consumers, such as:

- Payment declined
- Payment cannot be processed
- Payment failed

PayPal provides ready-made answers to these questions online for customers to help them solve these issues.

At the same time, the merchants need the checkout systems to work, and need to be protected against fraud. For merchants, PayPal's seamless service means accepting all types of credit or debit cards, payment via digital wallets and facilitating credit services. PayPal adds value for their merchants and helps them grow by providing insights, based on customer data, that identify potential opportunities; for example, upselling other products, targeting consumers in the geographical area or offering other products. PayPal also offers 'easier exchanges and returns, to help merchants drive increased conversion through higher consumer engagement' (PayPal, 2023a: 3). This is part of its seamless customer experience.

To encourage a wide range of merchants, including well-known brands, to adopt PayPal, the business also offers 'branded checkout' options (PayPal, 2023a: iii). This ensures the checkout process feels like part of the brand website, rather than moving backwards and forwards to PayPal.

CASE QUESTIONS

- PayPal believes that customer experience is the main reason why consumers remain loyal to a business. To what extent do you agree or disagree with this and why? What other factors may contribute to customer loyalty?
- What challenges might PayPal face when trying to keep both consumers and merchants happy?
- PayPal has championed digital wallets for a seamless checkout experience. What challenges exist with a reliance on digital payment systems?

FURTHER EXERCISES

1. Evaluate the potential for chatbots in a sports or food business. Identify the types of questions which may be asked, the required responses and the benefits of the chatbot for the business.

2. Apply the phygital customer experience (PH-CX) framework to an organisation of your choice. Identify the driving forces behind the connectors and pillars.

3. For an organisation of your choice analyse the role of social media in digital customer experience.

4. The phygital customer experience is only available from larger stores and means smaller stores will eventually close. Discuss and justify your response.

(Continued)

SUMMARY

This chapter has explored:

- The different elements in digital customer experience
- Phygital customer experience management
- The role of the metaverse in customer experience
- Digital customer journeys

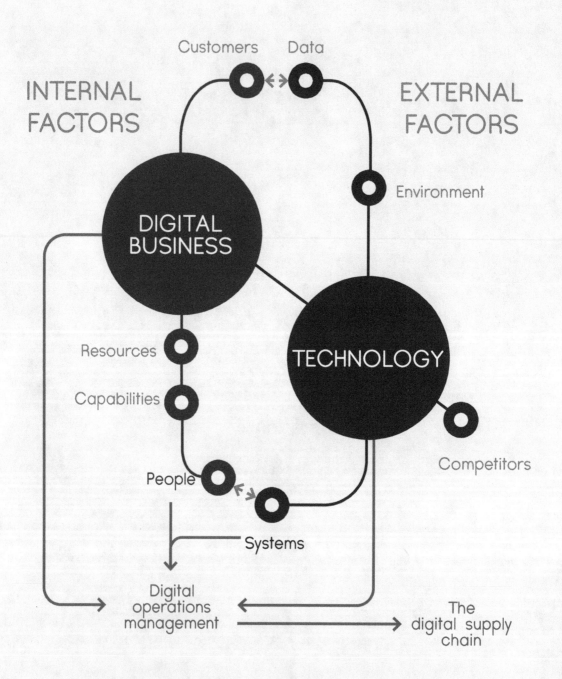

12

DIGITAL OPERATIONS MANAGEMENT

LEARNING OUTCOMES

When you have read this chapter, you will be able to:

Understand digital operations management

Apply the virtual value chain

Analyse digital operations

Evaluate the application of cobots

Create a supply chain map

PROFESSIONAL SKILLS

When you have worked through this chapter, you should be able to:

- Assess key issues in supply chain management
- Identify, recognise and understand internal and external factors that may impact future operations

12.1 INTRODUCTION TO DIGITAL OPERATIONS MANAGEMENT

Operations management is about managing inputs and outputs. Inputs may be raw materials (e.g. steel) or unstructured data (e.g. social media feedback), and outputs may be finished goods (e.g. cars) or ordered information (e.g. datasets). At a basic level, operations management involves:

- Process – joining up the inputs and outputs, fulfilling requests and orders
- Planning and control – ensuring the physical layout of the facility is efficient and effective, plus organising inventory is where it is needed, when it is needed and that it is of the right quality
- People – who is needed to deliver the inputs and outputs, and when
- Strategy and measures – an overall plan to make it happen, which is reviewed against agreed metrics

Historically operations management was about manufacturing, although this extends to services that require the same systems. For example, the hospitality sector is all about service, whether in a hotel, a restaurant or a destination. In this case the inputs are the staff and the outputs are happy customers sharing great feedback. Digital operations is using technology to adapt or enhance a business and its operations (Holopainen et al., 2022).

The greatest change in operations management has been the introduction of **Industry 4.0** (see Chapters 7 and 8). Industry 4.0 enabled many operations processes to be digitised and facilitated the **Internet of Things** (see Key Term). These connected devices provide smarter operations systems.

KEY TERM   INTERNET OF THINGS

The Internet of Things (IoT) 'is used as an umbrella keyword for covering various aspects related to the extension of the Internet and the Web into the physical realm, by means of the widespread deployment of spatially distributed devices with embedded identification, sensing and/or actuation capabilities' (Miorandi et al., 2012: 1497). IoT means that any device with smart components (such as sensors, RFID) and connectivity (such as Wi-Fi enabled) can be linked. The devices are often referred to as smart devices, operating in smart systems.

This chapter looks at how technology has changed operations management, rather than covering the entire subject (see Discover More: **On Operations Management**), and the key issues for business.

> ### DISCOVER MORE ON OPERATIONS MANAGEMENT
>
> Read the latest edition of *Operations Management* by Nigel Slack, Alistair Brandon-Jones & Nicola Burgess, published by Pearson, or the latest edition of *Operations Management, Managing Global Supply Chains* by Ray R. Venkataraman and Jeffrey K. Pinto, published by Sage.

12.2 DIGITAL OPERATIONS MANAGEMENT TOOLS

Digital operations management tools range from process software such as MRP, ERP and iBPM systems, to planning and control systems such as CAD, CIM, RFID, IoT and people tools – or robots. These are explained in Table 12.1 with examples and the challenges involved.

Table 12.1 Digital operations management tools

Tools	What this means	Example	Challenges
Material requirements planning (MRP) systems	MRP systems are used to identify the raw materials or other components are needed in the manufacturing process and may automate order placing to ensure they arrive on time	Manufacturing a smartphone needs 100s of parts from many different countries and MRP systems can identify what is needed and when	MRP systems vary in capability and cost as some provide an integrated solution across the entire factory, others focus on production only
Computer-aided design (CAD) systems	Using computers to create designs, instead of pen and paper	CAD systems are used to design smartphones, smart watches, cars and houses as the drawings can be stored, amended and shared	Not all CAD designs are easy to share as the recipient may need the same software
Computer-integrated manufacturing (CIM) systems	Using computers to control the production process which may involve design, optimisation of materials, manufacturing and assembly	Often used in automotive production where the car chassis moves around the production line and is built piece by piece	If one piece is missing or fails the quality control process, the entire system may be stopped which causes delays
Enterprise resource planning (ERP) systems	ERP systems integrate all aspects of planning in an organisation, from the MRP to people and other processes that need planning	Hotel chains use ERP systems to plan who and what is needed when and where	The planning systems require data from people to be entered accurately so any errors result in big mistakes
Intelligent business process management (iBPM) systems	Business process management systems model and analyse what is needed to achieve the business goals and iBPM uses artificial intelligence such as machine learning	Used in many sectors including healthcare where iBPM systems can automate repetitive tasks, such as securely collecting and filing forms with patient information and respond to requests for healthcare	All clinical users need to update patient appointments using the same system or the records will be incomplete

(Continued)

Table 12.1   (Continued)

Tools	What this means	Example	Challenges
Radio-frequency identification (RFID)	RFID involves tags which are attached to an item and readers which can see where they are	Widely used in many sectors such as Amazon self-service stores which can assess when goods are taken off the shelves, placed into baskets and leave the store	In manufacturing, 2 tags could collide, resulting in the wrong information being read, and RFID focuses on short-range tracking
Artificial intelligence (AI)/advanced analytics	AI provides machine learning as processes can be optimised based on past experience	Intel (the computer chip maker) uses AI to improve its manufacturing processes which means speeding up production with fewer errors	AI can be costly to introduce to a business and can be subject to cyberattacks
Internet of Things (IoT) and Big Data	IoT devices have embedded sensors where all the elements in the supply chain can be connected and visible on a dashboard; this feeds into big data to show where there may be issues to be resolved	Smart speakers are IoT devices, as are **digital twins** (see Chapter 11)	If the internet stops working it is impossible to see the IoT devices
Advanced self-guided robotics	Robots or **cobots** (see Key Term) which operate independently on the factory floor	Many factories and warehouses use robots, from Samsung when building washing machines, to Amazon distribution hubs	The biggest challenge is the high cost to adopt robotics and acceptance by workers

Many of the digital tools have been available for several years – such as MRP systems – but technology has made these easier to use and more affordable for smaller businesses. Some of these tools are in our daily lives, such as tags – we can use these to find luggage at airports, or find where a car has been parked, or even track a family member!

KEY TERM   COBOTS

Cobots are collaborative robots or 'the robots which are specifically made for working along with the people in the open environment' (Gupta et al., 2022: 195). Examples are warehouse cobots picking items and delivering to human 'colleagues', and healthcare robots such as Moxi (see diligentrobots.com/moxi) which collects samples and delivers supplies to enable healthcare workers to focus on patient care.

Activity 12.1   Evaluate the application of cobots

In groups evaluate how cobots could be used to streamline a process at your university. Consider the advantages and disadvantages, as well as any challenges they may bring. Make recommendations to introduce cobots in the next 12 months.

DIGITAL TOOL   Visualcapitalist.com

VisualCapitalist shares infographics on many topics, such as technology and smartphones, and this includes sharing how many parts there are in an iPhone and the countries where these are manufactured.

- You can explore it here: visualcapitalist.com/every-single-part-inside-iphone

Improved technology has created a significant difference in the relationship between the human operators and the tools used, as the roles have been reversed. From the 1970s to 2015 the tools provided support for the humans, but as the technology has evolved, humans are supporting the digital tools. For example, early robots were programmed and needed to be 'fed' the raw materials. In an automotive factory, the robots would be loaded with rivets to fix pieces of the engine together. Advanced robotics means the robots know when their supplies are running low, and they can either collect them or command another robot to bring supplies. Table 12.2 shows the digital evolution in operations management.

Table 12.2   Digital evolution in operations management (OM)

	1970–1995	1995–2015	2015 onwards
Role of digital technology	Digital tools provide functional support for humans in OM	Digital tools provide process-wide support for humans in OM	Humans provide support for digital tools in OM
Typical technologies	• Material requirements planning (MRP) • Computer-aided design (CAD) • Computer-integrated manufacturing (CIM)	• Enterprise resource planning (ERP) • Intelligent business process management (iBPM) • Radio-frequency identification (RFID)	• Artificial intelligence (AI)/advanced analytics • Internet of Things (IoT) and Big Data • Advanced self-guided robotics
Genre of technology	Standalone tools to aid in function-specific information access	Integrated tools for OM across business functions and supply chain entities	Autonomous tools to automate OM decision making

Source: Angelopoulos et al. (2023: 878). Printed with permission of John Wiley

DISCOVER MORE ON DIGITAL OPERATIONS MANAGEMENT

Read 'Digital transformation in operations management: Fundamental change through agency reversal' by Angelopoulos et al. (2023), published in the *Journal of Operations Management*. This is an extended article by many academics which examines many different aspects of the metaverse.

12.2.1 ADVANCED ROBOTICS

Another major change in digital operations management is the use and development of robots. According to the International Federation of Robotics (IFR Press Room, 2023) over 500,000 industrial robots were installed in 2022 and the market is expected to grow to over 700,000 a year by 2026. However, moving from a manual to a robotic production line is a major investment. A single robotic arm which performs an assembly task such as on an iPhone production line could cost up to US$400,000 each and many would be needed. Yet autonomous mobile robots (AMRs), which can move around a warehouse selecting goods and bringing them to the despatch area, can cost $30,000 each.

Robots are moving into every part of our lives. For example, surgical robots are used in healthcare, such as hip and knee replacements. The surgeons working with them may act in a supervisory capacity and they can also be used as teaching tools. Robots are in business and education, with Pepper, the humanoid robot, being widely used. The company's website notes, 'Pepper is the world's first social humanoid robot able to recognize faces and basic human emotions. Pepper was optimized for human interaction and is able to engage with people through conversation and his touch screen' (Aldebaran, 2023: 1). Pepper helps in schools to support teachers and acts as a concierge in offices providing people with information such as directions. In a domestic setting, robots such as self-driving (robotic) cars, automatic lawnmowers, vacuum cleaners, security cameras are widely available – at a price!

The main advantages of using advanced robotics are reduced labour costs, fewer accidents at work, fewer workers with musculoskeletal disorders (neck, back and shoulder injuries), lower absenteeism and greater efficiency as robots don't stop for a coffee break or take holidays (Jacob et al., 2023). The downsides are the initial investment required and acceptance by users (see technology acceptance model in Chapter 6). User acceptance raised concerns by workers, including psychological stress and the idea of working with robots, who won't have conversations about the latest football matches. There were also worries about job losses and the loss of autonomy or personal independence (Jacob et al., 2023).

Looking at acceptance within consumers, Song & Kim (2022: 489) have explored Retail Service Robots (RSR), which are 'humanoid robots that use AI service automation to provide customized shopping assistance'. Their research found that RSRs are accepted when considered useful. They also identified that as robots lack natural language and may not be able to respond to all consumer queries, this reduces the benefit. Plus, their appearance can also cause anxiety which may be why more humanlike robots are being created (Song & Kim, 2022). These examples show the need to assess the introduction of new technology, which could be achieved using the technology acceptance model (see Chapter 6).

But robots are only one of the tools used in digital operations. Sometimes, it just takes an app, as Case Example 12.1 explains.

CASE EXAMPLE 12.1   Wasoko

The African continent has over 2.5 million small shops which consumers use to buy over 70% of their food and beverages (Ivers et al., 2022: 1). The challenge of the small stores is getting goods delivered when they are needed, which is being addressed by Wasoko.

Launched in 2016 as Sokowatch and rebranded to Wasoko in 2022 (Kene-Okafor, 2022), the name means 'people of the market' in Swahili and reflects how Wasoko is acting as a wholesaler – or market – for small shops. Wasoko has over 1,000 employees and operates across East Africa. The business has 'delivered 2.5 million orders to more than 50,000 active retail customers in its network' by applying digital operations. The goods delivered include everything you may find in a larger supermarket, such as food cupboard items (tinned goods), baking goods (oil, flour, sugar), fruit and vegetables, and home care (cleaning, laundry and personal items). Wasoko has digitised the supply chain for these small shops. Previously shopkeepers might have had to visit several wholesalers to buy the goods and transport back to their shops. As a digital wholesaler Wasoko also addressed the challenge of how long the goods could taker to arrive. They have introduced delivery of goods on the same day.

The user journey has been simplified as customers simply log on to the app, view the products and check the prices and then place their order. This has removed the need for multiple shopkeepers visiting multiple wholesalers and waiting for different deliveries to arrive, which is neither efficient nor climate friendly. Plus, Wasoko uses artificial intelligence to optimise its logistics to ensure greater sustainability with its deliveries.

Research by the Boston Consulting Group has found that 'The proprietors of traditional African retailers are generally young and educated' (Ivers et al., 2022: 1). Wasoko continues to innovate and understand its market. For example, as access to formal credit for small businesses remains a challenge (GeoPoll Africa 118 and the African Talent Company, 2023: 14), Wasoko has introduced buy now, pay later (see Chapter 4) for the shopkeepers 'who need working capital to order more goods' (Kene-Okafor, 2022: 1).

Wasoko has gained much attention as a tech start-up in a novel area and has raised over $125 million in venture capital funding (Kene-Okafor, 2022). Originally the business had a back-end focus as a distributor, but soon realised this model did not work for the customer base. The move to the front-end as a wholesaler has seen the development of an app so that shopkeepers can order and get same day delivery. This addresses a market need, as The Africa MSME Pulse Survey Report 2023 notes that 64% of businesses use 'mobile apps for at least some business functions' (GeoPoll Africa 118 and the African Talent Company, 2023: 11).

Case questions

- Wasoko has added a level of digital operations management for shopkeepers across Africa – what would be the next step to digitalise more of their operations?
- Wasoko uses artificial intelligence to map their delivery routes. How else can AI help Wasoko?
- User acceptance of the app has been high. Why is this? Where would the business encounter more challenges?

12.2.2 UNMANNED AERIAL VEHICLES – DRONES

According to Akbari & Hopkins (2022: 693), 'Drones were originally designed for military purposes but have emerged as a prospective solution to supply chain challenges such as urban parcel delivery, stockpiling, surveillance, inspection vehicle, traffic congestion, and pollution'. Commercial drones are already used in warehouses to move goods around. They have been considered a cost-effective and more sustainable solution for **last-mile delivery** (see Key Term), to replace trucks. But the type and use of drones varies based on the location and need (Eskandaripour & Boldsaikhan, 2023). Table 12.3 shows the different types of drones and examples of application.

Table 12.3 Types of drones and examples of application

Types of drones	Advantages and disadvantages	Examples of application
Single-rotor helicopter (looks like a small helicopter)	• Strong and durable • Useful hover features so they can deliver goods • Complex and need regular maintenance	Can carry larger packages and are often used to deliver humanitarian aid (medicines) in disaster zones and hard-to-reach places
Multi-rotor	• Short flight times • Good camera control • Works well in small areas	Aerial photography and surveying areas such as checking the state of a roof or difficult-to-access buildings
Fixed-wing (looks like a small aeroplane)	• Fast and can cover a large area • Significant training needed • Significant training needed	Aerial photography, mapping and surveying larger areas such as power-line inspection
Fixed-wing hybrid VTOL (Vertical Take-Off and Landing)	• Long flight time • Hovering can be a challenge • Still in development	Many commercial uses including agriculture monitoring to provide insights into crops and vegetation, as well as ecommerce package delivery by Amazon and Walmart

> **KEY TERM** LAST-MILE DELIVERY
>
> Last-mile delivery is the expression used to describe the final step in the supply chain, where the goods are taken from the warehouse or store and delivered to the end customer. The final distance may be less than a mile, or much more in rural settings. This is why parcel lockers and central delivery hubs are popular as they enable many parcels to be delivered to a single location, reducing carbon emissions.

Table 12.3 shows the disadvantages, yet many of these will be addressed as drone technology improves. For example, challenges include swapping batteries to extend distance capability, but the introduction of drone charging stations may reduce this. Another issue is acceptance in society. Yet in cases such as search and rescue operations, where it is too dangerous to send people, drones provide a useful solution and are soon accepted.

The biggest hurdle is government permission to use commercial drones in our towns and cities. This is because, similar to AI, drone technology was developed before the usage guidance was in place. As a result many countries have imposed strict conditions on drone application, as it could interfere with commercial air traffic and cause major accidents. For example, Amazon launched Prime Air (Amazon, 2022) intending to use fixed-wing hybrid VTOL drones to deliver parcels for the last mile. They selected 2 locations (California and Texas), flying over private land. But Prime Air was stopped by the Federal Aviation Authority due to permissions needed to fly over public areas such as roads. In the future, increased awareness about sustainability and our environment may facilitate the use of drones, in e-commerce operations management.

DISCOVER MORE ON DRONES AND LAST-MILE DELIVERY

Read 'Last-mile drone delivery: Past, present, and future' by Eskandaripour & Boldsaikhan (2023), published in *Drones*. This article provides background to the development of drones, their usage and potential opportunities.

Activity 12.2   Create solutions for last-mile delivery

Last-mile delivery can be the most expensive and least sustainable part of the supply chain. While drones are still being approved for last-mile delivery, parcel lockers are available. Create a campaign to encourage consumers to use single locations such as parcel lockers or central delivery hubs.

12.3 THE DIGITAL SUPPLY CHAIN

The digital supply chain encompasses the steps or processes involved in producing and distributing goods. This is complex; as Shafiq et al. (2020: 1) observed: 'supply chains have increasingly become more complex, multi-tiered, and geographically spread'. This is because it involves moving goods from multiple countries at different stages of production and at different times when needed. For example, smartphones contain over 1,000 parts sourced from around 40 countries which all need to come together to make 1 phone.

12.3.1 SUPPLY CHAIN CHALLENGES

To add to the complexity of the processes in the supply chain, there are additional factors to consider, such as:

- Geopolitical issues; for example, the war in Ukraine resulting in material shortages such as palladium, a raw material also used in mobile phones
- Economic issues; for example, unexpected increased costs such as more expensive freight prices due to rising energy costs

- Climate change issues; for example, reducing river levels in Germany and China, causing freight ships to reduce the volume of containers carried
- Ethical issues; for example, consumer pressures on poor welfare practice such as child labour being discovered in fast fashion factories
- Cultural issues; for example, consumers wanting to know the origin of their goods resulting in greater supply chain transparency, such as the Norwegian clothing manufacturer Helly Hansen adopting best practice and sharing details of all their suppliers on their website
- Socio-environmental issues; for example, healthcare crises which impact on production time, such as the 2020–2021 pandemic where many businesses closed due to government regulations or staff sickness
- Regulatory issues; for example, government rules and regulations on importing and exporting certain goods, such as US sanctions on microchips for some smartphone companies
- Technical issues; for example, incidents causing major delays, such as the Ever Given container ship that got stuck in the Suez canal

12.3.2 SUPPLY CHAIN MAPPING

To address these issues, many suppliers conduct **supply chain mapping** (see Key Term). Supply chain mapping provides 'managers with required level of understanding about the configuration of their supply chain to address its impact on supply chain planning, management and control processes' (MacCarthy et al., 2022: 2). It also allows managers to identify where there may be risks in the system; for example, raw materials near a geopolitical hotspot or a reliance on one mode of transport for delivery.

Figure 12.1 provides an example of a simplified smartphone supply chain. This does not show all 1,000 parts sourced from around 40 countries, but provides a starting point where each element could be expanded.

The process of creating these maps is complex. Some companies might not know where part of their products come from. You may think this is surprising, but Mars, who make brands such as Snickers, M&Ms and Dolmio, shared their challenges with tracing the source of their palm oil on their website (Mars, 2022: 1):

> Over the past several years, Mars has been on a journey to map our palm oil supply chain. Since 2018, we have published our full mill lists to show our progress. We had more than 1,500 mills supplying raw material, a number far too complex to manage, especially for a company that uses only 0.1% of the world's palm oil.
>
> In 2019 we announced our ambition is to significantly simplify our palm oil supply chain. This will be coupled with meaningful engagement on human rights, and on-the-ground and satellite verification processes to monitor deforestation.

Figure 12.1   Simplified smartphone supply chain map

Mars has taken some time (years) to create these maps and identified the risks. This is why supply chain mapping has become a professional service offered to many manufacturers.

KEY TERM   SUPPLY CHAIN MAPPING

Supply chain mapping illustrates 'the organization's chains of supply' (Khan et al., 2022: 3744). The maps were initially considered to be a linear process and evolved to recognise the different tiers involved across the 'upstream' suppliers and 'downstream' end clients. So every business or process involved from start to finish would be graphically illustrated on a supply chain map to show the connections and identify potential risks.

Smartphone Sixty Seconds® – Discover supply chain mapping

- Take out your mobile phone and search for 'supply chain mapping' AND 'cocoa' or 'supply chain mapping' AND 'palm oil' in images.
- Select one of these maps and note the different processes or countries involved.
- Calculate the time involved from gathering the raw materials to final delivery.
- How many stakeholders are involved in the different processes? Don't forget to add in transport if that's not included!

According to Garay-Rondero et al. (2020), the traditional approach to supply chains was designed to manage logistics and the manufacturing operations. Digitalised supply chains provide more depth and detail of the processes and stakeholders involved. They also identify the potential risks and ethical issues, such as the use of child labour.

ETHICAL INSIGHTS   Made by children

Child labour means using those who are 'too young to work or are involved in hazardous activities that may compromise their physical, mental, social or educational development' (UNICEF, 2023: 1). Traditional supply chain mapping did not always identify where child labour was used. With multiple stakeholders in different markets, it was difficult to identify where some tasks (embroidery on jeans or sewing buttons) had been outsourced to cheaper suppliers. Moving towards digital supply chain maps, many businesses worldwide were found to be using child labour, for example in the production of clothing. These fast-fashion companies were shocked as they did not (and do not) support the practice.

- Swedish fashion chain H&M used clothing factories in Myanmar where children worked over 12 hours a day – H&M have since adopted a zero-tolerance policy to child labour
- UK fashion chain Primark's suppliers were outsourcing work to children in India – Primark have banned the use of child labour
- US retailer The Gap found that the governments of Uzbekistan and Turkmenistan employed child labour to harvest cotton used in their clothing – The Gap has procedures in place to ensure this no longer happens

The practice is illegal and is declining, but still exists. According to UNICEF (2023), the United Nations organisation that protects the rights of children, there are more than 1 in 5 child labourers in the world's poorest countries. As consumers want cheaper and cheaper clothing (the t-shirt for €2, $2 or £2), how else can the producers deliver these goods?

- What action can shoppers take to ensure they are not buying goods made by children?
- Poverty often leads to child labour – what are the alternatives for child labour in poorer communities?
- The use of child labourers has existed for years – how can this practice be eradicated?

12.3.3 ADDING VALUE ALONG THE SUPPLY CHAIN

Better understanding the supply chain provides opportunities to add value at each process. For example, a 1,000kg (metric ton or the size of a large elephant) of cocoa beans costs around $3,600. That's 36 cents for 100g, yet a finished luxury chocolate bar containing 50% cocoa (18 cents) costs $2.00. Each stage in the supply chain, from harvesting the beans, roasting and processing, and sending to the factory for mixing and packaging, adds value and the price increases. This is known as the value chain. In a digital context we also consider the **virtual value chain** (see Key Term).

KEY TERM   VIRTUAL VALUE CHAIN

A virtual value chain (VVC) is 'defined as the value chain system formed by information-based value activities in which companies engages in virtual world, is the extensibility and development of traditional value chain' (Liu & Wu, 2010: 1467). E-commerce has potential to add value as retailers cross-sell databases of consumers who may be interested in other goods. To create value in the VVC 'involves five activities: gathering, organizing, selecting, synthesizing and distributing information' (Liu & Wu, 2010: 1468).

12.4 ENHANCING DIGITAL OPERATIONS

The ability to map supply chains digitally highlighted weaknesses for many businesses, such as weak practices and ethical concerns, resulting in policy changes. Digital operations can be enhanced with technological developments, including technologies discussed in Chapters 5 and 6; 5G to 6G technology, the Internet of Things, blockchain, additive printing and artificial intelligence. Table 12.4 shows how digital technology can enhance operations management at different stages of the operations management.

Table 12.4   Digital technology enhancing operations management

Technology	Stage	Enhancement	Examples
Additive printing	Prototyping	Speeds up the development of new products	Prototypes for new pieces of cast jewellery may take weeks to create; using additive printing, this can be achieved in a single day
5G to 6G and the Internet of Things	Stock management	Stock with RFID or other sensors can be easily located and recorded	Zara, the Spanish retailer, uses RFID tags on its clothing
Additive printing	Manufacturing	Remove a manufacturing process	Where customisable goods are needed, such as in the dental sector, for dentures or teeth moulds.

(Continued)

Table 12.4 (Continued)

Technology	Stage	Enhancement	Examples
Artificial intelligence	Manufacturing	Recommending optimum use of materials	Typically factories using materials (fabric for clothing or furniture) would have 'wastage' where offcuts arose from the cutting and measuring process; using AI enables less wastage and better usage of the materials
Artificial intelligence	Manufacturing	Issues with quality can be identified earlier and resolved faster	Used in semi-conductor production to remove faulty chips in the process
Artificial intelligence	Delivery	Reviewing logistics arrangements and recommending more efficient routes	Major logistics companies already use AI to recommend the optimum routes
5G to 6G and the Internet of Things	Smart factories	Connecting all aspects of operations	The Tesla Gigafactory in Berlin, Germany is a smart factory and produces electric vehicle cars and batteries
Blockchain	Supply chain	Provides transparency across the supply chain	Walmart works with IBM for food products, to identify the growers and individual fields where produce is from

Source: Adapted from Choi et al. (2022)

THE INTERNET OF THINGS

The Internet of Things, which extends to the Internet of Everything and the Internet of Manufacturing, is enabled through 5G to 6G technology. The challenges are when aspects of the supply chain lack sensors and cannot be tracked, or when the Wi-Fi fails in local areas.

BLOCKCHAIN

Blockchain is still evolving and there have been attempts to make it work across operations management. Maersk, the global logistics company headquartered in Denmark, partnered with IBM to create TradeLens, 'an open and neutral supply chain platform' (Maersk, 2020: 9). But in 2022 it was discontinued because the business 'was unable to secure the necessary traction' (Maersk, 2022: 18). This is an example of **network effects** (see Chapter 4), as if the necessary number of participants was too small, the system fails to have value and may cost too much to operate. Maersk is a market leader in logistics and it may be that TradeLens is relaunched in the future when more partners are ready to be involved.

ADDITIVE PRINTING

Additive printing provides speedy solutions for prototyping, but uses significant plastic in the process. Other additives include fine metal alloy powder, but these are more expensive. This demonstrates the challenges in balancing a new technology with the costs of production.

Smartphone Sixty Seconds® – Find types of additive printing

- Take out your mobile phone and search for 'types of additive printing'.
- How many types of additives did you find?
- What are they used for and by which organisations?
- Discuss with classmates.

ARTIFICIAL INTELLIGENCE

Artificial intelligence is widely used in many parts of operations management, from providing insights that inform demand management to advanced robotics. This is an evolving area within manufacturing and needs an ecosystem in place to run effectively with engagement by all stakeholders in the supply chain.

Activity 12.3   Analyse digital operations

Last-mile delivery can be the most expensive and least sustainable part of the supply chain. While drones are still being approved for last-mile delivery, parcel lockers are available. Create a campaign to encourage consumers to use single locations such as parcel lockers or central delivery hubs.

12.5 CHALLENGES IN DIGITAL OPERATIONS MANAGEMENT

Operations management extends beyond global business to small and medium enterprises (SMEs), government and healthcare. For SMEs the main barriers to adoption Industry 4.0 are lack of resources. These are mainly gaps in knowledge (capability), with few people within the business that have the skills and infrastructure (capacity).

12.5.1 MANAGING RETURNS

Other issues are that operations management may run smoothly, but within e-commerce, challenges are consumer returns and **deshopping** (see Chapter 3). Operations management is geared up towards getting products out of the factory door, not taking them back. Amazon (2021: 1) has recognised this, following negative publicity about managing unwanted goods:

> Managing product returns and unsold stock is challenging, not just for Amazon, but for all retailers, both online and offline. Our approach is to build an extensive circular economy programme with the goal of reducing returns overall and increasing reuse and resale of products. We start by helping customers make informed purchase decisions to get what they want the first time – from detailed product information pages to customer reviews, and much more.

To address returns, some companies are charging shoppers to discourage the practice of consumers ordering 3 items with the intention of buying just 1, or those involved with deshopping and using and returning the goods.

CASE EXAMPLE 12.2   Zalando

Zalando is an online fashion and lifestyle retailer which was founded in Berlin in 2008. It has over 50 million active customers, it offers 7,000 brands, and manages over 260 million orders annually across 25 countries. You could describe it as Amazon for fashion.

Zalando stocks the products in its warehouses across Europe, delivers the goods and manages returns. Consumer experience is a key factor in the business's growth, as its website notes: 'Our customers are the focus of all of our activities. We are continuously improving our outstanding service and online shopping experience to better serve our growing customer base.' The number of returns is an issue for all e-commerce companies. Zalando notes about 50% of all products are returned. One way to address this is using the **mental model** (see Key Term) and ensuring that all possible questions about the product are answered online. This means that the customer is certain they require the product and it's right for them, before making the purchase. But with clothing this can be a challenge. To overcome challenges with returns and customers buying sizes that don't fit, Zalando has introduced size recommendations, based on customers providing photographs (these are deleted after the sizing exercise is completed) in the app. A further solution was to use 3D digital design software. This software creates an avatar of the person which means that online shoppers can try on the clothes and better assess whether it works with their height and shape. This is known as Zalando's virtual fitting room and is a form of AR. The business believes this is working, as 'More than 30,000 customers have previously interacted with the virtual fitting room with selected items of clothing' (Zalando, 2023: 1). They added that 'around half of the customers try more than one size on the avatar'.

Size and fit is such an important factor that the business has a 'vice president of size and fit'. They recognise that 'Zalando is the only European fashion e-commerce platform to have an in-house team dedicated to size and fit' and notes that:

> The team uses a combination of fitting models and machine learning, computer vision and other technologies to predict if items run big or small. It has also created personalised size recommendations based on customers' purchase and return history along with reference items customers can add to their size profile. For those items where Zalando provides size advice, size-related returns have decreased by 10 percent vs similar items where size advice is not provided.

The Zalando CRM system stores additional demographic details such as the customer's size, as well as their psychographics and behaviour, to understand what they have bought (purchase history) and goods that were returned. Merging the purchase and returns data with the customer profile in the CRM system enables Zalando to make other clothing recommendations that are more likely to be appropriate for their customers.

Yet returns remain a challenge. Goods returned may need laundering (if worn) or fixing (if damaged) or repackaging. In some cases this takes more time and investment than the value of the goods. This is an increasing issue and needs careful consideration.

Case questions

- Zalando is using AI to reduce its returns and improve the customer experience. What other technology could the business adopt to reduce returns?
- The value of data combined with AI will enable companies like Zalando to identify which customers are more likely to return goods. Should companies like Zalando block 'serial returners' from shopping with them?
- How can companies like Zalando better manage returns?

KEY TERM   MENTAL MODEL

The mental model is how people see things. It has been defined as 'knowledge structures employed by humans to describe, explain, and predict the world around them' (Andrews et al., 2023: 129). For example, consumers may think an item of clothing is too big or too short, or the right fit – when it isn't. This is why e-commerce retailers provide more measurement guidance.

12.5.2 CYBER SECURITY

According to *The Manufacturer* (Bush, 2023: 1) there were 'over 11 billion IoT devices worldwide in 2021 (rising to an estimated 29 billion by the end of the decade)'. Cyber threats include malware and ransomware attacks. In the UK, 'manufacturing had a reported 23.2% share of cyber attacks and a further 33% increase in the number of incidents caused by vulnerability exploitations from 2020 to 2021' (Bush, 2023: 1).

Cyberattacks can target products, equipment and ecosystems, with major effects, such as the following:

- Toyota's plastic parts and electronic component suppliers were attacked – resulting in the shutdown of operations in 28 production lines across 14 plants in Japan
- The Health Service Executive (HSE) of Ireland suffered a major ransomware cyber-attack – resulting in delays for citizens accessing vaccines
- UK-based KNP Logistics group had a major ransomware attack that impacted on key systems, processes and financial information – resulting in the firm's closure.

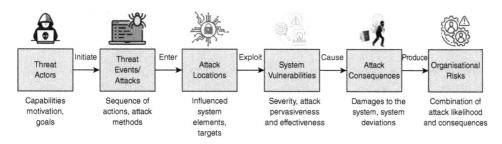

Figure 12.2   A generic risk model for attacks on cyber-physical manufacturing systems

Source: Rahman et al. (2023: 204)

To counter the different types of attacks, Rahman et al. (2023) propose a generic risk model for attacks on cyber-physical manufacturing systems, shown in Figure 12.2.

The generic risk model for attacks on cyber-physical manufacturing systems in Figure 12.2 takes a proactive perspective to identify who may wish to attack the system, how and where. When this information has been assessed, the business can consider where the weaknesses may be and the potential results. This enables businesses to take precautions before attacks occur. However, many attacks are due to social engineering where attackers pretend to be from the company and try to extract information to carry out phishing attacks.

DIGITAL TOOL   Social-engineer.org

Social-engineer.org is 'an online resource for security professionals, adversarial simulators (pentesters), as well as enthusiasts'. It provides more details about social engineering and more details about the types of attacks.

- You can explore it here: social-engineer.org

12.5.3 ETHICS

A major challenge across digital operations management is ethics. Areas uncovered in operations concern reducing child labour, ensuring workers are well paid and operating in appropriate conditions, and managing the business in a sustainable way. Many businesses have environmental, social and governance (ESG) policies in place and are starting to report on their ESG performance, yet most focus on the environment and the information they provide is not always accurate.

In Chapter 1 we explored **greenwashing** where businesses claim to be environmentally friendly but do the opposite, and in Chapter 6 we considered **bluewashing** where businesses make misleading claims about their ethical credentials. There are no universal requirements for businesses to adopt ethical policies, yet those with shareholders are reviewed more often with the growth of social media. However, there is a growth in companies certifying as a **B-Corporation** (see Chapter 10) to benefit a wider group of stakeholders.

Digital business requires people with skills and values to reduce the risk to the business as well as the wider community. Being in a digital space provides greater visibility and more opportunity to help businesses that wish to adopt a sustainable attitude for their communities and take a responsible approach towards consumption and production.

JOURNAL OF NOTE

The Journal of Operations Management focuses on the 'management of operations: manufacturing operations, service operations, supply chain operations'. It is published on behalf of the Association for Supply Chain Management.

CASE STUDY
PAYPAL: MANAGING DIGITAL OPERATIONS

Operations management involves process, planning and control, people, strategy and metrics. As PayPal is not a manufacturer, but a service business, the process involves various stages; approving new merchants, providing them with the tools to offer PayPal services, offering additional support to grow their business, managing the accounts and ongoing monitoring to ensure the process is working well.

For consumers the process includes a risk assessment to ensure they are genuine consumers and that they are not building large debts that they may be unable to repay and which may cause them hardship. In both cases there is a risk assessment, and to do this PayPal uses AI combined with big data. As the annual report explains: 'proprietary risk models and other indicators are applied to assess merchants who desire to use our merchant financing offerings to help predict their ability to repay' (PayPal, 2023: 22). This is about mitigating risk in the process to ensure the merchants are valid and not hoax websites, fraudulent businesses or engaged in illegal activities which are not acceptable. The risk models have been developed over many years, but simplified through big data, AI and machine learning. So if a merchant seems to represent a risk, it may be that they possess similar characteristics to other merchants who were weak. But the company recognises that:

> These risk models may not accurately predict the creditworthiness of a consumer or merchant due to inaccurate assumptions, including those related to the particular consumer or merchant, market conditions, economic environment, or limited transaction history or other data.

> The accuracy of these risk models and the ability to manage credit risk related to our credit products may also be affected by legal or regulatory requirements, changes in consumer behavior, changes in the economic environment, issuing bank policies, and other factors. (PayPal, 2023: 22)

This protects both PayPal and consumers. For consumers, there is a similar process:

> The credit decision-making process for our consumer credit products uses proprietary methodologies and credit algorithms and other analytical techniques designed to analyze the credit risk of specific consumers based on, among other factors, their past purchase and transaction history with PayPal or Venmo and their credit scores. (PayPal, 2023: 22).

(Continued)

The 'proprietary methodologies' refer to the in-house **API** (see Chapter 9) that has been developed which runs a risk rating in seconds. In the same way that consumers are protected from weak merchants, PayPal protects merchants from consumers who may pose a risk and fail to pay. PayPal also enables consumers to access and download their data from the settings area in their PayPal account. This enables consumers to take control where they believe there may be errors in the data.

In terms of the planning and control, as a financial services business, PayPal is subject to significant legal control procedures. It has a corporate duty to report on these issues and has a dedicated Audit and Risk Committee (ARC) which 'is primarily responsible for the oversight of the Company's risk framework and reports to the full Board on … a regular basis' (PayPal, 2023: 26).

As a service business, people are critical to its successful operation. Operating in over 200 markets with nearly 30,000 staff is complex and needs a clear structure. To ensure the strategy happens, PayPal has agreed key performance metrics: 'We measure the scale of our platform and the relevance of our products and services to our customers through certain metrics, including total payment volume, payment transactions, and active accounts' (PayPal, 2023: 4).

PayPal's business is more than finance. It is data as a service. While the actual data is not disclosed to third parties, this provides the business with a valuable resource that must be managed well to continue to thrive.

CASE QUESTIONS

- PayPal's risk assessment processes use AI and big data – what changes in consumer behaviour could result in the wrong conclusions and perhaps rejecting a consumer from signing up to PayPal?
- PayPal's proprietary methodologies are not shared. Is there a case to make these transparent? What benefits or risks could this create?
- In a service business, what are the main challenges in managing staff?

FURTHER EXERCISES

1. Evaluate 2 digital operations tools. Consider their advantages and disadvantages in a factory that makes sportswear.

2. For an organisation of your choice create a simplified supply chain map. Try to include as many stakeholders and processes as possible based on your research.

3. The virtual value chain (VVC) involves 5 activities: gathering, organising, selecting, synthesising and distributing information. For an organisation of your choice, apply value across the VVC.

4. In the future all factories will be run by robots. Discuss and justify your response.

SUMMARY

This chapter has explored:

- Digital operations management tools
- The digital supply chain framework
- Advanced robotics and drones
- Challenges in the digital supply chain

APPENDIX A

THE UNITED NATIONS SUSTAINABLE DEVELOPMENT GOALS

The 17 United Nations (UN) Sustainable Development Goals (SGDs) were adopted by all UN member states in 2015 as part of 'Agenda 2030' to end extreme poverty, protect the planet, and combat injustice and inequality.

The United Nations SDGS are not just for citizens and governments, but for businesses too, to 'do business responsibly and then pursue opportunities to solve societal challenges through business innovation and collaboration'.[1] The SDGs involve considering the wider societal impact of business. As the United Nations Global Compact noted, 'The Ten Principles of the UN Global Compact provide a common ethical and practical framework for operationalizing corporate responsibility'. Table A provides more guidance on how the UN SDGS relate to business.

---

[1]https://unglobalcompact.org/sdgs/about

APPENDIX A

Table A   The United Nations Sustainable Development Goals and how they relate to business

Focus	Goal	How the goal relates to business[2]
No Poverty	Goal 1. End poverty in all its forms everywhere	Work is a major route for many to escape poverty. Breaking the cycle of poverty involves decent and productive jobs, sustainable enterprises and economic transformation.
Zero Hunger	Goal 2. End hunger, achieve food security and improved nutrition and promote sustainable agriculture	Every actor along the agriculture supply chain, including farmers, producers, traders, retailers, investors and consumers has a critical role to play to establish sustainable food systems that advance food security, protect the environment and ensure economic opportunity.
Good Health and Well-being	Goal 3. Ensure healthy lives and promote well-being for all at all ages	Global health issues impact all aspects of business from supply chains to customers.
Quality Education	Goal 4. Ensure inclusive and equitable quality education and promote lifelong learning opportunities for all	Investing in education creates a generation of skilled people.
Gender Equality	Goal 5. Achieve gender equality and empower all women and girls	Empowering women and girls helps expand economic growth, promote social development and establish more stable and just societies.
Clean Water and Sanitation	Goal 6. Ensure availability and sustainable management of water and sanitation for all	Global water challenges, such as water scarcity and pollution, have a negative impact on businesses. Companies need to assess their water performance to address these challenges and ultimately stay in business.
Affordable and Clean Energy	Goal 7. Ensure access to affordable, reliable, sustainable and modern energy for all	Climate change poses both risks and opportunities to businesses of all sizes, sectors and regions of the world. It is in the best interest of the business community, to take an active role in low-carbon technologies, increase energy efficiency and reduce carbon emissions.
Decent Work and Economic Growth	Goal 8. Promote sustained, inclusive and sustainable economic growth, full and productive employment and decent work for all	Decent work and raising the living standards of all workers requires companies to adopt sustainable, responsible and inclusive workplace practices, and for companies with supply chains to use their leverage with suppliers to contribute to the realization of decent work globally.
Industry, Innovation, and Infrastructure	Goal 9. Build resilient infrastructure, promote inclusive and sustainable industrialization and foster innovation	Sustainable industrialization can lift communities out of poverty but needs to be managed carefully to avoid additional pressures on people and planet.
Reduced Inequalities	Goal 10. Reduce inequality within and among countries	Reducing inequalities benefits businesses as it helps create a more stable and predictable business environment. It also introduces greater diversity of thought into the workplace, boosting innovation and profitability.

---

[2]https://unglobalcompact.org/sdgs/17-global-goals

Focus	Goal	How the goal relates to business[2]
Sustainable Cities and Communities	Goal 11. Make cities and human settlements inclusive, safe, resilient and sustainable	Cities are centres of commerce and boost the productivity needed for economic development. Many cities in developing countries face unplanned urban sprawl as infrastructure has not kept pace with population growth. Better urban planning and management is needed to make the world's urban spaces more inclusive, safe, resilient and sustainable.
Responsible Consumption and Production	Goal 12. Ensure sustainable consumption and production patterns	A company's entire supply chain can make a significant impact in promoting human rights, fair labour practices, environmental progress and anti-corruption policies.
Climate Action	Goal 13. Take urgent action to combat climate change and its impacts	Climate breakdown is already affecting lives and livelihoods, especially among the most vulnerable in the Global South. Businesses can send strong market signals and develop innovative solutions to build trust and present credible plans towards a zero-carbon economy, do their part to increase society's resilience and unlock climate finance, while advocating for a green and just recovery.
Life Below Water[1]	Goal 14. Conserve and sustainably use the oceans, seas and marine resources for sustainable development	Life below water supports many livelihoods and businesses. Leading companies can implement policies and practices to protect ocean ecosystems affected by their end-to-end operations.
Life on Land	Goal 15. Protect, restore and promote sustainable use of terrestrial ecosystems, sustainably manage forests, combat desertification, and halt and reverse land degradation and halt biodiversity loss	Businesses rely on the goods and services provided by Biodiversity and Ecosystem services, as input for their products and processes. They contribute to ecosystem change by generating impacts through their core operations, supply chains or investment choices.
Peace and Justice Strong Institutions	Goal 16. Promote peaceful and inclusive societies for sustainable development, provide access to justice for all and build effective, accountable and inclusive institutions at all levels	Governance is the systems and processes that ensure the overall effectiveness of an entity – whether a business, government or multilateral institution. Companies can engage with the UN Global Compact on the three critical governance topics: anti-corruption, peace, and rule of law.
Partnerships for the Goals	Goal 17. Strengthen the means of implementation and revitalize the global partnership for sustainable development	For businesses to succeed, they require access to energy, good governance and sustainable economic development. The business community can work alongside the public sector to develop more integrated solutions to global challenges.

[3]https://unglobalcompact.org/library/139

REFERENCES

Abhari, K., & McGuckin, S. (2023). Limiting factors of open innovation organizations: A case of social product development and research agenda. *Technovation*, *119*(May 2022), 102526. https://doi.org/10.1016/j.technovation.2022.102526

Adamson, B. (2019). CSO update: The new B2B buying journey and its implication for sales. In *Gartner for Sales*. www.gartner.com/en/sales/insights/cso-update (This Gartner report is archived and is included for historical context only)

Africa ClimAccelerator. (2022). Wastezon's app helps promote the reuse, remake and repair of e-waste products. Africaclimaccelerator.com. https://africaclimaccelerator.com/wastezons-app-helps-promote-the-reuse-remake-and-repair-of-e-waste-products/

Akbari, M., & Hopkins, J. L. (2022). Digital technologies as enablers of supply chain sustainability in an emerging economy. *Operations Management Research*, *15*(3–4), 689–710. https://doi.org/10.1007/s12063-021-00226-8

Aldebaran. (2023). Pepper. www.aldebaran.com. www.aldebaran.com/en/pepper

Almansour, M. (2023). Artificial intelligence and resource optimization: A study of Fintech start-ups. *Resources Policy*, *80*(December 2022), 103250. https://doi.org/10.1016/j.resourpol.2022.103250

Alnuaimi, B. K., Kumar, S., Ren, S., & Budhwar, P. (2022). Mastering digital transformation: The nexus between leadership, agility, and digital strategy. *Journal of Business Research*, *145*(March), 636–648. https://doi.org/10.1016/j.jbusres.2022.03.038

Alstyne, M. W. Van, Parker, G. G., & Choudary, S. P. (2016). Pipelines, platforms, and the new rules of strategy. *Harvard Business Review*, *94*(4), 54–62. http://web.b.ebscohost.com.uplib.idm.oclc.org/ehost/pdfviewer/pdfviewer?vid=1&sid=775e3c09-4be9-456d-8d20-e3135111888d%40sessionmgr103%0Ahttp://web.a.ebscohost.com.esc-web.lib.cbs.dk/ehost/detail/detail?vid=2&sid=dfe63f02-9445-4549-a7b5-892fe035a253%40ses

Amazon. (2021). What happens to unwanted or damaged products at Amazon? https://blog.aboutamazon.co.uk/company-news/what-happens-to-unwanted-or-damaged-products-at-amazon

Amazon. (2022). Amazon reveals the new design for Prime Air's delivery drone. Amazon. www.aboutamazon.com/news/transportation/amazon-prime-air-delivery-drone-reveal-photos

Andrews, R. W., Lilly, J. M., Srivastava, D., & Feigh, K. M. (2023). The role of shared mental models in human-AI teams: A theoretical review. *Theoretical Issues in Ergonomics Science*, *24*(2), 129–175. https://doi.org/10.1080/1463922X.2022.2061080

Ang, T., Wei, S., & Anaza, N. A. (2018). Livestreaming vs pre-recorded: How social viewing strategies impact consumers' viewing experiences and behavioral intentions. *European Journal of Marketing*, *52*(9–10), 2075–2104. https://doi.org/10.1108/EJM-09-2017-0576

Angelopoulos, S., Bendoly, E., Fransoo, J., Hoberg, K., Ou, C., & Tenhiälä, A. (2023). Digital transformation in operations management: Fundamental change through agency reversal. *Journal of Operations Management*, *69*(6), 876–889. https://doi.org/10.1002/joom.1271

Apple. (2021). App Store stopped more than $1.5 billion in potentially fraudulent transactions in 2020. www.apple.com/newsroom/2021/05/app-store-stopped-over-1-5-billion-in-suspect-transactions-in-2020/

Appley, D. G., & Winder, A. E. (1977). An evolving definition of collaboration and some implications for the world of work. *The Journal of Applied Behavioral Science*, *13*(3), 279–291. https://doi.org/10.1177/002188637701300304

Armstrong Soule, C. A., & Sekhon, T. S. (2022). Signaling nothing: Motivating the masses with status signals that encourage anti-consumption. *Journal of Macromarketing*, *42*(2), 308–325. https://doi.org/10.1177/02761467221093228

Arogyaswamy, B. (2020). Big tech and societal sustainability: An ethical framework. *AI and Society*, *35*(4), 829–840. https://doi.org/10.1007/s00146-020-00956-6

Asli Demirgüç-Kunt, Klapper, L., Singer, D., & Ansar, S. (2021). *The Global Findex Database 2021*. World Bank Group.

Aubert-Hassouni, C., & Cloarec, J. (2022). Privacy regulation in the age of artificial intelligence. In A. Hanlon & T. L. Tuten (Eds.), *The Sage Handbook of Digital Marketing*. Sage Publications.

Australian Competition & Consumer Commission. (2023). *Online product and service reviews*. accc.gov.au. www.accc.gov.au/business/advertising-and-promotions/online-product-and-service-reviews

Avula, V., Nanditha, R., Dhuli, S., & Ranjan, P. (2021). The Internet of Everything: A survey. *Proceedings – 2021 IEEE 13th International Conference on Computational Intelligence and Communication Networks, CICN 2021*, 72–79. https://doi.org/10.1109/CICN51697.2021.9574695

Aw, E. C. X., Tan, G. W. H., Cham, T. H., Raman, R., & Ooi, K. B. (2022). Alexa, what's on my shopping list? Transforming customer experience with digital voice assistants. *Technological Forecasting and Social Change*, *180*(April), 1–13. https://doi.org/10.1016/j.techfore.2022.121711

Azuma, R. T. (1997). A survey of augmented reality. *Presence: Teleoperators and Virtual Environments*, *6*(4), 355–385. https://doi.org/10.1561/1100000049

B Labs. (2023). B Lab is the nonprofit network transforming the global economy to benefit all people, communities, and the planet. Bcorporation.Net. www.bcorporation.net/en-us/movement/about-b-lab

Banjo, S., Yap, L., Murphy, C., & Chan, V. (2020, February). The coronavirus outbreak has become the world's largest work-from-home experiment. *Time*. https://time.com/5776660/coronavirus-work-from-home/

Barney, J. B. (1991). Firm resources and sustained competitive advantage. *Journal of Management*, *17*(1), 99–120. https://doi.org/10.1177/014920639101700108

Barney, J. B. (1995). Looking inside for competitive advantage. *Academy of Management Executive*, *9*(4), 49–61.

Batat, W. (2022). What does phygital really mean? A conceptual introduction to the phygital customer experience (PH-CX) framework. *Journal of Strategic Marketing*, 1–24. https://doi.org/10.1080/0965254X.2022.2059775

Becker, L., & Jaakkola, E. (2020). Customer experience: Fundamental premises and implications for research. *Journal of the Academy of Marketing Science*, *48*(4), 630–648. https://doi.org/10.1007/s11747-019-00718-x

Becker, W. J., Belkin, L. Y., Conroy, S. A., & Tuskey, S. (2021). Killing me softly: Organizational e-mail monitoring expectations' impact on employee and significant other well-being. *Journal of Management, 47*(4), 1024–1052. https://doi.org/10.1177/0149206319890655

Belo, R., & Li, T. (2022). Social referral programs for freemium platforms. *Management Science, 68*(12, December), 8933–8962. https://doi.org/10.1287/mnsc.2022.4301

Berners-Lee, T. (1989). *Information Management: A Proposal.* www.w3.org/History/1989/proposal.html

Bharadwaj, A., Sawy, O. El, Pavlou, P. A., & Venkatraman, N. (2013). Digital business strategy: Toward a next generation of insights. *MIS Quarterly, 37*(2), 471–482. Retrieved from www.misq.org/misq/downloads/download/editorial/581/

Bingley, W. J., Curtis, C., Lockey, S., Bialkowski, A., Gillespie, N., Haslam, S. A., Ko, R. K. L., Steffens, N., Wiles, J., & Worthy, P. (2023). Where is the human in human-centered AI? Insights from developer priorities and user experiences. *Computers in Human Behavior, 141*, 1–8. https://doi.org/10.1016/j.chb.2022.107617

Blomsma, F., Bauwens, T., Weissbrod, I., & Kirchherr, J. (2023). The 'need for speed': Towards circular disruption—What it is, how to make it happen and how to know it's happening. *Business Strategy and the Environment, 32*(3), 1010–1031. https://doi.org/10.1002/bse.3106

Bokolo Jnr, A., & Petersen, S. A. (2023). Using an extended technology acceptance model to predict enterprise architecture adoption in making cities smarter. *Environment Systems and Decisions, 43*(1), 36–53. https://doi.org/10.1007/s10669-022-09867-x

Booms, B. H., & Bitner, M. J. (1980). New management tools for the successful tourism manager. *Annals of Tourism Research, 7*(3), 337–352.

Bowman, C., & Ambrosini, V. (2000). Value creation versus value capture: Towards a coherent definition of value in strategy. *British Journal of Management, 11*, 1–15. https://doi.org/10.1111/1467-8551.00147

Boyes, H., & Watson, T. (2022). Digital twins: An analysis framework and open issues. *Computers in Industry, 143*(June), 103763. https://doi.org/10.1016/j.compind.2022.103763

Brennan, B. (2022). The relationship between ecommerce and social commerce: Subset, evolution or new paradigm? In A. Hanlon & T. L. Tuten (Eds.), *The Sage Handbook of Digital Marketing.* Sage Publications.

Brown, T. (2008). Design thinking. *Harvard Business Review, 86*(June), 85–92.

Brunetti, F., Matt, D. T., Bonfanti, A., De Longhi, A., Pedrini, G., & Orzes, G. (2020). Digital transformation challenges: Strategies emerging from a multi-stakeholder approach. *TQM Journal, 32*(4), 697–724. https://doi.org/10.1108/TQM-12-2019-0309

Bruno, I., Lobo, G., Covino, B. V., Donarelli, A., Marchetti, V., Panni, A. S., & Molinari, F. (2020). Technology readiness revisited: A proposal for extending the scope of impact assessment of European public services. *ACM International Conference Proceeding Series*, 369–380. https://doi.org/10.1145/3428502.3428552

Bujor, A., & Avasilcai, S. (2018). Open innovation in creative industries. Part I: Innovation and design. *IOP Conference Series: Materials Science and Engineering, 400*(6), 1–9. https://doi.org/10.1088/1757-899X/400/6/062007

Buttle, F., & Maklan, S. (2019). *Customer Relationship Management: Concepts and Technologies* (4th ed.). Routledge.

Bush, J. (2023, March 14). Manufacturing under attack: Cyber security on the agenda. *The Manufacturer*. www.themanufacturer.com/articles/manufacturing-under-attack-cyber-security-on-the-agenda/

Caesarius, L. M., & Hohenthal, J. (2022). Big data marketing: Context and affordances. In A. Hanlon & T. L. Tuten (Eds.), *The Sage Handbook of Digital Marketing*. Sage Publications.

Calvin Ong, H. L., & Jeyaraj, S. (2014). Work–life interventions: Differences between work–life balance and work–life harmony and its impact on creativity at work. *Sage Open*, *4*(3). https://doi.org/10.1177/2158244014544289

Carrasco-Carvajal, O., Castillo-Vergara, M., & García-Pérez-de-Lema, D. (2023). Measuring open innovation in SMEs: An overview of current research. In *Review of Managerial Science*, 17(2). Springer Berlin Heidelberg. https://doi.org/10.1007/s11846-022-00533-9

Carrefour. (2021). *Universal Registration Document – Annual Financial Report*.

Carvalho, P., & Alves, H. (2022). Customer value co-creation in the hospitality and tourism industry: A systematic literature review. *International Journal of Contemporary Hospitality Management*. https://doi.org/10.1108/IJCHM-12-2021-1528

Chen, J., Yang, L., & Hosanagar, K. (2022). To brush or not to brush: Product rankings, customer search and fake orders. *Information Systems Research, November*. https://doi.org/10.2139/ssrn.3468363

Chen, L., Tong, T. W., Tang, S., & Han, N. (2022). Governance and design of digital platforms: A review and future research directions on a meta-organization. In *Journal of Management*, *48*(1). https://doi.org/10.1177/01492063211045023

Chen, S. W., Chen, P. H., Tsai, C. T., & Liu, C. H. (2022). An intelligent based symmetrical classification of online shop selling counterfeit products. *Symmetry*, *14*(10), 1–12. https://doi.org/10.3390/sym14102132

Cheng, R., Wu, N., Chen, S., & Han, B. (2022). Reality check of metaverse: A first look at commercial social virtual reality platforms. *Proceedings – 2022 IEEE Conference on Virtual Reality and 3D User Interfaces Abstracts and Workshops, VRW 2022*, 141–148. https://doi.org/10.1109/VRW55335.2022.00040

Cherney, M. R., Fetherston, M., & Johnsen, L. J. (2018). Online course student collaboration literature: A review and critique. In *Small Group Research*, *49*(1). https://doi.org/10.1177/1046496417721627

Chesbrough, H. (2012). Open innovation: Where we've been and where we're going. *Research Technology Management*, *55*(4), 20–27. https://doi.org/10.5437/08956308X5504085

Chesney, R., & Citron, D. (2019). Deepfakes and the new disinformation war: The coming age of post-truth geopolitics. *Foreign Affairs*, *98*(1), 147–155. https://search.proquest.com/docview/2161593888?accountid=14777

Chevalier, S. (2022). Global retail e-commerce sales worldwide from 2014 to 2026. Statista. www.statista.com/statistics/379046/worldwide-retail-e-commerce-sales/%0Aemarketer.com

Chitturi, R., Raghunathan, R., & Mahajan, V. (2008). Delight by design: The role of hedonic versus utilitarian benefits. *Journal of Marketing*, 72(May), 48–63. https://doi.org/10.1509/jmkg.72.3.48

Choi, T. M., Kumar, S., Yue, X., & Chan, H. L. (2022). Disruptive technologies and operations management in the Industry 4.0 era and beyond. *Production and Operations Management*, 31(1), 9–31. https://doi.org/10.1111/poms.13622

Christensen, C. M. (1997). *The Innovator's Dilemma: When New Technologies Cause Great Firms to Fail*. Harvard Business School Press.

Christensen, C. M., McDonald, R., Altman, E. J., & Palmer, J. E. (2018). Disruptive innovation: An intellectual history and directions for future research. *Journal of Management Studies*, 55(7), 1043–1078. https://doi.org/10.1111/joms.12349

Chung, J., & Lee, Y. S. (2022). The evolving impact of robots on jobs. *ILR Review*, 76(March), 290–319. https://doi.org/10.1177/00197939221137822

Competition and Markets Authority. (2016). Giving a balanced picture: Do's and don'ts for online review sites. gov.uk. https://assets.publishing.service.gov.uk/government/uploads/system/uploads/attachment_data/file/512880/Giving_a_balanced_picture_-_dos_and_don_ts_for_online_review_sites.pdf

Competition and Markets Authority. (2021, June 25). Press release CMA to investigate Amazon and Google over fake reviews. gov.uk. www.gov.uk/government/news/cma-to-investigate-amazon-and-google-over-fake-reviews

Conger, K., Fausset, R., & F. Kovaleski, S. (2019). San Francisco Bans Facial Recognition Technology. *The New York Times*. www.nytimes.com/2019/05/14/us/facial-recognition-ban-san-francisco.html

Cookson, C. (2023, August 1). Glasgow university spinout raises $43mn to 'digitise chemistry'. *Financial Times*. www.ft.com/content/be25204a-6ad6-4db5-bbf5-f819954d0ce5

Coppola, D. (2022a, March 10). Market share of the digital subscription economy worldwide 2020. Statista.Com. www.statista.com/statistics/1295125/digital-subscription-economy-global-market-share-by-sector/

Coppola, D. (2022b, March 10). Market size of the digital subscription economy worldwide 2020-2025. Statista.Com. www.statista.com/statistics/1295064/market-size-digital-subscription-economy-worldwide-by-segment/

Curry, D. (2023). Venmo revenue and usage statistics. Business of Apps. www.businessofapps.com/data/venmo-statistics/

David-West, O., Iheanachor, N., & Umukoro, I. O. (2019). Mobile money as a frugal innovation for the bottom of the pyramid – Cases of selected African countries. *Africa Journal of Management*, 5(3), 274–302. https://doi.org/10.1080/23322373.2019.1652023

Davis, F. D. (1989). Perceived usefulness, perceived ease of use, and user acceptance of information technology. *MIS Quarterly*, 13(3), 319–340. https://doi.org/10.2307/249008

Dayaram, S. (2023). The metals inside your iphone are more precious than you thought: Here's why. CNET. www.cnet.com/tech/mobile/the-metals-inside-your-iphone-are-more-precious-than-you-thought-heres-why/

De Keyser, A., Lemon, K. N., Klaus, P., & Keiningham, T. L. (2015). A framework for understanding and managing the CX. In *Working Paper Series*, 15(121).

REFERENCES

Deng, Y., Lambrecht, A., & Liu, Y. (2022). Spillover effects and freemium strategy in mobile app market. *SSRN Electronic Journal*, December, 1–24. https://doi.org/10.2139/ssrn.3149550

Department of Defense. (2022). *DoD Zero Trust Strategy*.

Devagiri, J. S., Paheding, S., Niyaz, Q., Yang, X., & Smith, S. (2022). Augmented reality and artificial intelligence in industry: Trends, tools, and future challenges. *Expert Systems with Applications*, *207*(June), 118002. https://doi.org/10.1016/j.eswa.2022.118002

Dwivedi, Y. K., Hughes, L., Baabdullah, A. M., Ribeiro-Navarrete, S., Giannakis, M., Al-Debei, M. M., Dennehy, D., Metri, B., Buhalis, D., Cheung, C. M. K., Conboy, K., Doyle, R., Dubey, R., Dutot, V., Felix, R., Goyal, D. P., Gustafsson, A., Hinsch, C., Jebabli, I., … Wamba, S. F. (2022). Metaverse beyond the hype: Multidisciplinary perspectives on emerging challenges, opportunities, and agenda for research, practice and policy. *International Journal of Information Management*, *66*(July), 1–55. https://doi.org/10.1016/j.ijinfomgt.2022.102542

Dwivedi, Y. K., Ismagilova, E., Hughes, D. L., Carlson, J., Filieri, R., Jacobson, J., Jain, V., Karjaluoto, H., Kefi, H., Krishen, A. S., Kumar, V., Rahman, M. M., Raman, R., Rauschnabel, P. A., Rowley, J., Salo, J., Tran, G. A., & Wang, Y. (2020). Setting the future of digital and social media marketing research: Perspectives and research propositions. *International Journal of Information Management*, May, 102168. https://doi.org/10.1016/j.ijinfomgt.2020.102168

E-Estonia. (2021). This is the story of the world's most advanced digital society. Retrieved August 20, 2023, from https://e-estonia.com/story/

E-Estonia. (2023). *Enter e-Estonia*.

Eisenhardt, K. M., & Martin, J. A. (2000). Dynamic capabilities: What are they? *Strategic Managment Journal*, *21*, 1105–1121. http://dx.doi.org/10.1016/j.jaci.2012.05.050

Ellen MacArthur Foundation. (2023). Circular economy introduction. https://ellenmacarthurfoundation.org/topics/circular-economy-introduction/overview

Enholm, I. M., Papagiannidis, E., Mikalef, P., & Krogstie, J. (2022). Artificial intelligence and business value: A literature review. *Information Systems Frontiers*, *24*, 1709–1734. https://doi.org/10.1016/j.jfo.2021.11.002

Entur. (2023a). About Entur. https://om.entur.no/om-entur

Entur. (2023b). About the travel planner. https://om.entur.no/om-entur

Eskandaripour, H., & Boldsaikhan, E. (2023). Last-mile drone delivery: Past, present, and future. *Drones*, *7*(2), 1–19. https://doi.org/10.3390/drones7020077

European Commission. (2018). Behavioural study on the transparency of online platforms. https://doi.org/10.2818/637090

European Commission. (2021a). Ethics by design and ethics of use approaches for artificial intelligence (November). https://ec.europa.eu/digital-single-market/en/news/ethics-guidelines-trustworthy-ai

European Commission. (2021b). Fostering solidarity and responsibility between generations. In *Green Paper on Ageing*.

European Commission. (2022a). Commission welcomes political agreement on new rules to ensure the safety of machinery and robots. Europa.Eu.

European Commission. (2022b). Digital Economy and Society Index (DESI) 2022 Norway. https://digital-strategy.ec.europa.eu/en/library/digital-economy-and-society-index-desi-2022

European Commission. (2023). What is a data breach and what do we have to do in case of a data breach? Retrieved September 3, 2023, from https://commission.europa.eu website: https://ec.europa.eu/info/law/law-topic/data-protection/reform/rules-business-and-organisations/obligations/what-data-breach-and-what-do-we-have-do-case-data-breach_en

European Environment Agency. (2020). *Circular Economy System Diagram*. Circular Economy System Diagram. /www.ellenmacarthurfoundation.org/circular-economy/interactive-diagram

European Parliament. (2023). Circular economy: definition, importance and benefits. European Parliament. www.europarl.europa.eu/news/en/headlines/economy/20151201STO05603/circular-economy-definition-importance-and-benefits

Ewers, K., Baier, D., & Höhn, N. (2020). Siri, do I like you? Digital voice assistants and their acceptance by consumers. *Journal of Service Management Research*, 4(1), 52–68. https://doi.org/10.15358/2511-8676-2020-1-52

Fauville, G., Luo, M., Queiroz, A. C. M., Bailenson, J. N., & Hancock, J. (2021). Zoom exhaustion & fatigue scale. *Computers in Human Behavior Reports*, 4(July), 100119. https://doi.org/10.1016/j.chbr.2021.100119

Federal Ministry for Economic Affairs and Climate Action. (2023). *Industrie 4.0*. www.bmwk.de/Redaktion/EN/Dossier/industrie-40.html

Fernandes, T., & Oliveira, E. (2021). Understanding consumers' acceptance of automated technologies in service encounters: Drivers of digital voice assistants adoption. *Journal of Business Research*, 122, 180–191. https://doi.org/10.1016/j.jbusres.2020.08.058

Fernandez-Vidal, J., Perotti, F. A., Gonzalez, R., & Gasco, J. (2022). Managing digital transformation: The view from the top. *Journal of Business Research*, 152(July), 29–41. https://doi.org/10.1016/j.jbusres.2022.07.020

Flew, T. (2021). *Regulating Platforms*. Polity Press.

Floridi, L. (2019). Translating principles into practices of digital ethics: Five risks of being unethical. *Philosophy & Technology*, 185–193. https://doi.org/10.1007/s13347-019-00354-x

Foehr, J., & Germelmann, C. C. (2020). Alexa, Can I Trust You? Exploring consumer paths to trust in smart voice-interaction technologies. *JACR*, 5(2), 181–205.

Forti, V., Baldé, C. P., Kuehr, R., Bel, G., Jinhui, L., Khetriwal, D. S., Linnell, J., Magalini, F., Nnororm, I. C., Onianwa, P., Ott, D., Ramola, A., Silva, U., Stillhart, R., Tillekeratne, D., Van Straalen, V., Wagner, M., & Yamamoto, T., & Zeng, X. (2020). The Global E-waste Monitor 2020: Quantities, flows, and resources. In *Ensure healthy Lives and Promote Well-being for All. Experiences of Community Health, Hygiene, Sanitation and Nutrition*. https://ewastemonitor.info/gem-2020/

Fowler, B. (2023). Cyberattack on PayPal exposes user social security numbers looking for great deals? CNET. www.cnet.com/tech/services-and-software/social-security-numbers-stolen-in-paypal-cyber-attack/

Fowler, C., Jiao, J., & Pitts, M. (2022). Frustration and ennui among Amazon MTurk workers. *Behavior Research Methods*, *August*. https://doi.org/10.3758/s13428-022-01955-9

Friedman, M. (1970, September 13). The social responsibility of business is to increase its profits. *The New York Times*, 17. http://link.springer.com/chapter/10.1007/978-3-540-70818-6_14

Fuller, J. B., & Kerr, W. R. (2022). The Great Resignation didn't start with the pandemic. *Harvard Business Review*. https://hbr.org/2022/03/the-great-resignation-didnt-start-with-the-pandemic

Fundación Cibervoluntarios. (2021). Press Kit.

Fundación Cibervoluntarios. (2022). Can we help you? www.cibervoluntarios.org/

Garay-Rondero, C. L., Martinez-Flores, J. L., Smith, N. R., Omar, S., Morales, C., & Aldrette-Malacara, A. (2020). Digital supply chain model in Industry 4.0. *Journal of Manufacturing Technology Management*, *31*(5), 887–933. https://doi.org/10.1108/JMTM-08-2018-0280

Garcia-Ortega, B., Galan-Cubillo, J., Llorens-Montes, F. J., & de-Miguel-Molina, B. (2023). Sufficient consumption as a missing link toward sustainability: The case of fast fashion. *Journal of Cleaner Production*, *399*(February), 136678. https://doi.org/10.1016/j.jclepro.2023.136678

Gartner. (2022a). Digital business. gartner.com. www.gartner.com/en/information-technology/glossary/business-analytics

Gartner. (2022b). Hype Cycle for Emerging Technologies. This Gartner report is archived and is included for historical context only. GARTNER and HYPE CYCLE are registered trademarks of Gartner, Inc. and/or its affiliates and are used herein with permission. All rights reserved.

Gartner. (2023). Hype Cycle Methodology. https://www.gartner.com/en/research/methodologies/gartner-hype-cycle

Gebhardt, M., Kopyto, M., Birkel, H., & Hartmann, E. (2022). Industry 4.0 technologies as enablers of collaboration in circular supply chains: A systematic literature review. *International Journal of Production Research*, *60*(23), 6967–6995. https://doi.org/10.1080/00207543.2021.1999521

GeoPoll Africa 118 and the African Talent Company. (2023). *The Africa MSME Pulse Survey Report 2023*.

Gielens, K., & Steenkamp, J. B. E. M. (2019). Branding in the era of digital (dis)-intermediation. *International Journal of Research in Marketing*, *36*(3), 367–384. https://doi.org/10.1016/j.ijresmar.2019.01.005

Google. (2023). PayPal leverages Google Cloud to flawlessly manage surges in financial transactions. https://cloud.google.com/customers/paypal

Gupta, A., Dixit, A. K., Kumar, K. S., Lavanya, C., Chakravarthi, M. K., & Gangodkar, D. (2022). Analyzing robotics and computer integrated manufacturing of key areas using cloud computing. *Proceedings of 5th International Conference on Contemporary Computing and Informatics, IC3I 2022*, 194–199. https://doi.org/10.1109/IC3I56241.2022.10072581

Gurca, A., Bagherzadeh, M., & Velayati, R. (2023). Aligning the crowdsourcing type with the problem attributes to improve solution search efficacy. *Technovation*, *119*(July 2022), 102613. https://doi.org/10.1016/j.technovation.2022.102613

H&M. (2023). Repair & remake. www2.hm.com/en_gb/sustainability-at-hm/take-care/repair-remake.html

Habib, G., Sharma, S., Ibrahim, S., Ahmad, I., Qureshi, S., & Ishfaq, M. (2022). Blockchain technology: Benefits, challenges, applications, and integration of blockchain technology with cloud computing. *Future Internet, 14*(11), 1–22. https://doi.org/10.3390/fi14110341

Hamid, R. A., Albahri, A. S., Alwan, J. K., Al-Qaysi, Z. T., Albahri, O. S., Zaidan, A. A., Alnoor, A., Alamoodi, A. H., & Zaidan, B. B. (2021). How smart is e-tourism? A systematic review of smart tourism recommendation system applying data management. *Computer Science Review, 39*, 100337. https://doi.org/10.1016/j.cosrev.2020.100337

Hamilton, R., Ferraro, R., Haws, K. L., & Mukhopadhyay, A. (2021). Traveling with companions: The social customer journey. *Journal of Marketing, 85*(1), 68–92. https://doi.org/10.1177/0022242920908227

Hanlon, A. (2022a). *Digital Marketing: Strategic Planning & Integration* (2nd ed.). Sage Publications.

Hanlon, A. (2022b). Metaverse – together alone ? *LSE Business Review.* https://blogs.lse.ac.uk/businessreview/2022/06/01/metaverse-together-alone/

Hanlon, A., & Jones, K. (2023). Ethical concerns about social media privacy policies: Do users have the ability to comprehend their consent actions? *Journal of Strategic Marketing*, 1–18. https://doi.org/10.1080/0965254X.2023.2232817

Hanlon, A., & Laasch, O. (2024). Digitalizing. In *Principles of Business & Management Practicing Ethics, Responsibility, Sustainability* (3rd edn).

Hasan, M. H., Osman, M. H., Admodisastro, N. I., & Muhammad, M. S. (2023). Legacy systems to cloud migration: A review from the architectural perspective. *Journal of Systems and Software, 202*, 111702. https://doi.org/10.1016/j.jss.2023.111702

He, S., Hollenbeck, B., & Proserpio, D. (2022). The market for fake reviews. *Marketing Science, 41*(5), 468–493. https://doi.org/10.1287/mksc.2022.1353

Hein, A., Schreieck, M., Riasanow, T., Setzke, D. S., Wiesche, M., Böhm, M., & Krcmar, H. (2020). Digital platform ecosystems. *Electronic Markets, 30*(1), 87–98. https://doi.org/10.1007/s12525-019-00377-4

Hirschman, E. C., & Holbrook, M. B. (1982). Hedonic consumption: Emerging concepts, methods and propositions. *Journal of Marketing, 46*(3), 92–101. https://doi.org/10.2307/1251707

Högberg, K., & Willermark, S. (2022). Strategic responses to digital disruption in incumbent firms – a strategy-as-practice perspective. *Journal of Computer Information Systems, 63*(2), 1–12. https://doi.org/10.1080/08874417.2022.2057373

Holopainen, M., Ukko, J., & Saunila, M. (2022). Managing the strategic readiness of industrial companies for digital operations. *Digital Business, 2*(2), 100039. https://doi.org/10.1016/j.digbus.2022.100039

Hoyer, W. D., Kroschke, M., Schmitt, B., Kraume, K., & Shankar, V. (2020). Transforming the customer experience through new technologies. *Journal of Interactive Marketing, 51*, 57–71. https://doi.org/10.1016/j.intmar.2020.04.001

Hsu, P. F., Nguyen, T. K., & Huang, J. Y. (2021). Value co-creation and co-destruction in self-service technology: A customer's perspective. *Electronic Commerce Research and Applications, 46*(101), 101029. https://doi.org/10.1016/j.elerap.2021.101029

Hufnagel, G., Schwaiger, M., & Weritz, L. (2022). Seeking the perfect price: Consumer responses to personalized price discrimination in e-commerce. *Journal of Business Research, 143*(September 2021), 346–365. https://doi.org/10.1016/j.jbusres.2021.10.002

Hylland, O. M. (2022). Tales of temporary disruption: Digital adaptations in the first 100 days of the cultural Covid lockdown. *Poetics, 90*, 1–11. https://doi.org/10.1016/j.poetic.2021.101602

IBM. (2023). Cost of a data breach report. *Computer Fraud & Security*. https://doi.org/10.1016/s1361-3723(21)00082-8

IEA. (2022). *Data Centres and Data Transmission Networks – Tracking Report*. www.iea.org/reports/data-centres-and-data-transmission-networks

IFR Press Room. (2023). *World Robotics 2023 Report*.

Innovation Fund Denmark. (2018). *Societal Readiness Levels (SRL) defined according to Innovation Fund Denmark*. https://innovationsfonden.dk/sites/default/files/2019-03/societal_readiness_levels_-_srl.pdf

International Telecommunication Union, I. (2021). *Facts and Figures 2021: 2.9 billion people still offline*. www.itu.int/hub/2021/11/facts-and-figures-2021-2-9-billion-people-still-offline/

Inuwa-Dutse, I. (2023). FATE in AI: Towards algorithmic inclusivity and accessibility. *ArXiv, 01*(01590), 1–19. https://arxiv.org/abs/2301.01590v1

iSG Provider Lens. (2022). *Future of work – services and solutions* (October). www.unisys.com/siteassets/collateral/analyst-report/ar-futureofwork-servicesandsolutions-quadrpt-au-20220916.pdf

Ivers, L., Niavas, S., Mitchell, C., Sqalli, Z., & Frikha, O. (2022). The future of traditional retail in Africa. BCG.com. www.bcg.com/publications/2022/the-future-of-traditional-retail-in-africa

Jacob, F., Grosse, E. H., Morana, S., & König, C. J. (2023). Picking with a robot colleague: A systematic literature review and evaluation of technology acceptance in human–robot collaborative warehouses. *Computers and Industrial Engineering, 180*(February). https://doi.org/10.1016/j.cie.2023.109262

Jandyal, A., Chaturvedi, I., Wazir, I., Raina, A., & Ul Haq, M. I. (2022). 3D printing – A review of processes, materials and applications in industry 4.0. *Sustainable Operations and Computers, 3*(September 2021), 33–42. https://doi.org/10.1016/j.susoc.2021.09.004

Jeske, D. (2022). Remote workers' experiences with electronic monitoring during Covid-19: Implications and recommendations. *International Journal of Workplace Health Management, 15*(3), 393–409. https://doi.org/10.1108/IJWHM-02-2021-0042

Jin, K. (2021). Virtual technology in the real world of COVID-19. *XRDS: Crossroads, The ACM Magazine for Students, 28*(2), 79. https://doi.org/10.1145/3495270

Jung, S., Shin, H. W., Gohary, A., & Chan, E. Y. (2023). Benefits and challenges of online collaborative learning from the perspectives of non-traditional event management students: A comparison between asynchronous and synchronous learning. *Journal of Teaching in Travel and Tourism, 2*, 109–129. https://doi.org/10.1080/15313220.2022.2109553

Kaplan, A., & Haenlein, M. (2019). Siri, Siri, in my hand: Who's the fairest in the land? On the interpretations, illustrations, and implications of artificial intelligence. *Business Horizons, 62*(1), 15–25. https://doi.org/10.1016/j.bushor.2018.08.004

Kaplan, A., & Haenlein, M. (2020). Rulers of the world, unite! The challenges and opportunities of artificial intelligence. *Business Horizons, 63*(1), 37–50. https://doi.org/10.1016/j.bushor.2019.09.003

Kasten, A. (2023). AI, tighter budgets, and rise of evil digital twins: UMGC cyber trends for 2023. UMGC Global Media Center.

Katz, M. L., & Shapiro, C. (1985). Network externalities, competition and compatibility. *American Economic Review, 75*(3), 424–440.

Katz, M. L., & Shapiro, C. (1994). Systems competition and network effects. *Journal of Economic Perspectives, 8*(2), 93–115. https://doi.org/10.1257/jep.8.2.93

Kene-Okafor, T. (2022). Sokowatch Rebrands to Wasoko as it raises $125M Series B from Tiger Global and Avenir. TechCrunch.com. https://techcrunch.com/2022/03/16/sokowatch-rebrands-to-wasoko-as-it-raises-125m-series-b-from-tiger-global-and-avenir/

Khan, S. A., Mubarik, M. S., Kusi-Sarpong, S., Gupta, H., Zaman, S. I., & Mubarik, M. (2022). Blockchain technologies as enablers of supply chain mapping for sustainable supply chains. *Business Strategy and the Environment, 31*(8), 3742–3756. https://doi.org/10.1002/bse.3029

Kim, N., Montreuil, B., & Klibi, W. (2022). Inventory availability commitment under uncertainty in a dropshipping supply chain. *European Journal of Operational Research, 302*(3), 1155–1174. https://doi.org/10.1016/j.ejor.2022.02.007

King, T., & Dennis, C. (2006). Unethical consumers: Deshopping behaviour using the qualitative analysis of theory of planned behaviour and accompanied (de)shopping. *Qualitative Market Research, 9*(3), 282–296. https://doi.org/10.1108/13522750610671699

Kirk, J., Bandholm, T., Andersen, O., Husted, R. S., Tjørnhøj-Thomsen, T., Nilsen, P., & Pedersen, M. M. (2021). Challenges in co-designing an intervention to increase mobility in older patients: a qualitative study. *Journal of Health Organization and Management, 35*(9), 140–162. https://doi.org/10.1108/JHOM-02-2020-0049

Klotz, A. C., & Bolino, M. C. (2022). When quiet quitting is worse than the real thing. *Harvard Business Review, September*, 1–6. https://hbr.org/2022/09/when-quiet-quitting-is-worse-than-the-real-thing

Koc, I., & Arslan, E. (2021). Dynamic ticket pricing of airlines using variant batch size interpretable multi-variable long short-term memory. *Expert Systems with Applications, 175*(March), 114794. https://doi.org/10.1016/j.eswa.2021.114794

Kock, N. (2005). What is e-collaboration? in *International Journal of E-collaboration, 1*(1), 1–7. http://cits.tamiu.edu/kock/pubs/journals/2005JournalIJeC/Kock2005.pdf

Kranzbühler, A. M., Kleijnen, M. H. P., Morgan, R. E., & Teerling, M. (2018). The multilevel nature of customer experience research: An integrative review and research agenda. *International Journal of Management Reviews, 20*(2), 433–456. https://doi.org/10.1111/ijmr.12140

Kraus, S., Jones, P., Kailer, N., Weinmann, A., Chaparro-Banegas, N., & Roig-Tierno, N. (2021). Digital transformation: An overview of the current state of the art of research. *Sage Open, 11*(3). https://doi.org/10.1177/21582440211047576

Lacoste. (2021). Lacoste textile product durability protocol. file:///C:/Users/annma/Downloads/Sustainable-development-progress-report-2022.pdf

Laffey, D. (2022). Price comparison websites. In A. Hanlon & T. L. Tuten (Eds.), *The Sage Handbook of Digital Marketing*. Sage Publications.

Lapalme, J., Gerber, A., Van Der Merwe, A., Zachman, J., Vries, M. De, & Hinkelmann, K. (2016). Exploring the future of enterprise architecture: A Zachman perspective. *Computers in Industry*, *79*, 103–113. https://doi.org/10.1016/j.compind.2015.06.010

Lemon, K. N., & Verhoef, P. C. (2016). Understanding customer experience throughout the customer journey. *Journal of Marketing*, *80*(6), 69–96. https://doi.org/10.1509/jm.15.0420

Lewis, M. (2022). Market guide for subscription and recurring billing management solutions (April). www.gartner.com/en/documents/4013597

Li, T. T., Wang, K., Sueyoshi, T., & Wang, D. D. (2021). ESG: Research progress and future prospects. *Sustainability (Switzerland)*, *13*(21). https://doi.org/10.3390/su132111663

Libai, B., Bart, Y., Gensler, S., Hofacker, C. F., Kaplan, A., Kötterheinrich, K., & Kroll, E. B. (2020). Brave new world? On AI and the management of customer relationships. *Journal of Interactive Marketing*, *51*, 44–56. https://doi.org/10.1016/j.intmar.2020.04.002

Liu, L., & Wu, J. N. (2010). Virtual value chain and competitive advantages in the context of e-commerce. *Proceedings – 2010 IEEE 17th International Conference on Industrial Engineering and Engineering Management, IE and EM2010*, 1467–1472. https://doi.org/10.1109/ICIEEM.2010.5646044

Lobschat, L., Mueller, B., Eggers, F., Brandimarte, L., Diefenbach, S., Kroschke, M., & Wirtz, J. (2021). Corporate digital responsibility. *Journal of Business Research*, *122*(July 2018), 875–888. https://doi.org/10.1016/j.jbusres.2019.10.006

López-Ramírez, C. A., García-Cáceres, R. G., & Herrera-Rodríguez, J. M. (2022). Taxonomy of outsourcing alternatives through systematic literature review. *Tecnura*, *26*, 124–144.

Luo, B., Lau, R. Y. K., Li, C., & Si, Y. W. (2022). A critical review of state-of-the-art chatbot designs and applications. *Wiley Interdisciplinary Reviews: Data Mining and Knowledge Discovery*, *12*(1), 1–26. https://doi.org/10.1002/widm.1434

Luo, Y. (2022). A general framework of digitization risks in international business. *Journal of International Business Studies*, *53*(2), 344–361. https://doi.org/10.1057/s41267-021-00448-9

MacCarthy, B. L., Ahmed, W. A. H., & Demirel, G. (2022). Mapping the supply chain: Why, what and how? *International Journal of Production Economics*, *250*(August), 1–20. https://doi.org/10.1016/j.ijpe.2022.108688

Maddahi, A., Leach, T. R., Saeedi, M., Dhannapuneni, P. R., Maddahi, Y., Choukou, M. A., & Zareinia, K. (2022). Roboethics in remote human interactions and rehabilitative therapeutics. *Applied Sciences (Switzerland)*, *12*(12). https://doi.org/10.3390/app12126033

Maersk. (2020). Annual report. https://investor.maersk.com/news-releases/news-release-details/annual-report-2020

Maersk. (2022). Annual report. https://ml-eu.globenewswire.com/Resource/Download/2f63098a-d33e-41d9-9eb0-068bb0c3eb04

Mariani, M. M., Machado, I., & Nambisan, S. (2023). Types of innovation and artificial intelligence: A systematic quantitative literature review and research agenda. *Journal of Business Research*, *155*(PB), 113364. https://doi.org/10.1016/j.jbusres.2022.113364

Mars. (2022). Simplification & verification. www.mars.com/about/policies-and-practices/palm-oil-policy/simplification-and-verification

Marsh, E. (2018). Understanding the effect of digital literacy on employees' digital workplace continuance intentions and individual performance. *International Journal of Digital Literacy and Digital Competence*, *9*(2), 15–33. https://doi.org/10.4018/ijdldc.2018040102

Martynov, V. V., Shavaleeva, D. N., & Zaytseva, A. A. (2019). Information technology as the basis for transformation into a digital society and Industry 5.0. *Proceedings of the 2019 IEEE International Conference Quality Management, Transport and Information Security, Information Technologies IT and QM and IS 2019*, 539–543. https://doi.org/10.1109/ITQMIS.2019.8928305

McMillan, H. S., Morris, M. L., & Atchley, E. K. (2011). Constructs of the work/life interface: A synthesis of the literature and introduction of the concept of work/life harmony. *Human Resource Development Review*, *10*(1), 6–25. https://doi.org/10.1177/1534484310384958

Mell, P., & Grance, T. (2011). *The NIST Definition of Cloud Computing*: Vol. September (p. 7). National Institute of Standards and Technology.

Merriam-Webster. (2016). Definition of Innovation. Merriam-Webster.Com Dictionary. www.merriam-webster.com/dictionary/innovation

Mikalef, P., Pappas, I. O., Krogstie, J., & Giannakos, M. (2018). Big data analytics capabilities: A systematic literature review and research agenda. *Information Systems and E-Business Management*, *16*(3), 547–578. https://doi.org/10.1007/s10257-017-0362-y

Miorandi, D., Sicari, S., De Pellegrini, F., & Chlamtac, I. (2012). Internet of things: Vision, applications and research challenges. *Ad Hoc Networks*, *10*(7), 1497–1516. https://doi.org/10.1016/j.adhoc.2012.02.016

Mishra, S., & Tripathi, A. R. (2020). Literature review on business prototypes for digital platform. *Journal of Innovation and Entrepreneurship*, *9*(23), 1–19.

Mondal, S., Das, S., & Vrana, V. G. (2023). How to bell the cat? A theoretical review of generative artificial intelligence towards digital disruption in all walks of life. *Technologies*, *11*(2). https://doi.org/10.3390/technologies11020044

Moore, G. E. (1965). Cramming more components onto integrated circuits. *Electronics*, *38*(8), 33–35. papers3://publication/uuid/8E5EB7C8-681C-447D-9361-E68D1932997D

Mortara, L., & Minshall, T. (2011). How do large multinational companies implement open innovation? *Technovation*, 31(10–11), 586–597. https://doi.org/10.1016/j.technovation.2011.05.002

Murciano-Hueso, A., Martín-García, A. V., & Cardoso, A. P. (2022). Technology and quality of life of older people in times of COVID: A qualitative study on their changed digital profile. *International Journal of Environmental Research and Public Health*, *19*(16). https://doi.org/10.3390/ijerph191610459

Murinde, V., Rizopoulos, E., & Zachariadis, M. (2022). The impact of the FinTech revolution on the future of banking: Opportunities and risks. *International Review of Financial Analysis*, *81*(March), 102103. https://doi.org/10.1016/j.irfa.2022.102103

Nadkarni, S., & Prügl, R. (2021). Digital transformation: A review, synthesis and opportunities for future research. In *Management Review Quarterly*, *71*(2). Springer International Publishing. https://doi.org/10.1007/s11301-020-00185-7

Nadler, R. (2020). Understanding "Zoom fatigue": Theorizing spatial dynamics as third skins in computer-mediated communication. *Computers and Composition*, *58*, 102613. https://doi.org/10.1016/j.compcom.2020.102613

Nambisan, S., Lyytinen, K., Majchrzak, A., & Song, M. (2017). Digital innovation management: Reinventing innovation management research in a digital world. *MIS Quarterly: Management Information Systems*, *41*(1), 223–238. https://doi.org/10.25300/MISQ/2017/411.03

Nargesian, F., Zhu, E., Miller, R. J., Pu, K. Q., & Arocena, P. C. (2019). Data lake management: Challenges and opportunities. *Proceedings of the VLDB Endowment*, *12*(12), 1986–1989. https://doi.org/10.14778/3352063.3352116

NASA. (2012). Technology readiness level. NASA.gov. www.nasa.gov/directorates/heo/scan/engineering/technology/txt_accordion1.html

National Science Foundation. (2023). Cyber-physical systems. www.nsf.gov/news/special_reports/cyber-physical/

Netflix. (2022). Annual Report. https://ir.netflix.net/financials/annual-reports-and-proxies/default.aspx

Netflix Help Center. (2023). How Netflix's Recommendations System Works. Netflix. https://help.netflix.com/en/node/100639

Neves, B. B., & Mead, G. (2021). Digital technology and older people: Towards a sociological approach to technology adoption in later life. *Sociology*, *55*(5), 888–905. https://doi.org/10.1177/0038038520975587

Niu, Y., Ying, L., Yang, J., Bao, M., & Sivaparthipan, C. B. (2021). Organizational business intelligence and decision making using big data analytics. *Information Processing and Management*, *58*(6), 102725. https://doi.org/10.1016/j.ipm.2021.102725

O'Reilly, T. (2005). What is Web 2.0. Design patterns and business models for the next generation of software. O'Reilly Blog. http://oreilly.com/web2/archive/what-is-web-20.html

Ogunbodede, O., Papagiannidis, S., & Alamanos, E. (2022). Value co-creation and co-destruction behaviour: Relationship with basic human values and personality traits. *International Journal of Consumer Studies*, *46*(4), 1278–1298. https://doi.org/10.1111/ijcs.12757

OpenAI. (2022). ChatGPT: Optimizing language models for dialogue. https://openai.com/blog/chatgpt/

Ounvorawong, N., Breitsohl, J., Lowe, B., & Laffey, D. (2022). Outcomes of cyber-victimization and bystander reactions in online brand communities. *International Journal of Electronic Commerce*, *26*(2), 200–221. https://doi.org/10.1080/10864415.2022.2050582

PayPal. (2021). Building a digital economy that powers a more inclusive and resilient world. https://s202.q4cdn.com/805890769/files/doc_downloads/global-impact/PayPal-2021-Global-Impact-Report.pdf

PayPal. (2022a). 2022 Notice of Annual Meeting of Stockholders and Proxy Statement 2021 Annual Report. https://s201.q4cdn.com/231198771/files/doc_financials/2022/ar/PayPal-Holdings-Inc.-2022-Combined-Proxy-Statement-and-Annual-Report.pdf

PayPal. (2022b). One PayPal. Many locations. https://careers.pypl.com/locations/default.aspx

PayPal. (2022c). Opening opportunities for all. https://careers.pypl.com. https://careers.pypl.com/home/

PayPal. (2023a). 2022 Annual Report. https://investor.pypl.com/financials/annual-reports/default.aspx

PayPal. (2023b). Careers. https://careers.pypl.com/home/default.aspx

PayPal. (2023c). PayPal's 2022 Task Force on Financial Disclosures (TCFD) Index (May). https://s202.q4cdn.com/805890769/files/doc_downloads/global-impact/TCFD-Index-2022.pdf

PayPal Editorial Staff. (2022). Finding the business value in customer values. PayPal.com. www.paypal.com/us/brc/article/customer-values

PayPal Editorial Staff. (2023a). 7 ways your business could accelerate digital transformation with PayPal. www.paypal.com/sg/brc/article/enterprise-accelerate-business-digital-transformation

PayPal Editorial Staff. (2023b). What are popular digital wallets and their benefits to businesses? PayPal.com. www.paypal.com/us/brc/article/accept-digital-wallets

Peteraf, M. A., & Bergen, M. E. (2003). Scanning dynamic competitive landscapes: A market-based and resource-based framework. *Strategic Management Journal*, *24*(10 SPEC ISS.), 1027–1041. https://doi.org/10.1002/smj.325

Pew Research Center. (2022). Public more likely to see facial recognition use by police as good, rather than bad for society. Pew Research Center. www.pewresearch.org/internet/2022/03/17/public-more-likely-to-see-facial-recognition-use-by-police-as-good-rather-than-bad-for-society/#:~:text=In%20terms%20of%20potential%20impact,widely%20use%20facial%20recognition%20technology.

Plé, L., & Cáceres, R. C. (2010). Not always co-creation: Introducing interactional co-destruction of value in service-dominant logic. *Journal of Services Marketing*, *24*(6), 430–437. https://doi.org/10.1108/08876041011072546

Poniatowski, M., Lüttenberg, H., Beverungen, D., & Kundisch, D. (2021). Three layers of abstraction: A conceptual framework for theorizing digital multi-sided platforms. *Information Systems and E-Business Management*, *20*, 257–283. https://doi.org/10.1007/s10257-021-00513-8

Port of Turku. (2023). SecurePax- hankkeessa tähdätään tietoliikenteen ja turvallisuuden kehittämiseen. www.portofturku.fi/2019/04/12/securepax-hankkeessa-tahdataan-tietoliikenteen-ja-turvallisuuden-kehittamiseen/

Prahalad, C. K., & Ramaswamy, V. (2004). Co-creating unique value with customers. *Strategy & Leadership*, *32*(3), 4–9. https://doi.org/10.1108/10878570410699249

Precedence Research. (2023). Augmented reality market. PrecedenceResearch.com. www.precedenceresearch.com/augmented-reality-market

QuickLizard. (2023). Understanding your AI. www.quicklizard.com/wp-content/uploads/2022/01/eBook-Understanding-Your-AI.pdf

Rahman, M. H., Wuest, T., & Shafae, M. (2023). Manufacturing cybersecurity threat attributes and countermeasures: Review, meta-taxonomy, and use cases of cyberattack taxonomies. *Journal of Manufacturing Systems*, *68*(October 2022), 196–208. https://doi.org/10.1016/j.jmsy.2023.03.009

Raja Santhi, A., & Muthuswamy, P. (2023). Industry 5.0 or industry 4.0S? Introduction to industry 4.0 and a peek into the prospective industry 5.0 technologies. *International Journal on Interactive Design and Manufacturing*, *17*(2), 947–979. https://doi.org/10.1007/s12008-023-01217-8

Rauschnabe, P. A., Babin, B. J., tom Dieck, M. C., Krey, N., & Jung, T. (2022). What is augmented reality marketing? Its definition, complexity, and future. *Journal of Business Research*, *142*, 1140–1150. https://doi.org/10.1016/j.jbusres.2021.12.084

Rehman, H. M., Nee, A. Y. H., Yuen Onn, C., & Rehman, M. (2021). Barriers to adoption of Industry 4.0 in manufacturing sector. *International Conference on Computer and Information Sciences: Sustaining Tomorrow with Digital Innovation (ICCOINS)*, July, 59–64. https://doi.org/10.1109/ICCOINS49721.2021.9497171

Republic of Rwanda. (2016). National E-Waste Management Policy for Rwanda (August). http://197.243.22.137/rwamagana/fileadmin/user_upload/National_e-Waste_Management_Policy_for_Rwanda.pdf

Riess, R., & Sottile, Z. (2023, July 29). Uber self-driving car test driver pleads guilty to endangerment in pedestrian death case. CNN Business. https://edition.cnn.com/2023/07/29/business/uber-self-driving-car-death-guilty/index.html

Rita, P., & Ramos, R. F. (2022). Global research trends in consumer behavior and sustainability in e-commerce: A bibliometric analysis of the knowledge structure. *Sustainability (Switzerland)*, *14*(15). https://doi.org/10.3390/su14159455

Ritter, T., & Pedersen, C. L. (2020). Digitization capability and the digitalization of business models in business-to-business firms: Past, present, and future. *Industrial Marketing Management*, *86*(November 2019), 180–190. https://doi.org/10.1016/j.indmarman.2019.11.019

Rogers, E. M. (1962). *Diffusion of innovations* (3rd ed.). Free Press of Glencoe. https://doi.org/citeulike-article-id:126680

Rojanakit, P., Torres de Oliveira, R., & Dulleck, U. (2022). The sharing economy: A critical review and research agenda. *Journal of Business Research*, *139*(February 2021), 1317–1334. https://doi.org/10.1016/j.jbusres.2021.10.045

Ronayne, D. (2021). Price comparison websites. *International Economic Review*, *62*(3), 1081–1110. https://doi.org/10.1111/iere.12504

Rosário, A., & Raimundo, R. (2021). Consumer marketing strategy and e-commerce in the last decade: A literature review. *Journal of Theoretical and Applied Electronic Commerce Research*, *16*(7), 3003–3024. https://doi.org/10.3390/jtaer16070164

Rotman, B. D. (2020). We're not prepared for the end of Moore's Law. *MIT Technology Review*. www.technologyreview.com/2020/02/24/905789/were-not-prepared-for-the-end-of-moores-law/

Roy, S. K., Gruner, R. L., & Guo, J. (2022). Exploring customer experience, commitment, and engagement behaviours. *Journal of Strategic Marketing*, *30*(1), 45–68. https://doi.org/10.1080/0965254X.2019.1642937

Rudmark, D., Lindman, J., Tryti, A., & Dammen, B. (2023). Beyond procurement: How Entur navigated the open source journey to advance public transport. *IEEE Software*, *40*(4), 62–70. https://doi.org/10.1109/MS.2023.3266482

Runge, J., Levav, J., & Nair, H. S. (2022). Price promotions and "freemium" app monetization. *Quantitative Marketing and Economics*, *20*(2), 101–139. https://doi.org/10.1007/s11129-022-09248-3

Saarikko, T., Westergren, U. H., & Blomquist, T. (2020). Digital transformation: Five recommendations for the digitally conscious firm. *Business Horizons*, *63*(6), 825–839. https://doi.org/10.1016/j.bushor.2020.07.005

Saha, V., Goyal, P., & Jebarajakirthy, C. (2022). Value co-creation: A review of literature and future research agenda. *Journal of Business and Industrial Marketing*, *37*(3), 612–628. https://doi.org/10.1108/JBIM-01-2020-0017

Sahakiants, I., & Dorner, G. (2021). Using social media and online collaboration technology in expatriate management: Benefits, challenges, and recommendations. *Thunderbird International Business Review*, *63*(6), 779–789. https://doi.org/10.1002/tie.22233

Salminen, J., Kamel, A. M. S., Jung, S. G., Mustak, M., & Jansen, B. J. (2022). Fair compensation of crowdsourcing work: The problem of flat rates. *Behaviour and Information Technology*, 1–22. https://doi.org/10.1080/0144929X.2022.2150564

Sanders, S. (2022). Does the paradox of choice exist in theory? A behavioral search model and pareto-improving choice set reduction algorithm. *AI and Society*, *0123456789*. https://doi.org/10.1007/s00146-022-01612-x

Sarker, I. H. (2021). Machine learning: Algorithms, real-world applications and research directions. *SN Computer Science*, *2*(3), 1–21. https://doi.org/10.1007/s42979-021-00592-x

Sasu, D. D. (2022). Internet usage in Nigeria – statistics & facts. Statista. www.statista.com/topics/7199/internet-usage-in-nigeria/#topicHeader__wrapper

Saxena, N., Rastogi, E., & Rastogi, A. (2021). 6G use cases, requirements, and metrics. In Y. Wu, S. Singh, T. Taleb, A. Roy, H. S. Dhillon, M. R. Kanagarathinam, & A. De (Eds.), *6G Mobile Wireless Networks* (pp. 7–24). Springer. https://doi.org/10.1007/978-3-030-72777-2_2

Schneider, F., & Enste, D. (2002). Hiding in the shadows: The growth of the underground economy. *Economic Issues*, *30*(March), 1–11. www.imf.org/external/pubs/ft/issues/issues30/

Schraudner, M., Schroth, F., Jütting, M., Kaiser, S., Millard, J., & Shenja, van der G. (2018). Social innovation: The potential for technology development, RTOs and industry. *RTO Innovation Summit*, November. https://doi.org/10.46692/9781447353805

Schultze, U., & Avital, M. (2011). Designing interviews to generate rich data for information systems research. *Information and Organization*, *21*(1), 1–16. https://doi.org/10.1016/j.infoandorg.2010.11.001

Scully, D. (2022). Marketing automation: A design perspective. In A. Hanlon & T. L. Tuten (Eds.), *The Sage Handbook of Digital Marketing*. Sage Publications.

Seele, P., Dierksmeier, C., Hofstetter, R., & Schultz, M. D. (2021). Mapping the ethicality of algorithmic pricing: A review of dynamic and personalized pricing. *Journal of Business Ethics*, *170*(4), 697–719. https://doi.org/10.1007/s10551-019-04371-w

Shaalan, A., Tourky, M. E., & Ibrahim, K. (2022). The chatbot revolution: Companies and consumers in a new digital age. In A. Hanlon & T. L. Tuten (Eds.), *The Sage Handbook of Digital Marketing*. Sage Publications.

Shafiq, A., Ahmed, M. U., & Mahmoodi, F. (2020). Impact of supply chain analytics and customer pressure for ethical conduct on socially responsible practices and performance: An exploratory study. *International Journal of Production Economics*, *225*(October 2019), 107571. https://doi.org/10.1016/j.ijpe.2019.107571

Shirmohammadi, M., Chan Au, W., & Beigi, M. (2022). Antecedents and outcomes of work-life balance while working from home: A review of the research conducted during the COVID-19 Pandemic. *Human Resource Development Review*, 21(4), 473–516. https://doi.org/10.1177/15344843221125834

Short, J., Williams, E., & Christie, B. (1976). The social psychology of telecommunications. *Journal of Chemical Information and Modeling*, *53*(9). https://doi.org/10.1017/CBO9781107415324.004

Shulman, D. (2016). Being a Customer Champion = Delivering Choice & Opportunity. Stay up to date. https://newsroom.paypal-corp.com/Being-a-Customer-Champion-Delivering-Choice-Opportunity

Si, S., & Chen, H. (2020). A literature review of disruptive innovation: What it is, how it works and where it goes. *Journal of Engineering and Technology Management*, *56*(April), 1–21. https://doi.org/10.1016/j.jengtecman.2020.101568

Simms, A., & Nichols, T. (2014). Social loafing: A review of the literature. *Journal of Management Policy*, *15*(1), 58–67.

Sinclair, J., & Wilken, R. (2009). Sleeping with the enemy: Disintermediation in internet advertising. *Media International Australia*, *132*, 93–104. https://doi.org/10.1177/1329878x0913200110

Skog, D. A., Wimelius, H., & Sandberg, J. (2018). Digital disruption. *Business and Information Systems Engineering*, *60*(5), 431–437. https://doi.org/10.1007/s12599-018-0550-4

Smith, K. T. (2020). Marketing via smart speakers: What should Alexa say? *Journal of Strategic Marketing*, *28*(4), 350–365. https://doi.org/10.1080/0965254X.2018.1541924

Solberg, E., Traavik, L. E. M., & Wong, S. I. (2020). Digital mindsets: Recognizing and leveraging individual beliefs for digital transformation. *California Management Review*, *62*(4), 105–124. https://doi.org/10.1177/0008125620931839

Song, C. S., & Kim, Y. K. (2022). The role of the human–robot interaction in consumers' acceptance of humanoid retail service robots. *Journal of Business Research*, *146*(April), 489–503. https://doi.org/10.1016/j.jbusres.2022.03.087

Speare-Cole, R., & Mitevska, T. (2018, November 21). Europe's 100 digital champions. FT.com. www.ft.com/content/6d68a236-e153-11e8-8e70-5e22a430c1ad

Statista. (2021). Distribution of internet users worldwide as of 2021, by age group (p. 8). www.statista.com/statistics/272365/age-distribution-of-internet-users-worldwide/

Statista. (2022). Global waste generation – statistics & facts. Statista.com. www.statista.com/topics/4983/waste-generation-worldwide/

Statista. (2023a). Barriers to voice technology adoption worldwide as of 2020. www.statista.com/statistics/1134244/barriers-to-voice-technology-adoption-worldwide/

Statista. (2023b). Video streaming worldwide. www.statista.com/topics/7527/video-streaming-worldwide/#topicOverview

Steils, N., & Hanine, S. (2022). Creative crowdsourcing: A marketing strategy for innovative companies. In A. Hanlon & T. L. Tuten (Eds.), *The Sage Handbook of Digital Marketing*. Sage Publications.

Stephenson, N. (2011). *Snow Crash* (Re-issue). Penguin.

Stocchi, L. (2022). The role of mobile technologies in digital marketing and sales. In A. Hanlon & T. L. Tuten (Eds.), *The Sage Handbook of Digital Marketing*. Sage Publications.

Stocchi, L., Pourazad, N., Michaelidou, N., Tanusondjaja, A., & Harrigan, P. (2022). Marketing research on mobile apps: Past, present and future. *Journal of the Academy of Marketing Science*, *50*(2). Springer US. https://doi.org/10.1007/s11747-021-00815-w

Taecharungroj, V. (2023). "What can ChatGPT do?" Analyzing early reactions to the innovative AI chatbot on Twitter. *Big Data and Cognitive Computing*, *7*(1). https://doi.org/10.3390/bdcc7010035

Teece, D. J. (2007). Explicating dynamic capabilities: The nature and microfoundations of (sustainable) enterprise performance. *Strategic Management Journal*, *28*, 1319–1350. https://doi.org/10.1002/smj

Thakur, R., Alsaleh, D., & Hale, D. (2023). Digital disruption: A managers' eye view. *Journal of Business and Industrial Marketing*, *38*(1), 53–70. https://doi.org/10.1108/JBIM-05-2021-0273

The Global Compact. (2004). Who cares wins: Connecting financial markets to a changing world. www.unepfi.org/fileadmin/events/2004/stocks/who_cares_wins_global_compact_2004.pdf

The Insight Partners. (2022). Workplace services market size to gain $193+bn by 2028 globally, at a CAGR of 10.6 %; says The Insight Partners. Newswires. www.einnews.com/pr_news/601170756/workplace-services-market-size-to-gain-193-bn-by-2028-globally-at-a-cagr-of-10-6-says-the-insight-partners

The Open Group. (2023). *The TOGAF® Standard, 10th Edition*. www.opengroup.org/togaf

Theoharakis, V., & Wong, V. (2002). Marking high-technology market evolution through the foci of market stories: The case of local area networks. *Journal of Product Innovation Management*, *19*(6), 400–411. https://doi.org/10.1016/S0737-6782(02)00176-5

Thomas, S. M., & Baddipudi, V. (2022). Changing nature of work and employment in the gig economy: The role of culture building and leadership in sustaining commitment and job satisfaction. *NHRD Network Journal*, *15*(1), 100–113. https://doi.org/10.1177/26314541211064735

Thorp, H. H. (2023). ChatGPT is fun, but not an author. *Science*, *379*(6630), 313–313. https://doi.org/10.1126/science.adg7879

Ting, T. Z. T., & Stagner, J. A. (2021). Fast fashion – wearing out the planet. *International Journal of Environmental Studies*, *80*(4), 856–866. https://doi.org/10.1080/00207233.2021.1987048

Törhönen, M., Giertz, J., Weiger, W. H., & Hamari, J. (2021). Streamers: The new wave of digital entreprenurship? Extant corpus and future research agenda. *Electronic Commerce Research and Applications*, *46*(December 2020). https://doi.org/10.1016/j.elerap.2020.101027

Tóth, Z., Caruana, R., Gruber, T., & Loebbecke, C. (2022). The dawn of the AI robots: Towards a new framework of AI robot accountability. *Journal of Business Ethics*, *178*(4), 895–916. https://doi.org/10.1007/s10551-022-05050-z

Tsoukalas, G. (2022). PayPal gets employees invested in innovation from idea to implementation. *Harvard Business Review*, *July*(12), 1–6. https://hbr.org/2022/07/how-paypal-gets-employees-invested-in-innovation

Tuzovic, S. (2022). Talk to me – the rise of voice assistants and smart speakers: A balance between efficiency and privacy. In A. Hanlon & T. L. Tuten (Eds.), *The Sage Handbook of Digital Marketing*. Sage Publications.

Ubank. (2023). *Why ubank? About us*. www.ubank.com.au/why-ubank

UBS Editorial Team. (2021). Investing in digital subscriptions (March). www.ubs.com/global/en/wealth-management/our-approach/marketnews/article.1525238.html

UNICEF. (2023). Child labour statistics. https://data.unicef.org/topic/child-protection/child-labour/

Unisys. (2021). *Unisys Corporation 2021 Annual Report*. www.unisys.com/common/investors/annuals/2013_Unisys_Annual_Report.pdf

Unitar – United Nations Institute for Training and Research. (2023). E-Waste Monitor. https://ewastemonitor.info/

United Nations. (2015). The SDGS in action. www.undp.org/sustainable-development-goals

United Nations. (2020a). Roadmap for digital cooperation. In *Report of the Secretary-General* (June). www.un.org/en/content/digital-cooperation-roadmap/assets/pdf/Roadmap_for_Digital_Cooperation_EN.pdf

United Nations. (2020b). Secretary-General's roadmap for digital cooperation. Undocs. Org. www.un.org/en/content/digital-cooperation-roadmap/

United Nations. (2021). Technology and innovation 2021. https://unctad.org/system/files/official-document/tir2020_en.pdf

United Nations. (2022). *The Sustainable Development Goals Report*. https://unstats.un.org/sdgs/report/2022/

United Nations Conference on Trade and Development (UNCTAD). (2021). Data protection and privacy legislation worldwide. https://unctad.org/page/data-protection-and-privacy-legislation-worldwide

United Nations Conference on Trade and Development (UNCTAD). (2022). eCommerce Week 2022 Outcome Report (April). https://unctad.org/eweek2022

Unni, R. M. (2022). Programmatic advertising. In A. Hanlon & T. L. Tuten (Eds.), *The Sage Handbook of Digital Marketing*. Sage Publications.

Vailshery, L. S. (2022). Microsoft teams: Number of daily active users 2019–2022. Statista. www.statista.com/statistics/1033742/worldwide-microsoft-teams-daily-and-monthly-users/

Varadarajan, R., Welden, R. B., Arunachalam, S., Haenlein, M., & Gupta, S. (2022). Digital product innovations for the greater good and digital marketing innovations in communications and channels: Evolution, emerging issues, and future research directions. *International Journal of Research in Marketing*, *39*(2), 482–501. https://doi.org/10.1016/j.ijresmar.2021.09.002

Vargo, S. L., & Lusch, R. F. (2004). Evolving to a new dominant logic for marketing. *Journal of Marketing*, *68*(1), 1–17. https://doi.org/10.1080/13552600410001470973

Vargo, S. L., & Lusch, R. F. (2017). Service-dominant logic 2025. *International Journal of Research in Marketing*, *34*(1), 46–67. https://doi.org/10.1016/j.ijresmar.2016.11.001

Vial, G. (2019). Understanding digital transformation: A review and a research agenda. *Journal of Strategic Information Systems*, *28*(2), 118–144. https://doi.org/10.1016/j.jsis.2019.01.003

VISA. (2022). Annual Report. www.ptonline.com/articles/how-to-get-better-mfi-results

VISA Direct. (2022). VISA Direct. VISA Developer Center. https://developer.visa.com/capabilities/visa_direct/docs

Vyas, L. (2022). "New normal" at work in a post-COVID world: Work–life balance and labor markets. *Policy and Society*, *41*(1), 155–167. https://doi.org/10.1093/polsoc/puab011

W3Techs. (2022). W3Techs – World Wide Web technology surveys. https://w3techs.com/

Wang, H., Huang, J., & Zhang, Z. (2019). The impact of deep learning on organizational agility. *ICIS*, 1–9. https://aisel.aisnet.org/icis2019

Waqas, M., Hamzah, Z. L. B., & Salleh, N. A. M. (2021). Customer experience: A systematic literature review and consumer culture theory-based conceptualisation. In *Management Review Quarterly*, *71*(1). Springer International Publishing. https://doi.org/10.1007/s11301-020-00182-w

Warnke, J. (2022). Going beyond with extended reality. accenture.com. www.accenture.com/de-de/about/going-beyond-extendcd-reality

Wastezon. (2022). Redefine the future of urban mining. Wastezon.com. https://wastezon.com/

Waters, R. (2023). Man beats machine at Go in human victory over AI. Ars Technica. https://arstechnica.com/information-technology/2023/02/man-beats-machine-at-go-in-human-victory-over-ai/

Weizenbaum, J. (1966). ELIZA – A computer program for the study of natural language communication between man and machine. *Communications of the ACM*, *9*(1), 36–45. https://doi.org/10.1145/365153.365168

Wernerfelt, B. (1984). A resource-based view of the firm. *Strategic Management Journal*, *5*, 171–180. https://doi.org/10.1002/smj.4250050207

Whittaker, Z. (2023). Toyota Japan exposed millions of vehicles' location data for a decade. https://techcrunch.com/2023/05/12/toyota-japan-exposed-millions-locations-videos/

Wielgos, D. M., Homburg, C., & Kuehnl, C. (2021). Digital business capability: Its impact on firm and customer performance. *Journal of the Academy of Marketing Science*, *49*(4), 762–789. https://doi.org/10.1007/s11747-021-00771-5

Wilson, C., & Mergel, I. (2022). Overcoming barriers to digital government: Mapping the strategies of digital champions. *Government Information Quarterly*, *39*(2), 101681. https://doi.org/10.1016/j.giq.2022.101681

Wilson, M., Robson, K., & Pitt, L. (2022). Consumer subversion and its relationship to anti-consumption, deviant and dysfunctional behaviors, and consumer revenge. *Psychology and Marketing*, *39*(3), 598–611. https://doi.org/10.1002/mar.21583

Wolny, J., & Charoensuksai, N. (2014). Mapping customer journeys in multichannel decision-making. *Journal of Direct, Data and Digital Marketing Practice*, *15*(4), 317–326. https://doi.org/10.1057/dddmp.2014.24

World Habitat. (2003). *The Impact of the Grameen Bank Mobile Phone Programme*. https://world-habitat.org/publications/the-impact-of-the-grameen-bank-mobile-phone-programme/

Wrigley, C., Nusem, E., & Straker, K. (2020). Implementing design thinking: Understanding organizational conditions. *California Management Review*, *62*(2), 125–143. https://doi.org/10.1177/0008125619897606

Xu, X., Lu, Y., Vogel-Heuser, B., & Wang, L. (2021). Industry 4.0 and Industry 5.0—Inception, conception and perception. *Journal of Manufacturing Systems*, *61*(September), 530–535. https://doi.org/10.1016/j.jmsy.2021.10.006

Zaggl, M. A., Malhotra, A., Alexy, O., & Majchrzak, A. (2023). Governing crowdsourcing for unconstrained innovation problems. *Strategic Management Journal*, August 2020, 1–35. https://doi.org/10.1002/smj.3505

Zalando. (2023). Zalando brings a virtual fitting room pilot to millions of customers. https://corporate.zalando.com/en/technology/zalando-brings-virtual-fitting-room-pilot-millions-customers

Zaman, R., Jain, T., Samara, G., & Jamali, D. (2022). Corporate governance meets corporate social responsibility: Mapping the interface. *Business and Society*, *61*(3), 690–752. https://doi.org/10.1177/0007650320973415

Zandt, F. (2021). Turning teamwork into profit. statista.com. www.statista.com/chart/12977/countries-with-the-best-work-life-balance/

Zhong, Y., Oh, S., & Moon, H. C. (2021). Service transformation under Industry 4.0: Investigating acceptance of facial recognition payment through an extended technology acceptance model. *Technology in Society*, *64*(January), 1–10. https://doi.org/10.1016/j.techsoc.2020.101515

Zimand-Sheiner, D., & Lahav, T. (2022). Plain old Bess in a different dress? Disruptions of public relations in the digital age. *Public Relations Review*, *48*(5), 102250. https://doi.org/10.1016/j.pubrev.2022.102250

Zoghaib, A. (2022). Voice marketing. In A. Hanlon & T. L. Tuten (Eds.), *The Sage Handbook of Digital Marketing*. Sage Publications.

INDEX

Page numbers followed by *f* indicate figures; those followed by *t* indicate tables.

Printed in the USA
CPSIA information can be obtained
at www.ICGtesting.com
CBHW080931170524
8518CB00013B/48

9 781529 624229